THE ILIAD

BRISTOL CLASSICAL PAPERBACKS

THE ILIAD

SECOND EDITION

Martin Mueller

Bristol Classical Press

Second edition published in 2009 by
Bristol Classical Press
an imprint of
Gerald Duckworth & Co. Ltd.
90-93 Cowcross Street, London EC1M 6BF
Tel: 020 7490 7300
Fax: 020 7490 0080
info@duckworth-publishers.co.uk
www.ducknet.co.uk

First edition published by Allen & Unwin in 1984

A catalogue record for this book is available
from the British Library

ISBN 978 1 85399 715 0

Typeset by Ray Davies
Printed and bound in Great Britain by
CPI Antony Rowe, Chippenham, Wiltshire

Contents

Contents

Preface to the Second Edition

This book was first published in 1984, but its roots go back to the sixties, and its central ideas appeared in my essay on 'Knowledge and Delusion in the Iliad' (1970). It is in many ways a German book and deeply shaped by my engagement with Wilamowitz's *Ilias und Homer* and Schadewaldt's *Iliasstudien*, but above all with Karl Reinhardt's searching inquiries into the nature of the 'Iliadic'. Reinhardt's posthumous and fragmentary book about the *Iliad* has the title *The Iliad and its Poet*. More recently Mark Edwards has written a very sensible and sensitive book with the title *The Poet of the Iliad*. These are programmatic titles that ask the interpreter to see the work in relationship to a single maker about whose life we know nothing but whose voice and 'take' on the world can be heard in the work. My book is an attempt to make modern readers hear that voice more clearly.

In a recent essay on 'Rhapsodes, Bards, and Bricoleurs: Homerizing Literary Theory', Egbert Bakker has divided Homeric scholars into those who look for a 'transcendental' or an 'immanent' Homer. According to this useful distinction my book falls squarely in the 'transcendental' camp. But there are two different ways in which one might challenge too sharp a division between a 'divine creator outside the scope of any historical research' and 'the poems themselves [and] the mechanisms that not only were instrumental in their development but that also sustained their transmission and survival' (Bakker 2007, 1).

The first challenge comes from Shakespeare's Sonnet 111 in which the speaker says:

> my nature is subdued
> To what it works in, like the dyer's hand.

Auden took the title for his collection of essays *The Dyer's Hand* from this phrase. The dyer's hand questions the dualism of immanent and transcendent. The poet will always get his hands dirty, and his poems will reek of the stuff from which they are made. You may call this an incarnational theory of poetry, but every 'embodiment' has its unique aspect.

The second challenge is probabilistic. In a conventional system of any size there is for all practical purposes no limit to the different ways of combining conventional elements for new effects. Bach and Handel or Haydn and Mozart worked within strongly defined harmonic, melodic, and rhythmic conventions. If we say that within two quite different period styles each of these composers speaks with an unmistakable voice, we are not moving from the 'mechanisms ... instrumental in their development' to a 'divine creator'. The unmistakable voice of Bach speaks in, with, and through those mechanisms, and the listener's pleasure consists in hearing that voice and being able to distinguish it from others. Nor is this desire a modern hankering after individuality as Milman Parry thought. Something very like it appears in a famous and charming passage from the Apollo Hymn:

Hail and farewell to you, maidens, remember me kindly hereafter
When anybody of men upon earth, say a wayfaring stranger
Come to this island, should ask your opinion and pose you this question,
'Who, do you think, is the man that is sweetest of singers, O maidens,
Of those that visit you here? And in which do you take the most pleasure?'
Answer him then well together, unanimously in my favour:
'He is a blind man whose home is on Chios, that rugged and rockbound
Island, and all of his poems are excellent, now and hereafter.'

Pope's 'grace beyond the reach of art' need not take us into a world of transcendence; it may be a matter of searching the probabilities that are immanent in the conventions. As the mad Ophelia says: 'You may wear your rue with a difference' (*Hamlet* 4.5.182).

A search for immanent difference is the major cause of change in this edition. In the nineties, Ahuvia Kahane and I became interested in computationally assisted analysis of Homeric repetitions. With the help of two gifted programmers, Craig Berry and Bill Parod, we built the *Chicago Homer*, a database that in a crude but consistent way recorded all instances of word sequences that occurred more than once. The very mechanical definition of a repetition in that database is not the same as the definition of a Homeric formula. On the other hand, it created a robust quantitative framework for analysing the distribution of various types of repetitive phenomena across Early Greek epic. Questions of the type 'how many of this occur here rather than there?' can now be answered in minutes rather than hours. Moreover, the Chicago Homer lets you quickly execute searches that are very difficult to do with other lexical tools, such as 'show me all repetitions that occur in Iliad 16 and 22 but nowhere else'.

*

The framing chapters of this book have been substantially rewritten in the light of the quantitative inquiries supported by the data in the Chicago Homer. While I have made minor changes in the central chapters on plot, fighting, similes, and the gods, I have rewritten the introduction and the chapter on the composition of the *Iliad*. I have added a new and quite long chapter on Homeric repetitions, which starts from the premise that frequency is a very important property of style. In ordinary conversation we are acutely sensitive to things other people say often, rarely, or never. Turning this natural and informal sensitivity into systematic attention is a good procedure, especially with the Homeric poems, where repetition is the central stylistic phenomenon readers have to come to terms with.

The chapter on repetitions is somewhat more technical than the rest of the book, and some readers may feel like Odysseus, caught between the Scylla of Greek and the Charybdis of statistics. But the other chapters of the book do not depend on a command of its detail. The opening chapter now includes a section on 'Reading Homeric repetitions', which is less quantitative in its orientation.

We will never know for sure just how the *Iliad* and *Odyssey* came into being. But the classification of different types of repetition provides substantial corroborative evidence for some version of the hypothesis that the poems result from the consequential encounter of two language technologies. We are living through a very different stage of such an encounter today and are familiar with the uncertainties and possibilities of hybrid technologies. But then every child is a hybrid.

In the preface to the first edition I thanked Brook Manville, Claude Rawson, Herbert Tucker, and John Wright for their advice, and I repeat those thanks here. I thank Marianne Hopman for the excellent advice on how to approach the task of revision a quarter century later. But where this version improves on the first edition, the largest thanks are due to four individuals who helped me gain some footing in the business of digitally assisted text analysis, which for better or for worse will come to play an increasingly important role in scholarly work with texts. Gregory Crane's Morpheus or morphological parser of ancient Greek was a critical tool in the process of extracting Homeric repetitions. Mark Olsen may not even remember that almost 15 years ago he wrote some perl scripts for me that made it seem possible to tackle repetitions in a systematic fashion. Bill Parod helped me explore the potential of relational database technology for certain kinds of philological queries. And Craig Berry wrote the program that extracted the repetitions for the Chicago Homer on which my analyses depend. I am deeply grateful for their support on these particular, and many general, matters.

1

Introduction

History and the *Iliad*

In *Troy and Homer: Towards a Solution of an Old Mystery*, Joachim Latacz embeds the *Iliad* in a rich context of archaeological and other evidence taken from Greek and Near Eastern sources. In this regard he follows such milestones of Homeric scholarship as Whitman's *Homer and the Heroic Tradition*, Page's *History and the Homeric Iliad*, Kirk's *The Songs of Homer*, and Webster's *From Mycenae to Homer*. Compared with those books, the historical dimension of my study is marginal and in no way competes with any of their accounts. On the other hand, historically oriented scholars have often been complacent about examining the types of relationship one can plausibly assume between a fictional text and various levels of historical reality. My chief aim in the following pages, beyond sketching a minimal historical framework, is to set the stage for an extended analysis of the text by clarifying the network of temporal relations in which it exists. What is the relationship of the *Iliad* to the 'historical' events it purports to describe, to the contemporary world in which it originated, and to the 'heroic society' of which it is an image? And what is the relationship between the *Iliad* as a 'heroic poem' to the subsequent city culture in which it became a canonical text?

Herodotus, writing in the latter half of the fifth century BCE, expressed the conventional wisdom of his day when he dated Homer, the author of both the *Iliad* and the *Odyssey*, about 400 years before his own time. Most modern think that a later date is more likely: 'the *Iliad* at least, seems from the evidence of art and literature to have been in circulation by about 630' (West 1999, 364).

Modern archaeologists have reconstructed the history of settlements on the site of Troy beyond 3000 BCE. Homer's Troy to them is 'Troy VIIa'. This settlement came to a violent end around 1200 BCE and was in all probability destroyed by war, although a fire cannot be ruled out. Was it destroyed in the 'Trojan War', i.e. a collective expedition by mainland Greeks? The ancients had no doubt on this score. Even so sceptical a writer as Thucydides used the *Iliad* as a source for his review of early Greek history on the assumption that by discounting the elaborations of poetic fancy he could recover the historical truth about a pan-Hellenic expedition. Modern scholars are divided on the subject. Some think that the very existence of the *Iliad* is proof that such an expedition must have taken place, although it surely did not last ten years or have Helen as its cause. Others point to instances in which we have independent evidence about the event a heroic poem purports to celebrate and can only marvel at the gap between history and fiction. No heroic poem without ruins, Albin Lesky (1966, 12) has written. From our knowledge of other heroic poetry we may conclude that the mere ruins in the Troad were a sufficient factual irritant to produce in time the pearl of the *Iliad*. We may well believe that the ruins of Troy were the 'cause' of the *Iliad*, but we must not expect the *Iliad* to tell us much about the cause of those ruins.

1

Whether or not there was a 'Trojan War', the *Iliad* rests on a tradition of verse-making that goes back centuries beyond Homer and probably reaches into Mycenaean times. Homer's Greeks do not call themselves Hellenes as the Greeks of the classical period (and probably of Homer's day) did, and the political map of the *Iliad* reflects an old pattern of settlements that was radically altered with the population movements towards the end of the second millennium conveniently known as the Dorian invasion. The *Iliad* refers to some objects such as Nestor's cup or the boar's helmet that can be matched with Mycenaean artefacts discovered by modern archaeologists. In the case of the *phasganon arguroêlon*, the 'silver-studded sword', not only is there a corresponding artefact, but also the Homeric phrase can be matched with words that appear on the Mycenaean clay tablets inscribed in the Linear B script that represents an early form of Greek. Homer's poetic language also includes archaic words that predate the dialect divisions that took place centuries before his time. But Homer knew less about Mycenaean Greece than is taught today in a good undergraduate course. To illustrate his epics with Mycenaean pictures is a profound anachronism, even where the Homeric object has a Mycenaean origin, for it provides the verbal image with a pictorial equivalent that in most cases neither Homer nor his audience had ever seen. The past remembered in the *Iliad* and the Mycenae excavated by the twentieth-century archaeologist are two very different things.

Whatever the precise date of the *Iliad,* the story of the pan-Hellenic expedition against Troy has much more to do with Greece around 700 BCE than with the late Mycenaean age. The world of the Greek city states was characterised both by a propensity for internecine rivalry and by a strong sense of cultural identity and superiority. Greeks of whatever ethnic origin divided the world into those who 'talk Greek' (*hellênizein*) and all the others who make unintelligible noises and are therefore fitly called 'bar-bar-ians'. While Greece never achieved political unity, it developed common religious festivals and competitions that united, for the duration of the event, even cities that were at war. The institutions that maintained the sense of pan-Hellenic identity date back to the eighth century – above all, the Olympic Games, whose beginnings the Greeks dated back to 776 BCE by our calendar. The most powerful of these pan-Hellenic institutions is of course the *Iliad*. One may well ask whether the Greeks, who from the eighth century on established colonies in much of the eastern and some of the western Mediterranean, would have resisted the centrifugal tendencies of such geographical dispersal had it not been for the common past, the common religion and the common set of values that the *Iliad* 'created', if only by putting traditional materials in canonical form.

The story of the expedition of 'all the Achaeans' against Troy is not a poem 'about' Mycenaean Greece, but it is, in a different sense of 'about', a poem about the pan-Hellenic consciousness of the *polis* world in its earliest stage. In what sense is the *Iliad* about a 'heroic society' existing in a particular place at a particular time? Many scholars believe that, despite certain distortions due to poetic licence, the *Iliad* is a reliable description of a heroic society. A.W.H. Adkins in particular has provided elaborate analyses of the value system of Homeric heroic society, but his hypotheses have not gone unchallenged by philosophers or historians (Long 1970, Snodgrass 1974).

It is unquestionably true that the characters of the *Iliad* for the most part observe a warrior code that can be found in many real societies. Courage, physical strength, loyalty to friends and kinsmen, revenge, and hospitality to strangers are important elements of this code. It is an aristocratic code, and there is no reason to doubt that some version of it governed the lives of the landowners who were the normative part of Homer's audience. But it is one thing to say that the upper strata of Homer's audience lived according to a warrior code and another to claim that they formed the heroic society of which the *Iliad* is a description. Greek has given us the useful word *pornography* (writing about whores). One might coin the analogue *hero-graphy* and capture an essential aspect of heroic poetry: it is never a description but always a fiction of desire, born out of a fascination with, yearning for, and revulsion at, physical violence.

The modern reader, by which I mean the reader since the eighteenth century, has typically approached the *Iliad* from a perspective of nostalgic inferiority. The characters and actions of the *Iliad* breathe a fullness and simple strength that he lacks, and he mourns the loss of the glamorous world that produced such glamorous poetry. But there never was a world of heroic glamour to correspond to its poetic image. 'Heroic' is an adjective in the past tense. To the poet of the *Iliad* the present is inferior to an image of the past endowed with greater fullness. Men like Hektor or Aias, let alone Achilles, no longer exist. Three times he tells us that it would take two modern men to hoist the stones his heroes lift with ease (5.303, 12.447, 20.286.) And even the characters in the poem share in this regression towards a fuller past: in the first book Nestor in the presence of Agamemnon and Achilles reminisces about a time when he fought with men the like of which he will not see again (1.262). G.S. Kirk (1962, 135-8) has argued persuasively that the impoverished material conditions following the collapse of Mycenaean culture were a particularly rich breeding ground for the heroic tradition of which Homer is the culmination. But ultimately the heroic vision is the product of the more radical and metaphysical poverty that is the subject of meditation in Wallace Stevens's *Esthétique du mal*:

> Natives of poverty, children of malheur,
> The gaiety of language is our seigneur.

Homer, his contemporaries and his modern readers inhabit the first line, Achilles and Hektor the second. A failure to observe that crucial distinction will ruin our understanding of the sense in which the *Iliad* is a poem 'about' heroic society.

Occasionally in the *Iliad* we catch a glimpse of a less heroic everyday world. The most striking passages of this kind are the shield of Achilles (18.478) and Nestor's narrative of his role in the war with the Epeians (11.671). The latter is a story of greed and revenge and deals with a dispute of two villages over horses and cattle. It is a three-day affair, and perhaps more than any other part of the *Iliad* it gives a sense of what warfare in the eighth century may have been like. The former is an encyclopaedic tableau of the real world, telling us about marriage, justice, war, harvesting and celebration. It is an ordinary and 'realistic' world, made radiant, but not elevated, by the skill of Hephaistos. In the *Odyssey* such glimpses are more common; in particular, Odysseus' false accounts of his adventures describe an unheroic, almost mean-spirited world. It would be quite wrong to see in such passages the traces of a more 'modern' world. Rather, they reveal the everyday world that underlies both the *Iliad* and the *Odyssey*, and they tell us a great deal about the imaginative energy that wrested from this simple and poor world the austere and splendid vision of force that inspires the *Iliad*.

We know much less about the world in and for which Homer wrote than about the

3

world that made of his poems a kind of Scripture. Homer was 'the poet' par excellence in the world of the Greek city states, and the *Iliad* and *Odyssey* were what Eric Havelock has called a 'tribal encyclopaedia', through story and example conveying information about the entire range of human affairs. Is it surprising that classical Athens looked for guidance to poems celebrating a heroic society? The question loses its point as soon as we recognise the heroic world as a vision in the past rather than an image of a once existing world. Moreover, the vision is deeply rooted in a city culture. What differentiates the *Iliad* from other heroic poems is the significance of Troy as setting and theme. It is true that Priam's palace is all we ever see inside Troy. But one need only look at the banqueting-hall in *Beowulf* to recognise that Troy is much more than an extended royal palace. The walls of Troy enclose and define a city.

Historians of Greek moral thought like Adkins have made much of the distinction between the competitive values of the warrior and the cooperative values of the citizen. The distinction is real but it should not be bridged by a theory of evolution. The warrior code retained its relevance and appeal not only in the militaristic climate of Sparta, but also in the 'softer' Athens, which took no less pride in its citizen army than in its cultural accomplishments. And the fact that the warrior code dominates the *Iliad* to the seeming exclusion of everything else reflects less a historical stage of development than the poem's unremitting concentration on the marginal situation of war.

The warrior code is less foreign to the citizen reader than some evolutionary theories suggest. A similar point can be made about the aristocratic bent of the *Iliad*. Is there not a fundamental opposition between the democratic spirit of Athens and the exclusive spirit of the warrior caste in the *Iliad*? The exclusiveness is beyond question. The *Iliad* is rather like a club and bestows on its members privileges that persist in the face of grave moral shortcomings. Take Paris, a womaniser and fighter of dubious velour. Hektor is not afraid to scold him in public, but in the end even Paris remains a member in good standing and does not forfeit the privileges such standing confers. What those privileges are is made emphatically clear in the Thersites scene of the second book. Thersites is not a member – in fact, he is the only non-member in the *Iliad* – and he is the aristocrat's image of a perfect plebeian: an ugly loudmouth and coward. He stands up in the assembly and rails at Agamemnon. What he says is very similar to what Achilles had said, but it does not matter, for someone like him has no right to speak in the first place. His presumption must be brutally checked, and Odysseus does not hesitate to do so, first in words and then in deed (2.265-70):

> So he spoke and dashed the sceptre against his back and
> shoulders, and he doubled over, and a round tear dropped from him,
> and a bloody welt stood up between his shoulders under
> the golden sceptre's stroke, and he sat down again, frightened,
> in pain, and looking helplessly about wiped off the tear-drops.
> Sorry though the men were they laughed over him happily …

Once the distinction between members and non-members is made, however, the *Iliad* pays no further attention to it. In this it is very unlike, say, *Don Quixote* or Shakespearian plays, in which a high-low distinction is a recurring structural element. Those who gain admission to the narrator's world form a society of peers with little internal differentiation along hierarchic lines. There is a natural hierarchy of youth and age, and there are kings and priests to whom special respect is due by virtue of their office. There is also the pecking order maintained by the warriors' continuing rivalry among themselves. Nonetheless, it is fundamentally a society of equals with a remarkable ease and simplicity of manners. This state of affairs is mirrored on Olympus, where the gods, while mindful of the power and pre-eminence of Zeus, do not hesitate to answer back or quarrel with him.

Homer's Athenian audience was very receptive to an ethos that was exclusive and competitive but anti-hierarchic. Quite apart from the fact that the privilege of citizenship was beyond the reach of slaves and resident aliens, Athenian society was hardly egalitarian. With the great exception of Socrates, most famous Athenians came from 'good' families whose commitment to politics, inseparable from warfare, found a ready mirror in the image of the heroic world. In Athens, just as in Homer's day, the values of the upper class established the moral norms and canons of taste, even though Homer's audience was never restricted to that class. Those values and a commitment to competitive excellence governed the conception of the typical. If we think of the normative citizen reader as a young man of the class that produced Kimon, Miltiades, Perikles, and Alkibiades, the gap between the city and the heroic world narrows considerably.

The poet(s) of Homer

The word 'Homer' refers with great precision to the 15,693 lines of the *Iliad* and the 12,110 lines of the *Odyssey*. These poems must have been made by some human(s), but we know nothing about who s/he or they were. Nor do we know with any degree of precision just how they were made or how long it took to make the versions that we read today. Such facts as we know point to a paradox: the *Iliad* and *Odyssey* are deeply rooted in oral traditions of verse-making, but they have spent most of their lives as highly canonical texts in cultures dependent on writing. Without writing they would long have been lost. We do not know whether writing merely preserved them or whether it played a role in shaping them as well. It remains a tempting speculation that 'Homer' is the result of a highly consequential encounter of two language technologies during the transition from an 'oral' to a 'literate' culture – a transition in which, as in other major cultural shifts, the 'old' is never completely replaced but lives on in different ways and shapes the ways of the 'new'.

To begin with known facts, since the middle of the second century BCE the texts of the *Iliad* and *Odyssey* have been transmitted with remarkable fidelity. The editor of the recent and authoritative Teubner text, Martin West, has identified some 160 interpolated passages that add up to just over 200 lines or 1.25% of the text. By contrast, the quarto and folio editions of *King Lear* differ in more than 10% of their lines. Textual variance within a particular Homeric line is rarely of interest. Is there a single substantive disagreement about the interpretation of a Homeric scene that turns on choosing this rather than that reading?[1] We know from papyrus fragments that prior to the second century BCE the Homeric texts fluctuated considerably in the number of lines. By contrast later multi-line papyrus fragments overwhelmingly show the same

---

[1] Compare this with the large literature on the duals in *Iliad* 9, perhaps the most celebrated textual crux in Greek literature. The textual tradition unanimously uses a dual verb form to refer to the three men who try to assuage Achilles' anger. There has not been and probably will never be a fully persuasive solution.

number of lines in the same order. The texts of the *Iliad* and *Odyssey* have been extraordinarily stable for two millennia. We also know that from the early third century on successive generations of increasingly professional scholars spent much labour on those texts. The most famous of them was Aristarchus. Their work is known to us at third or fourth hand through the scholia or marginal notes that have survived in some manuscripts, notably Venetus A, the most important manuscript source for the *Iliad*. It is not entirely clear what impact their work had on the stabilisation of the Homeric vulgate, but stabilised it was.

Was that stabilisation an act of consolidation or creation? Do we have Homer's *Iliad* or that of Aristarchus? Plato is an important witness. When he cites a single Homeric line, it nearly always differs a little from what we read today – perhaps because he was quoting from memory. On the other hand, when he quotes multi-line passages they do not differ from the vulgate in the order of lines. Take this evidence with generous dashes of hope, and you conclude that the poets and philosophers of fifth- and fourth-century Greece read more or less the same Homer that we do.

As we move back from the classical to the archaic period of Greek history it becomes increasingly difficult to square the ideal of a faithfully preserved *Iliad* with the practical difficulties surrounding the accurate transmission across generations of a document of 16,000 lines in a world that had only recently re-acquainted itself with writing.

The Mycenaean Greeks used writing for administrative and commercial purposes (Linear B). After the collapse of their civilisation around 1200 BCE, writing disappeared from Greece for four centuries. Towards the end of the ninth century BCE, the Greeks adapted an alphabet from the Phoenicians. The date is suggested by the resemblance of the Greek alphabet to Phoenician scripts current during that period. We know very little about the spread or degree of literacy in Greece until roughly 600 BCE when inscriptions become more frequent. Only a handful of documents can with any confidence be dated before 700 BCE. The most famous of these, a cup found in 1953 in Ischia, is a plain piece of pottery with a three-line inscription, partly iambic and partly hexametric. The inscription is fragmentary; a plausible reading attributes aphrodisiac powers to the modest cup and therefore ranks it above the 'cup of Nestor' (*Nestoros potêrion*), about which Book 11 of the *Iliad* has much to say. It is a striking feature of the inscription that its orthography and punctuation imply a system of prosodic notation for hexametric verse. The few other inscriptions from around 700 BCE also are in hexameters.

The evidence, slender as it is, is sufficient to establish the fact that writing was known during the period 725-650 BCE that most scholars would agree on as a critical period for the genesis of the Homeric poems. There is, however, no positive evidence to suggest that the Greeks of that period had the document management technologies for coping with texts as long as the *Iliad*. I use modern computer terminology advisedly to draw attention to the 'scale' problems of a very new technology. The early fixing and transmission of the Homeric texts will forever remain a mystery.

Moving back in time deepens some problems but produces greater clarity about others. Internal evidence and analogies with other cultures suggest that the most striking features of Homeric verse-making are rooted in the practices of an oral culture. Indeed, in its general outlines this is as known a fact about the Homeric poems as the fact of their extraordinarily stable written transmission since the second century BCE.

1. Introduction

But this certainty only produces more uncertainties about the ways in which to relate the known and the unknown. Hypotheses about negotiating these relations have always been shaped less by evidence – of which there is very little – than by individual or generational dispositions. Hypotheses divide along answers to three somewhat overlapping questions.

The first question is whether in looking at human achievements, especially of a highly significant kind, you incline towards a 'strong author' or a 'weak author' view. The second question is whether you think of the *Iliad* and *Odyssey* as poems that largely stay within the parameters of their genre or whether you think of them as transformational works that relate to their generic backgrounds in roughly the ways in which the *Matthew Passion* or the *Marriage of Figaro* relate respectively to the musical genres of passion and *opera buffa*. You can see the traces of *opera buffa* in every scene of *The Marriage of Figaro,* but you cannot predict the opera from the genre.

The third question is whether in the creation of the Homeric poems you give to writing a role that goes beyond the mechanical preservation of documents that were generated in and for a different medium. Just about every theory about the composition and authorship of the Homeric poems since the days of F.A. Wolf can be defined very satisfactorily in terms of where it positions itself vis-à-vis these three questions.

The nineteenth-century division of German Homeric scholars into 'unitarians' and 'analysts' or, as they were known jocularly, *Einheitshirten* and *Liederjäger* (unity shepherds vs. song hunters) was very much a division between strong and weak views of authorship. F.A. Wolf in his *Prolegomena* set the agenda for this quarrel when he turned a casual remark by Cicero into a theory of a 'Pisistratean recension' according to which Homer consisted of separate and anonymous poems floating in a generic space of epic narrative until the tyrant Pisistratus in the middle of the sixth century ordered them to be stitched together. A very peculiar and distinctly German version of a 'strong author' theory appears in the many books and articles in which the author seeks to rescue a Homeric Gulliver from his Lilliputian copyists, redactors, imitators etc. Wilamowitz's *Ilias und Homer* is the most famous of these works and still worth reading despite or because of its wilful brilliance.

A powerful 'weak author' component is the reverse side of Milman Parry's interest in the systematic character of Early Greek epic diction. A very different kind of 'weak author' or 'strong tradition' theory appears in the Multitext Homer project by Gregory Nagy and his students. The focus here is not on the *ipsissima verba* of a putative single author but on a living tradition in which you see textual variance as the many eddies and cross-currents of a a river flowing through time. This view is strongly shaped by theories about *mouvance* in medieval French epic, and the eventual stabilisation of the text is something of a fall into fixity.

Milman Parry's son Adam took a markedly 'strong author' position in a famous essay with the programmatic title 'Have we Homer's *Iliad?* ' to which the answer is 'yes'. In a very declarative manner Martin West opens his Latin preface to 1998 Teubner edition of the *Iliad* with the sentence:

Ilias materiam continet iamdiu per ora cantorum diffusam, formam autem contextumque qualem nos novimus tum primum attinuit, cum conscripta est; quod ut fieret, unius munus fuit maximi poetae.

7

(The Iliad contains materials that had circulated among oral poets for a long time, but it received the form and context in which we know it when it was first written down, which was the work of a single and very great poet.)

West's strong author is a writer. Albert Lord and his student Richard Janko also posit a strong author, but they see him as dictating his poem. How much of a difference is there between having a secretary and knowing how to type? There may be less difference between Janko, Lord, and West than there is between any of them and G.S. Kirk's theory of the 'monumental composer' who changed the rules of the epic game but did not use writing directly or indirectly and whose poems were transmitted orally but in fixed form for almost two centuries.

The arguments about Homer and writing typically take the form of culture following commerce. The Greek alphabet resulted from contacts between Greek and Phoenician traders, but poets were quick to explore a new medium. Barry Powell reverses this causal chain and argues that it was the creation of the *Iliad* that spurred the introduction of writing into Greece. Here writing appears almost as the cause of a strong author position.

In the strong author theories surveyed here the emphasis is on the change of scale and on the role that writing did or did not play. A greater emphasis on qualitative change is found in Karl Reinhardt's famous essay of 1937 on the judgement of Paris. Reinhardt sees a tradition of straightforward stories with simple morals, whether the ruse of Penelope or the judgment of Paris, and he locates the genius of the poets of the *Iliad* and *Odyssey* in their ability to transform those stories into 'epic situations' of a scope and ethos that leave the source narratives far behind. Reinhardt and Kirk lived in very different worlds of classical scholarship, but there are interesting overlaps between Kirk's 'monumental composer' and Reinhardt's shaper of epic situations.

Compared with these big questions, it is a lesser and more practical question whether or not you assign the *Iliad* and *Odyssey* to the 'same author', however you understand 'author'. Internal evidence offers much support for and little resistance to reading the *Odyssey* as an intentional and complementary sequel to the *Iliad*. It is a little easier to see such an ambition as the work of a different author, and if one is concerned with articulating the very deep thematic and narrative differences between the two epics it is a convenient fiction to think of their authors as different as well. But no difference between the *Iliad* and *Odyssey* in terms of language, technique or perspective is so deep that it could not be contained within the work of a single author. There are also deep phrasal affinities between the *Odyssey* and some parts of the *Iliad*, notably the last book. These go well beyond commonality of a shared epic idiom. They have puzzled scholars since the mid-nineteenth century and remain a puzzle (see p. 185 for a fuller discussion).

What about the 'real' Homer, the person who certainly composed the *Iliad* and perhaps the *Odyssey* as well? If you are a 'weak author' person, the question makes little sense. Homer is just a name to personalise a tradition, and perhaps we would be better off not using the name (Nagy 1992, 28). But the 'strong author' scholars are just as sceptical on biographical matters. They no longer believe, as Wilamowitz or Schadewaldt did, that you can extract from the ancient sources about Homer's life a story that bears any semblance to what actually happened (Graziosi 2002, 14). The sources tell you much about the needs of people in some particular then and there, and from that perspective their informational value is far from trivial. But they tell you nothing about 'Homer'. Martin West, the strongest of 'strong author' proponents, has an essay on 'The Invention of Homer' in which he argues that there was indeed a *maximus poeta,* that he was responsible for the *Iliad* in very much the form in which we read it today, but that we know nothing about him except that his name was not 'Homer', which was instead a back formation from the name of a professional guild of rhapsodes called the Homeridae (West 1999).

Homo homericus and the question of oral poetry

For the Greeks, Homer was simply The Poet and as such a timeless authority. While the Homeric poems have maintained a highly canonical status through 2,500 years of Western culture, later ages have tended to put an existential divide between themselves and 'Homer'. You see some of this in a Plutarchan anecdote about the last meeting of Brutus and Portia. I quote from North's famous Elizabethan translation (Plutarch 1579, p. 1065):

> There *Porcia* being ready to depart from her husband *Brutus* and to returne to ROME did what she could to dissemble the griefe and sorow she felt at her hart: But a certaine paynted table bewrayed her in the ende, although vntill that time she always shewed a constant and pacient mind. The deuise of the table was taken out of the Greeke stories, howe *Andromachè* accompanied her husband *Hector* when he went out of the citie of TROY to goe to the warres, and how *Hector* deliuered her his litle sonne, and how her eyes were neuer of him. *Porcia* seeing this picture, and likening her selfe to be in the same case, she fell a weeping: and comming thither oftentymes in a day to see it, she wept still. *Acilius* one of *Brutus* friendes perceiuing that, rehearsed the verses *Andromachè* speaketh to this purpose in *Homer*:
>
> > Thou Hector art my father, and my mother, and my brother,
> > And husband eke, and in all: I mind not any other.
>
> Then *Brutus* smyling, aunswered againe: but yet (sayd he) I can not for my part say vnto *Porcia* as *Hector* aunswered *Andromachè* in the same place of the Poet:
>
> > Tush, meddle thou vvith vveying devvly owt
> > Thy mayds their task, and pricking on a clowt.

This is a classic instance of a belated perspective with its characteristic mix of inferiority, condescension, and regret. Some 1600 years later we encounter Alexander Pope reflecting on the scene in which Nausikaa does her laundry on the beach:

> It has been further objected, that the Poet gives an unworthy employment to Nausicaa, the daughter of a King; but such Critics form their idea of ancient, from modern greatness: It wou'd be now a meanness to describe a person of Quality thus employ'd, because custom has made it the work of persons of low condition: It would be now thought dishonourable for a Lady of high station to attend the flocks; yet we find in the most ancient history extant, that the daughters of Laban and Jethro, persons of power and distinction, were so employ'd, without any dishonour to their quality. In short, these passages are to be look'd upon as exact pictures of the old World, and consequently as valuable remains of Antiquity. (Note on Odyssey, 6.31; 6.35 in Pope's translation)

9

Between Plutarch and Pope, there is the sixteenth-century poet Ronsard who in the preface to his *Franciade* professes to emulate Homer's 'naïve facilité' rather than Vergil's 'curieuse diligence.' 'Naïf' here is closer to its etymological source *nativus* than to our 'naive', but the opposition is structurally related to Schiller's later opposition of 'naive' and 'sentimental' poetry.

That opposition turned out to be a powerful and deeply consequential ideological construct. We might turn for a moment to Gibbon, who in his discussion of the ancient Germans remarks that 'the use of letters is the principal circumstance that distinguishes a civilised people from a herd of savages incapable of knowledge or reflection.' There is an

> immense distance between the man of learning and the illiterate peasant. The former, by reading and reflection, multiplies his own experience, and lives in distant ages and remote countries; whilst the latter, rooted to a single spot, and confined to a few years of existence, surpasses but very little his fellow-labourer, the ox, in the exercise of his mental faculties. (*Decline and Fall*, 1.91)

In tone and substance this passage from 1776 stands at the other end of a position that is eloquently caught by the title of Herder's famous anthology of 1778, *Stimmen der Völker im Lied* or 'voices of the peoples in song'. What matters most is caught, not in speech, but in song, not by a learned individual, but by many voices of many peoples. One could do worse than see the history of Homeric criticism as an endless quarrel (sometimes friendly, often not) between readers whose habits of the heart or mind resonate more with Gibbon or with Herder. Evidence is very unlikely to settle the matter.

In his *Essay on Criticism* Pope envisages Virgil imitating Homer and attributes to him the discovery that 'Nature and Homer ... were the same.' 'Nature' here refers to universal standards, but it is easily modulates into Rousseau's 'Back to Nature', and some overtones of civilisation as 'dis-ease' are clearly audible in Pope's nostalgic evocation of Nausikaa and her laundry. And 'Homer' is the most iconic version of the poet as the child of nature. While the opposition of nature and art is an old idea, it is intensified in the late eighteenth century and adds a new twist to the Myth of the Two Poets, which in England found its best expression in the oppositions of Shakespeare and Milton or Homer and Vergil. The myth is a poetic version of the Fall and contrasts the self-effacing *naive* with the self-projecting *sentimental* poet. Homer had four great advantages over Shakespeare as the prototype of the self-effacing poet:

1. Nothing was known about his person, and it was not even clear whether his name was a real name. Thus he was more radically anonymous than Shakespeare, whose biography was never so mysterious as it was popular to assume.
2. Tradition pictured him blind, thus depriving him of a further powerful aspect of identity.
3. While Shakespeare in the opinion of Ben Jonson had small Latin and less Greek, Homer, according to the best knowledge of eighteenth-century historians, could not write at all.
4. He was original and spontaneous in the sense that nothing was known about his predecessors.

1. Introduction

Anonymous, blind, unlettered – what better image could there be of an original genius existing prior to the division of self and community, subject and object, thought and feeling, thing and meaning, concrete and abstract, or whatever other oppositions have been used to illustrate this particular ideological construct?

Homo homericus

A very important strand of twentieth-century Homeric scholarship is rooted in nine-teenth-century evolutionary theory, whether Hegelian or Darwinian, and sees Homer's world as a stage in the cultural evolution of mankind. The debts of that scholarship to the concept of a 'naive' Homer are obvious. Hermann Fränkel's *Ways and Forms of Early Greek Thought* or Bruno Snell's *Discovery of the Mind* are books that carry their story lines in their title. E.R. Dodds' argument about Homeric shame culture or A.W.H. Adkins' theories of the competitive structure of Homeric society are other distinctive scholarly contributions of this type, where 'not yet' or 'no longer' are important words. Equally significant is a tendency to draw a very sharp line not merely between us and Homer but between Homer and the Greek world for which the *Iliad* and *Odyssey* were the most canonical works.

The *reductio ad absurdum* of this approach is probably *The Origin of Conscious-ness in the Breakdown of the Bicameral Mind* by Julian Jaynes, who took the narrative conventions of divine intervention in the Homeric epics very literally and argued that the Greeks of Homer's day were wired differently and that the Socratic *daimonion* was the residue of an earlier age in which each human had a 'bicameral' mind in which one chamber could be addressed directly by the gods.

Homo homericus and oral poetry

Julian Jaynes' *homo homericus* never existed, but he demonstrates the temptations of pushing a hypothesis beyond any reasonable limits. Something similar can be said of what is sometimes called 'hard' Parryism, a very rigid insistence on the 'oral' nature of Homeric poetry. While few scholars any longer hold to its more doctrinaire forms, it is still helpful to review the basic assumptions of a method of inquiry that in its details is much too technical for the purposes of this inquiry.

It was known in the eighteenth century that the *Iliad* and *Odyssey* originated in a world that was unfamiliar with writing. In his *Prolegomena* of 1795, a milestone in the history of modern textual scholarship, F.A. Wolf made this conventional wisdom a point of departure for systematic reflections on the status of poetry in such a world and on the problems affecting its transmission. Wolf's *Prolegomena* set the agenda for a century or more of Homeric scholarship. Scholars furiously disagreed about whether the *Iliad* was the work of one or of many hands and whether a single hand should be posited at the beginning or end of the process of composition. But these disagreements did not affect a growing consensus that the poems employed a *Kunstsprache* or 'artistic dialect' (not unlike 'country' or 'blues' in popular music), and that the individual poet's art was steeped in his tradition to the point of disappear-ing in it.

It was the achievement of Milman Parry in the 1920s to rearrange the pieces of that consensus so as to give it the shape of a very strong theory. Parry was a peculiar

11

mixture of Herder and Henry Ford. He was more attracted to exploring how a collective and ethnically grounded creativity speaks through a particular maker than to tracing the ways in which such a maker plays with or reshapes a tradition. Thus in the final sentence of his MA thesis the *Iliad* and *Odyssey* are described as works in which 'the genius of the artist has blended with that of his race so inextricably that the two are hard to distinguish: they can only be realised in the perfection of the result'. In the same work the progressive individuality of the post-Homeric hymns strikes him as the cause of their poetic Fall: 'The later poems are graceful, charming, but they have not the greatness of the earlier hymn, which, losing nothing in grace or charm, has added to them a grave reverence and a spirit of universality ... The later hymns have allowed a definite impress of personality to creep in' (Parry 1971, 431, 430).

But Parry was also an American in the age of the assembly line and fascinated by the efficiency of systematic processes that eliminated redundancy. His new idea was not that Homeric poetry was oral or heavily conventional. Rather it was the hypothesis that the language of Early Greek epic is a system of metrical production that maximises both extension and economy: there was a solution or 'formula' for every contingency (the principle of extension), but there was only one solution for every contingency (the principle of economy). You might say that in Parry's vision of epic poetry *langue* and *parole* coincide.

Parry's writings do not always speak with quite the same voice. But at its most distinctive, that voice sits at the intersection of a deeply romantic and a deeply mechanical anti-individualism. The resultant hypotheses were immensely productive in terms of the insights they generated about stylistic and structural patterns in Early Greek epic. They were also troublingly totalising and at deep odds both with the poetry and the people described by it. Why would you want to describe a fundamentally ludic activity as a system with so little 'play' in it?

More significantly, how do you reconcile an aggressively self-denying theory of poetic production with the intensely self-seeking cast of characters that populate the world of Early Greek epic? The essence of parental advice in the *Iliad* is summed up in the line *aien aristeuein kai hupeirechon emmenai allôn* 'always excel and be ahead of the others' (6.208, 11.784). In the context of the *Iliad* the line refers to battle. But *aristeuein* literally means 'excel at whatever you do', and Hesiod's praise of 'good discord' in the opening of *Works and Days* may be seen as a gloss on the maxim and an explanation of how it works in the world of farmers, potters, builders, beggars, and – last but not least – poets:

> This is that Discord that stirs up even the helpless to hard work,
> Seeing a man gets eager to work on beholding a neighbour
> Who is exceedingly wealthy and makes haste ploughland and sowing,
> Putting his household in order: so neighbour competing with neighbour
> Runs after riches and therefore this Discord benefits mankind.
> Every potter begrudges another, and artists do likewise;
> Every beggarman envies a beggar, and poets are rivals.

A strongly competitive element is also present in a famous passage from the *Hymn to Apollo* (169-73):

1. Introduction

Hail and farewell to you, maidens, remember me kindly hereafter
When anybody of men upon earth, say a wayfaring stranger
Come to this island, should ask your opinion and pose you this question,
'Who, do you think, is the man that is *sweetest of singers*, O maidens,
Of those that visit you here? And in which do you take *the most pleasure?*'
Answer him then well together, unanimously in my favour:
'He is a blind man whose home is on Chios, that rugged and rockbound
Island, and all of his poems are excellent, now and hereafter.'

The Greek text of the last line read*s tou metopisthen aristeuousin aoidai* and uses the same verb that expresses the relentless quest for excellence and individual distinction that animates Homer's characters. This very explicit aspect of Early Greek culture is oddly erased by the most austere version of Parry's oral poetics.

It is important to remember that Parry made his decisive contributions to Homeric scholarship before he knew anything about the South Slavic guslars with which his name is often associated. They are the work of a linguist with a strong systematising urge, and they are entirely based on close scrutiny of the Homeric texts. They are also largely a theory of the microstructure of Homeric poetry – a point emphasised by Adam Parry when he edited his father's papers under the title *The Making of Homeric Verse*. On the other hand, Parry's theory was based on a division between oral and written literature, and it remains a paradigm of a theory that locates Homer on the other side of a very deep divide.

Important technical aspects of Parry's work were challenged by Hoekstra *in Homeric Modifications of Formulaic Prototypes* (1965) and by Hainsworth in *The Flexibility of the Homeric Formula* (1968). The titles of these quite technical monographs give a good indication of their aim to soften the rigid excesses of Parry's theory. In a recent monograph on *Formular Economy in Homer* (2007) Rainer Friedrich grounds a Homeric poetics on the 'breaches' of formular economy. The insights are good, but the terminology is awkward and points to the lingering survival of the greatest initial shortcoming of Parry's hypothesis, its failure to conceive of the conventions of oral poetry as a rule-governed but open-ended system whose normal output would always include unpredictable, playful, and redundant phenomena.

Parry's work was continued and extended by Albert Lord, who in 1960 published his *The Singer of Tales*, an anatomy of oral poetry that is based on Homeric and Serbo-Croatian heroic poetry but claims validity for all oral poetry. The Parry-Lord theory, for all its wealth of empirical observation, cannot deny its derivation from the Myth of the Two Poets. It posits oral poetry as far more than poetry produced, performed and transmitted without the aid of writing. It is the expression of a distinct *mentalité* radically opposed at all levels to the world of literacy. The dogmas of the theory may be stated as follows:

1. The oral poet has no 'style' of his own – the very word betrays its origin in a literary culture. He composes with the aid of a stock of formulas inherited from the tradition.
2. The oral poem is formulaic at every level of organisation. Stock phrases are combined into sentences; stock themes into larger narrative units, etc.
3. The oral poet improvises, and there is no distinction between the acts of composi-

13

tion and performance. The concepts of a fixed text and of individual authorship, fundamental to a literate culture, make no sense in an oral context in which singer, tale and audience are merged in a communal tradition.
4. An oral tradition cannot survive the advent of literacy.

From these principles one can deduce two additional methodological rules:

5. The 'reader' of oral poetry must unlearn the habits of literacy if he wants fully to enter into the spirit of oral poetry.
6. If you prove that a poem is oral at one level of organisation, you must read it as an oral poem at all levels of organisation.

The rigid application of these principles to the Homeric poems has always confronted critics with the dilemma of having to acknowledge the unquestionably oral nature of Homeric verse at the cost of rejecting many perceived qualities of the *Iliad* and *Odyssey* as figments of a literary imagination. Ruth Finnegan therefore did Homeric scholarship a great service by proving that the theory of oral poetry as different from literate poetry at every level of organisation is a myth that does not fit the facts. She surveyed a wide range of oral literature differing in genre, social function and geographical origin and demonstrated beyond any reasonable doubt that it is impossible to identify a set of traits common to all oral literature.

In some cultures, oral poems are a collective possession, but others have a distinct notion of individual authorship. Performance and composition often coincide, as they do in Serbo-Croatian poetry, but there is ample evidence for oral poems that are premeditated and recited on separate occasions, whether by the author or by someone else. There is considerable variety with regard to verbatim transmission. Above all, Finnegan showed that the relationship of oral to literate traditions is extremely flexible and that many oral traditions have co-existed with literacy and made use of it. The conclusion of her research is that the internal variety of oral traditions and the great flexibility of their relationship to literacy greatly weaken arguments from analogy. To say of a work that it is oral is to make a statement about its dominant mode of production and or transmission. Such a statement of itself says nothing about the organisation, complexity and spirit of a text so produced or transmitted. The proof that a poem is like a certain kind of oral poetry in some ways does not justify the inference that it will be like that poetry in other ways. 'Oral literature' is a vague concept with low explanatory power.

Since the eighties, the most productive approaches to style and language in the Homeric poems have moved away from the oral/literate divide and have instead focused on them as a special kind of speech. The guiding question has moved from 'How does this feature differ from literate poetry?' to 'How can we relate this feature to what we know about ordinary properties of spoken language?' The great advantage of such an approach is that it grounds the analysis of Homeric phenomena in what people know about how people talk. We can sidestep the conundrum of how people who are no longer 'oral' can understand a poetry that is not yet 'literate' and draw instead on common sense understandings of speech and performance as well as on the formal study of these phenomena in speech act theory, cognitive psychology, and such subdisciplines of linguistics as pragmatics and discourse analysis. Richard

Martin, Egbert Bakker, and Elizabeth Minchin have in their different ways explored these new avenues.

Oral and aural

The relationship between 'oral' and 'aural' deserves some comment. To base canons of interpretation on the capabilities of an audience and to define limits in terms of what can be heard seems much more plausible than to derive such canons and limits from the circumstances of composition, since nothing prevents us from attributing prodigious powers to an individual composer. On the other hand, Homer's audience must have been much like us in general ability, except that engrained dependence on the written word had not atrophied their memory and listening ability. Thus we can make a reasonably informed guess about the collective ability of Homer's audience. But if we base canons of interpretation on the putative ability of such an audience we run up against the awkward fact that its aural character does not distinguish it radically from the audiences of such unquestionably literate writers as Sophocles or Vergil.

The truth is that the dominant form of reception for all ancient literature was aural. Our notion of 'reading' is shaped by the technology of book production. But the modern form of the book, the codex consisting of leaves that are sewn together and permit direct access to any part of a text in any order, is an invention of late antiquity. Prior to the codex, readers followed a scroll, a cumbersome process that greatly restricted the freedom to move within a text. Add to this the difficulty of duplication and the resulting scarcity of texts and you have a culture that puts a high premium on the listener's ability to grasp and retain a text with as little recourse to written documents as possible. It is a reasonable assumption that a poet's work will be shaped by his sense of what an attentive audience can comprehend (though not necessarily at a first hearing). But, given the aural nature of classical culture, we cannot use this assumption to posit a radical difference between the audiences of Homer and Sophocles. Because aurality straddles the oral/literate divide we cannot use the facts of recitation and aural reception to posit canons of interpretation that differentiate the criticism of the *Iliad* from that of the *Oresteia* or *Oedipus Rex*. Because of the oral/aural equivocation I have freely and deliberately used the word 'reader' as the singular form of 'audience' wherever dealing with questions of response to the text of the *Iliad*. Modern audiences read the poem, ancient audiences listened to it. The difference is not trivial, and the modern reader must keep it in mind. But, whether audiences read the *Iliad* or listen to it, they must construe and respond to the meaning of the words, and this act of making sense may justly be called 'reading'.

The fact of recitation does, however, raise a serious problem when we consider the length of the *Iliad*. Assuming an average speed of ten lines a minute, a continuous recitation of the poem's 15,693 lines would last about twenty-six hours. A complete performance of the *Iliad*, therefore, takes at least three days. Such performances can be traced back as far as the Panathenaean festivals of the sixth century, and the possibility of a complete performance, however special the occasion, may have been in the poet's mind. But it is equally clear that most listeners got to know the *Iliad* in bits and pieces and many never heard it from beginning to end at all. In this regard they may not have differed from Wagner fans. Before the long-playing record, the privilege of listening to all of the *Ring of the Nibelung* in order was given only to a small percentage of the people who loved and admired that work.

It follows from these conditions that the poet had to think in narrative units that could be detached and would be intelligible and reasonably self-contained in recitation. The episodic nature of Homeric narrative amply meets this requirement: the Quarrel of Agamemnon and Achilles, the Duel of Menelaos and Paris, Hektor in Troy, the Embassy, etc., all are intelligible units of narrative for a listener who has a general knowledge of the Trojan War. But how did the poet create a sense of a whole in a narrative that his listeners would for the most part encounter piecemeal? Roughly speaking, the poet had a choice between two strategies. He could think of his work as a kind of encyclopaedia, in which case all he had to do was to find some way of arranging a set of quasi-autonomous songs in a plausible sequence. If, on the other hand, he thought of his work as an integrated whole, he had to shape his episodes in such a manner that the elements of unification would reside in the structure of the episodes rather than in their connection, since the connections would be absent from most performances. The choice, it cannot be emphasised too strongly, was Homer's, and the evidence is in the text. His tradition was no guide to him in this regard, nor is our knowledge of heroic poetry in general of much use in determining which of these strategies he did choose.

The *Iliad* and *Odyssey*

This is a book about the *Iliad,* but one cannot quite ignore the *Odyssey* because the two poems stand in so deeply a complementary and contrasting relationship to each other that important aspects become of either become intelligible only by looking at both. If there is such a thing as the 'Homeric', it is not equally diffused through the epics but exists as a powerful tension between the 'Iliadic' and the 'Odyssean'. The names of the protagonists have identical metrical properties, including a middle syllable whose length can bend to the requirements of the verse: Achi(l)leus or Ody(s)seus. Their characters could not be more different, as the opening lines of the epics make clear. In the first six words of the *Iliad* the hero's full patronymic name is framed by the destructive wrath that will engulf him:

> *mênin aeide thea Pêlêïadeô Achilêos*
> *oulomenên*

By contrast the hero of the *Odyssey* is not named: we learn about a man of many turns who is tossed about a lot:

> *andra moi ennepe, mousa, polutropon, hos mala polla*
> *planchthê*

Achilles is incapable of dissimulation and in his most famous speech says – not accidentally to Odysseus: 'I hate like hell a man who thinks one thing but says another' (9.312-13). Odysseus escapes from the cave of Polyphemus because in a lifesaving and clever word play he gives his name as *outis* or 'nobody'.

Achilles has always already made his choice between a short and glorious or long and inglorious life. He never marries and dies before Troy falls. Odysseus survives and returns home to his wife and son. On the other hand, Odysseus's troubles are all due to the fact that after his successful escape from the monster's cave he boasts loudly that he is not 'nobody' after all, but Odysseus, which allows Polyphemus to invoke the anger of Poseidon that will plague Odysseus during his long wanderings. And when Kalypso, the 'concealing' goddess, offers him anonymous immortality, he politely declines and chooses Penelope and death. In his own and more flexible way, the choice of Achilles is also his.

The complementary and contrasting relationship of the two epics is expressed not only by the very different ways in which the heroes make the same choice. It also emerges from the different verbal fabric of each epic. Consider the eighty most common nouns, verbs, and adjectives in Table 1. The words are arranged in five columns. All of them are very common, and most of them are used often in both epics. They may be thought of as the core vocabulary of Homeric epic. The words in the middle column are used at approximately the same rate in both epics. The words in the left and right columns are used respectively more often or much more often in the *Iliad* or *Odyssey*.

This table is quite informative, partly because it highlights striking differences between the two epics, but largely because it is so ordinary. It does not disclose any secrets, but it uses the language of numbers, which within its reductive domain has a peculiar clarity, to confirm what we know already in a vaguer way. When we look at texts from a remote culture, there is a strong tendency to exaggerate difference. But if we assume that the distribution of the most common words in a language is a good indicator of what matters to its speakers, the hierarchy of things, activities, and qualities that emerges from the list common Homeric words is remarkably intelligible to us.

Focusing on the middle column, which marks the common area of the two epics, we find 'man' and 'ship' at the top of the list of nouns: the masculine agent and the human artefact that extends human dominion beyond its original sphere. From a postmodern perspective we might theorise that humans have always already been 'transhuman'. At the next level we find the nouns for 'god' and 'hand', and *thumos*, here translated as 'heart', a peculiar psychological organ that is the seat of desire and the will to go after things but can also stand for life itself. Nouns 3-5 thus identify a power beyond man, the quality that makes him go after things, and the hand that enables him to execute his desire.

'All', somewhat more common in the *Odyssey*, is the most common of adjectives and is followed by 'much'. But a concern with quality is close behind. In addition to the ~ 300 occurrences of 'eus', usually in its adverbial form and closely corresponding to 'well', there are ~150 compounds with some 600 occurrences of the 'well-made' type. There is only one step from quality to competition, and it is a telling indicator of the centrality of competition that *aristos*, which occurs about once every thousand words in Early Greek epic, is twice as common as 'best' is in Shakespeare.

'Philos', used equally as noun or adjective, is perhaps best translated as 'near and dear'. Sometimes it is close in usage to a possessive pronoun, but it never quite loses its special force.

We also find two adjectives that can be translated as 'godlike', but are used quite differently. *Dios* attributes the power and beauty of gods to humans, while 'athanatos'

Table 1. Common Homeric nouns, verbs and adjectives

Iliad ++	Iliad +	shared	Odyssey+	Odyssey++
son (613)	big (735)	man (1039)	all (1110)	come (770)
horse (460)	throw (470)	ship (1003)	say (817)	hall (302)
war (281)	stand (455)	much (874)	dear (770)	house (271)
spear (261)	seize (415)	have (792)	word (440)	servant (266)
fight (248)	foot (289)	god (775)	bad (439)	household
lance (240)	charge (242)	heart (758)	companion	(266)
laos (230)	bronze (218)	hand (637)	(436)	woman (263)
forceful (191)	persuade	say (560)	father (420)	house (155)
	(204)	go (551)	arrive (330)	guest (212)
	fall (178)	give (486)	beautiful (319)	
		see (443)	earth (296)	
		earlier (407)	work (233)	
		godlike (406)		
		walk (405)		
		put (379)		
		carry (373)		
		know (341)		
		understanding		
		(341)		
		become (314)		
		lead (298)		
		want (294)		
		speak to (236)		
		follow (200)		
		speech (299)		
		child (298)		
		well (251)		
		town (237)		
		master (232)		
		quick (229)		
		best (225)		
		old man (218)		
		mother (210)		
		immortal (200)		
		goddess (199)		
		black (185)		
		broad (162)		
		alone (158)		

is only said of gods because gods are always and humans never 'deathless'. Homeric characters want to have all or much. They treasure things and people dear to them. They like quality, and they worry about the ways in which people are sometimes like and always unlike the gods.

1. Introduction

In the list of most common verbs we find much semantic overlaps, but we can construct from it a hierarchy of activities that goes something like this:

I walk
I speak
I have
I give
I see
I know
I lead
I want

If we now look at the columns to the left and the right, we see very clearly how the narrative priorities of the *Iliad* and *Odyssey* are reflected in the distribution of basic words. Simone Weil's famous characterisation of the *Iliad* as a poem of force shows up in the prominence of the adjective *megas* and *krateros*. Many critics have observed that the *Odyssey* is much more moralistic than the *Iliad,* and this shows up in the greater frequency of the ethico-aesthetic opposition of good/beautiful and bad/ugly.

It is not surprising that the more common verbs in the *Iliad* have to do with fighting and its associated activities, such as throwing, standing, seizing, or charging. By contrast, the *Odyssey* portrays a world of coming and going. It is also a world of more talk.

The clearest differences emerge at the level of nouns. The nouns that dominate the Iliad are 'son', 'horse', 'war', 'foot', various words for weapons, and *laos*, which in the *Iliad* typically refers to warriors *en masse*. Domestic nouns dominate the *Odyssey*. Indeed the survey of the Homeric base vocabulary articulates the sphere of gendered difference that is so bluntly expressed in Hektor's final words to Andromache (6.490-3):

> Go therefore back to our house, and take up your own work,
> the loom and the distaff, and see to it that your handmaidens
> ply their work also; but the men must see to the fighting,
> all men who are the people of Ilion, but I beyond others.

Samuel Butler's fanciful speculation that the *Odyssey* was composed by a woman is almost certainly wrong, but the perceptions on which it rests are deeply rooted in the lexical differences between the two epics.

From the distant perspective of a root vocabulary many differences of language and culture seem to disappear. What remains are things, concepts, qualities, and activities without which it is hard to imagine any human culture. On the other, even at so basic a level differences emerge. Consider the ten most common nouns in Homer and Shakespeare (Table 2). 'Lord', 'sir', 'king' speak to the more hierarchical structure of Shakespeare's world, while 'love' and 'time' mark out important semantic domains of Shakespearean and indeed of 'modern' literature as it has been theorised since the Quarrel of the Ancients and Moderns.

Table 2. Ten most common nouns in Homer and Shakespeare

Homer	Shakespeare
man (*anêr*)	lord
ship (*naus*)	man
god (*theos*)	sir
heart (*thumos*)	love
hand (*cheir*)	king
son (*huios*)	heart
horse (*hippos*)	eye
father (*patêr*)	time
word (*epos*)	hand
companion (*hetairos*)	father

The Homeric hexameter

'Hexameter' means literally 'six-measure'. In practice it is the name for the 'dactylic' hexameter. *Dactylos* is the Greek word for 'finger', and a dactyl is a metrical unit that, like a finger, combines a long with two short parts. All Greek epic poetry from Homer through Nonnos is written in hexameters. The Romans imitated many Greek verse forms, and all Latin epic poetry is written in hexameters as well.

As the universal metre of the most exalted ancient literary form, the hexameter has had enormous cultural prestige, but efforts to imitate it in European languages have not worked very well. In English and other Germanic languages, metre is stress-based rather than quantitative. Thus the dactylic measure, which from a musical perspective is in 2/4 time with a 'long-short-short' pattern, turns into a lilting and waltzlike measure that lacks *gravitas*.

The hexameter can be described by means of a three-digit code plus a hyphen and the space character. The first digit has values between 1 and 6 and locates the position of a measure in the verse as a whole. The second digit has the values of 1 or 2 and identifies the first or second 'element' of the measure. The third digit, with values 0, 1, or 2, states whether the second element consists of one long unit with a value of 0 or of two short units with the respective values of 1 or 2. If successive elements occur within a word they are linked by a hyphen. If they are not, they are separated by a space. Thus the first line of the *Iliad* looks as follows:

mênin	*aeide*	*thea*	*Pêlêïadeô*	*Achilêos*
110-121	122-210-221	222-310	320-410-421-422-510	521-522-610-620

The first element of a measure is always long. The second is typically divided into two short units but may be long. The resultant measure is called a 'spondee'. But there are two additional rules. First, in the fifth measure spondees are avoided or used only for special effect. Secondly, the sixth measure always consists of a spondee. The joint effect of these rules is that most hexameters end with the characteristic cadence 'long-short-short-long-long'.

Described in those terms, the hexameter is a rigidly defined structure. Variety enters through the tension between syntactic and prosodic patterns. Syntactic rules govern the sequence of words, while prosodic rules govern the sequence of measures. If syntactic and prosodic boundaries coincide, the respective patterns reinforce each other. If they do not coincide, they create tension. The former condition is called *diaeresis*, the latter *caesura*. These terms of art are respectively Greek and Latin words for 'cutting'. *Diaeresis* cuts or ends a word at a metrical boundary; *caesura* ends a word inside a measure.

The hexameter is a very long verse form. Each line consists of between 12 and 17 syllables. The Homeric average is 15.7 syllables per line, compared with 12 syllables for the iambic trimeter of Greek drama and the 10 syllables of English blank verse. Because it takes between five and six seconds to recite, a hexameter sits well above the three-second window within which human short-term memory can comfortably process things. For that reason, it is typically divided into two or more parts. Diaeresis after the third measure is strictly avoided because a symmetric division undermines hexametric identity. But caesuras after the first element or within the second element of the third measure are strongly favoured and divide the hexameter into nearly equal parts while avoiding destructive symmetry. The opening lines of the *Iliad* and *Odyssey* are respectively instances of the 'strong' and 'weak' caesura in the third measure:

1	2	3	4	5	6
mê-nin a-	*-eide the-*	*-a	Pê-*	*-lê-i-a-*	*-deô A-chi-*	*lê-os*
and-ra moi	en-ne-pe	Mou-sa	po-	-lut-ro-pon	hos ma-la	pol-la

Sixty per cent of Homeric hexameters have a *diaeresis* after the fourth measure so that the last third of the verse tends to be a phrase with a clear syntactic and metrical definition. *Colon* is the term of art for the metrical subunits that result from these typical segmentations of the hexameter. *Cola* of various types are the building blocks of hexametric composition, and for the most part the poet operates with pre-existing units that meet both syntactic and prosodic requirements. These are the 'formulae' of oral composition.

Interpreting Homeric repetitions

Homeric 'formulae' and Sinclair's 'idiom principle'

Homeric repetitions are discussed at greater length in Chapter 6, which is somewhat more technical and quantitative in its orientation than the rest of this book. In this section, I rely on the findings of that chapter and discuss the problems that confront modern readers when they try to gauge the extent of 'formulaic' language in Homer.

Although the Homeric poems are models of a literate culture in the fidelity of their transmission across more than two millennia, they differ markedly from other written texts in the extent and kind of phrasal repetition. Language is always shot through with repetitions at all levels of organisation, but contexts differ widely with regard to the threshold at which a repeated phenomenon is no longer taken for granted but attracts attention as a blunder, tic, or special effect. It appears that in Western writing the threshold values for phrasal repetition fluctuate in a remarkably narrow range. Such works as the *Republic*, the *Aeneid*, *Paradise Lost*, *Emma*, or *Das Kapital* differ in just about every other respect, but they do not differ much in their threshold values for repetition.

Homeric poetry consistently violates these threshold values. Imitators or parodists of Homer from Virgil through Fielding to Joyce have invariably focused on phrasal repetition as their point of departure. So did Milman Parry in his studies of the Homeric formula.

In looking a phrasal repetition in Homer, I follow the tendency of recent scholars, in particular Egbert Bakker, who look at Homeric verse as special kind of speech and sidestep the opposition of 'oral' and 'literate' with its attendant ideological baggage. My particular point of departure is what the linguist John Sinclair called the 'idiom principle'. Sinclair posited an 'open choice' principle according to which speakers at any point in an utterance may continue it any way they like, subject to the general rules of the language. But Sinclair argued that this principle does not sufficiently account for what happens in actual utterance and that a second principle is needed:

> The principle of idiom is that a language user has available to him or her a large number of semi-preconstructed phrases that constitute single choices, even though they might appear to be analyzable into segments. To some extent, this may reflect the recurrence of similar situations in human affairs; it may illustrate a natural tendency to economy of effort; or it may be motivated in part by the exigencies of real-time conversation. (Sinclair 1991, 110)

It is apparent from the slightest acquaintance with Homeric poetry that it depends in a particularly distinctive and extensive fashion on the idiom principle. 'Rosy-fingered Dawn' and 'swift-footed Achilles' are idioms of a special kind. Idioms of all kinds thrive on repetition. Their aesthetic is not that of the *mot juste*, exquisitely fitted to a particular context, but of what John Foley has called 'traditional reference'. C.S. Lewis in his *Preface to Paradise Lost* made a similar point when he compared our responses to Homeric phrases about the 'wine-dark sea' to our responses to the thing itself:

> Yes; but under all these, like a base so deep as to be scarcely audible, there is something which we might very lamely express by muttering 'same old sea' or 'same old morning'. (Lewis 1942, 21)

In this deceptively simple sentence Lewis gets close to an important part of Homer's charm and power. But while it is relatively easy to see the point of a network of frequently repeated phrases that gain their power in a global rather than local manner, it is much harder to come to terms with phrases that are repeated only once or twice. Should we think of such phrases as coined for a particular situation and explore the allusive structures created by them? Or are such allusive patterns mirages of random and fragmentary transmission? If more had survived would the supposed local effect of a specific relationship dissolve in the global pattern created by the many occurrences of a traditional phrase?

These are difficult questions, and it must be the case that quite a few unique phrases or low-frequency repetitions owe their rarity to the accidents of transmission. On the other hand, the consequences of combinatorial logic are daunting. Well over half of all repeated phrases in Homer are repeated only once, and 80% of all phrases are repeated three times or less. From other known facts about the distribution of linguistic phenomena, whether oral or literate, it seems quite unlikely that the relative frequency of rare repetitions or unique phrases would drop in a larger corpus. Scholars who emphasise the 'traditional' nature of Homeric diction may underestimate the almost infinite phrasal variance that is generated by the combination of a limited number of motifs. For instance, the striking opening theme of Mozart's *Jupiter Symphony* is accurately described as a sequence of two banal motifs: 'drum rolls' followed by 'sighs'. At a particularly haunting moment in *The Winter's Tale* (4.450-2) Perdita says:

> this dream of mine, –
> Being now awake, I'll queen it no inch farther,
> But milk my ewes and weep.

This is quite close to ordinary spoken language, and except for the use of 'queen' as a verb, there is nothing remarkable about the lexicon or syntax of this passage. Nor is there anything remarkable about its thematic structure, which Leo Spitzer might have seen as an instance of Baroque *desengaño* or disillusionment. But it is a sublime and unique moment in Shakespearean drama, and there is nothing quite like it across billions of words of English poetry.

It is worth repeating that the striking nature of this passage is not a function of particularly fancy words. The extraordinary effect is produced by the combinatorial potential of ordinary words, which across utterances of any length will always produce many rare or unique combinations. This is a general property of human language and sits well below the distinction between the spoken and the written.

Phusizoos aia

Let us now turn to three different examples that raise the question of specifically allusive or highly context-sensitive phrases. The first involves a famous disagreement between Ruskin and Arnold. When Helen says to Priam that she cannot see her brothers among the Achaean warriors, the poet comments (3.243-4):

> *hôs phato. tous d' êdê katechen phusizoos aia*
> *en Lakedaimoni authi philêi en patridi gaiêi.*

> So she spoke, but the teeming earth lay already upon them
> away in Lakedaimon, the beloved land of their fathers.

Ruskin commented: 'The poet has to speak of the earth in sadness; but he will not let that sadness affect or change his thought of it. No: though Castor and Pollux be dead, yet the earth is our mother still – fruitful, lifegiving.' In his essay 'On Translating Homer' Matthew Arnold (p. 102) made fun of Ruskin's comment as an instance of a modern and sentimental criticism that has lost sight of Homer's simplicity. Parry (p. 125) echoes Arnold when he quotes Ruskin scornfully and argues that his discovery has ruled such criticism out of court. For him *phusizoos aia* is a formula like *polumêtis Odusseus* or *podas ôkus Achilleus*, and to inquire into its meaning or special appropriateness is mere foolishness. But is it? Consider the facts. The adjective *phusizoos* appears in two other passages in Early Greek epic. In his flashback narrative Odysseus reports how he saw Kastor and Pollux in the underworld (*Od.* 11. 300-4):

> Castor the tamer of horses and Pollux good at boxing,
> The life-giving earth covers them both, alive,
> (*tous amphô zôous katechei phusizoos aia*)
> and even beneath the earth they have honour from Zeus,
> every other day they live, on the other day they die,
> and they've been granted honour equal to the gods.

In the other passage (*Il.* 21.60-3), *phusizoos* also modifies the noun for 'earth', but this time in a verse-initial phrase where the adjective follows the noun. Achilles sees the hapless Lykaon who got away from him once:

> But come now, he must be given a taste of our spearhead
> so that I may know inside my heart and make certain
> whether he will come back even from there, or the prospering
> earth will hold him, she who holds back even the strong man.
> (*gê phusizoos, hê te kata krateron per erukei.*)

The known facts are these:

1. The adjective 'life-nourishing' appears twice in the verse-terminal phrase *phusizoos aia* and once in the verse-initial phrase *gê phusizoos*.
2. In its three occurrences, the adjective occurs in a passage that contrasts the life-giving force of the earth with the death of a warrior.
3. The two occurrences of *phusizoos aia* are tied to the fate of Kastor and Pollux.

Now contrast these facts with the following hypothetical distribution of three occurrences of that adjective:

1. It occurs three times in the verse-terminal phrase *phusizoos aia*.
2. It occurs in three different works.
3. The ironic contrast of life-giving earth and the warrior's death occurs once.
4. The phrase is not tied to the same person on more than one occasion.

In this hypothetical and entirely unremarkable distribution, the phrase would occur always in the same metrical position, but it would not be tied strongly to any particular person or situation. It would be an economic hypothesis to assume that we are dealing with three unrelated occurrences of an idiomatic phrase. But in the actual distribution of *phusizoos* it bonds with 'earth' in two metrically distinct forms; it always involves

24

the contrast of life and death, and in two of three occurrences it applies to the same individuals. Moreover, those two passages stand to each other in a relation of variation or correction. The *Iliad* dwells on the death of the brothers, which makes sense in the context of the *teichoskopia*. The Odyssean scene is an odd elaboration of the manner in which Kastor and Pollux, now envisaged as constellations, are and are not 'dead'. The most economic explanation for these coincidences is that they are the product of an individual memory or allusive purpose.

Understanding always involves creating the ground that 'under-stands' and supports hermeneutical operations. When it comes to Homeric repetitions it is crucially important to create an initial ground of understanding that does not foreclose the range of valid interpretation. In Aristophanes' *Frogs,* Dionysos laments the fact that since the death of Euripides gone there have been no playwrights with the power to coin striking phrases like 'The airy hall of Zeus' or 'foot of time'. From this we may gather that Athenian audiences appreciated such phrases just as Italian audiences appreciated the turns of melody, rhythm, or harmony in *Rigoletto*.

There is a wonderful scene in the opening book of the *Odyssey* where the singer Phemios sings about the disasters of the Achaeans on their return from Troy and Penelope tells him to stop. Telemachos intervenes and tells his mother not to blame the singer. Suffering comes from Zeus, and as for people, they like the latest story (1.351-2):

> *tên gar aoidên mallon epikleious' anthrôpoi,*
> *hê tis akouontessi neôtatê amphipelêtai.*

> for people more applaud the song
> that's newest to float about the hearers.

Wordsworth in his *Preface to the Lyrical Ballads* deplored a modern desire for novelty and wrote with eloquent disgust about the 'degrading thirst after outrageous stimulation' that led readers to neglect 'the invaluable works of our elder writers' for 'frantic novels, sickly and stupid German tragedies, and deluges of idle and extravagant stories in verse':

> For a multitude of causes unknown to former times are now acting with a combined force to blunt the discriminating powers of the mind, and unfitting it for all voluntary exertion to reduce it to a state of almost savage torpor. The most effective of these causes are the great national events which are daily taking place, and the encreasing accumulation of men in cities, where the uniformity of their occupations produces a craving for extraordinary incident which the rapid communication of intelligence hourly gratifies. (Wordsworth, 1.129)

But was there ever an age in which the 'discriminating powers of the mind' were not 'blunted'? Telemachos' poet is not that different from the Hermes-like Autolycus, thief, pedlar, and purveyor of ballads for a news-starved audience in Shakespeare's *Winter's Tale* (4.4. 257ff.). Dr Johnson said of Pope's *Rape of the Lock*:

> In this work are exhibited, in a very high degree, the two most engaging powers of an author. New things are made familiar, and familiar things are made new. (Johnson, 295)

This is less a comment about the matter than the art of poetry, but in its balanced emphasis on the 'familiar' and the 'new' it may be a more tolerant and accurate assessment of the psychological needs that poetry satisfies, whether in the days of Telemachos or now.

Returning to *phusizoos,* we shall never for certain whether this adjective was a traditional epithet for 'earth' before its appearance in *Iliad* 3. But given the competitive spirit of epic verse-making and the audience's delight in novelty, it is a safe assumption that Homeric audiences did not differ from the audiences of Euripides or Verdi in their appreciation of striking turns of phrase. The modern reader's decision to read a rare or unique phrase as specific and local will always be probabilistic subject to varying degrees of uncertainty. But the possibility of the rare or unique must always be kept alive.

The more closely we look at *phusizoos aia* the more reasons we find to support the argument that it aims at a special effect of the kind Ruskin described. The lines about Kastor and Polydeukes are very like the necrologues on fallen warriors, which are often suffused with irony and compassion. Moreover, the lines counterpoint the fate of Helen with that of her brothers: she is alive, although in exile and misery; they are dead, but buried in their own country. To be alive and happy in one's own country is a destiny denied to the progeny of Leda. Such is the fate of those on whom the gods bestow beauty and attention. *Phusizoos aia* resonates strongly in this context, just as the fate of Helen and her brothers resonates in the context of the fate of Achilles.

At the same time, what Ruskin heard is not necessarily the effect of a unique phrase. Charles Segal wrote that 'the unique and poignant expression, *'phusizoos aia'*, stands over against the formulaic *'philêi en patridi gaiêi'*. The special appropriateness and freshness of the former phrase heighten the tragic factuality and stern inflexibility of the latter, and vice versa' (Segal, 4). Perhaps he is right, but the poignancy of the passage does not depend on *'phusizoos aia'* being a special coinage. *Phusizoos* may well have been a typical epithet for the earth. What counts is its effective deployment in this context, which plays life and death, home and abroad against each other in a haunting fashion. As with the theme of the Jupiter Symphony, the power of lines derives not from familiar motifs in isolation (drum rolls, sighs), but from their juxtaposition.

Warriors quarrelling over a wife

The second example is offered as a friendly amendment to a very interesting essay by Seth Schein in which he argues that the fight between the beggar Iros and the disguised Odysseus is a transposition of the duel between Paris and Menelaos. In both cases the prize is a woman: Helen or Penelope. Schein's point of departure is the line:

hoppoteros de ke nikêsêi kreissôn te genêtai
Whichever of the two is stronger and conquers
$$(3.71 = 3.92 = Od. \ 18.46 \sim Od. \ 18.83)$$

This line is metrically anomalous in that it lacks a caesura in the third foot – a condition that is found only once every 200 lines. Schein argues that the line 'is associated in

26

the poetic tradition specifically' with 'a battle between two warriors over a "wife" ' (Schein 1991, 351). He adds that despite the many textual resemblances between the Paris/Menelaos Hektor/Aias and Hektor/Achilles duels in *Iliad* 3, 7, and 22 this particular line is not echoed in the later Iliadic duels because these do not include a quarrel over a wife.

It is a very attractive speculation to see the Iros-Odysseus scene as a transposition of the Paris-Menelaos duel, with the loudmouth coward Iros standing in for the suitors' desire to possess Penelope. But is it necessary or even probable to invoke a pre-existing association with a particular line and a particular theme? Considered as a bag of words the line consists of very common parts, with the exception of *hoppoteros*, which occurs eleven times in the *Iliad,* twice in the *Odyssey,* and once in the *Theogony.* The Iliadic occurrences strongly cluster: seven of the eleven occurrences are found in *Iliad* 3.

Table 3. Components of *Iliad* 3.71

hoppoteros	de	ke	nikêsêi	kreissôn	te	nikêsêi	3x
	de	ke					178x
	de	ke	nikêsêi (3) nikêsanti (2)				5x
			nikêsêi	kreissôn	te	genêtai	4x
					te	genêtai (7) variants (15)	22x

If we decompose the line into its phrasal components we discover an interesting pattern of what is and is not there (Table 3). It is not surprising that the very common phrase *de ke* combines with a form of the verb *nikaô* on two other occasions. But if you look up the locations, you see that all instances of *de+ke+nikaô* occur in *Iliad* 3 or *Odyssey* 18. You would think that from a semantic and metrical perspective *kreissôn te genêtai* ('turns out to be stronger') is just the kind of phrase that would be plastered all over the *Iliad.* But in fact it does not occur elsewhere. The closest analogue, semantically and metrically identical, but with marginal lexical and morphological variance, is *kreissôn ge genômai* (if I prevail), which is spoken by Eumaios to Odysseus when the 'battle over a wife' has become real (*Od.* 22.167).

If we approach this evidence with the expectation that rare or unique phrases are normal rather than exceptional, we may want to strengthen Schein's argument by questioning the 'traditional' status of the line in question. There certainly was a tradition of stories about the warrior's return to his wife. But in all probability *hoppoteros de ke nikêsêi kreissôn te genêtai* was never a pre-existing line traditionally associated with a battle between two warriors over a wife. The line was created by the poet who composed *Iliad* 3 in accordance with traditional practices of oral verse-making. This poet on that occasion was fond of *hoppoteros,* whose frequency in *Iliad* 3, whether by accident or design, acquires a strong thematic function: 'which of the two' will win?

The composer of the fight between Iros and Odysseus picked up this line, perhaps because of its striking metrical character, and used it in his transposition of a heroic motif into a fight between the two beggars. What conscious purpose one should associate with an intertextual operation of this kind is a question that is very difficult and perhaps unnecessary to answer. Effects are more readily seen than intentions, and the effects are very clear: The high heroic duel with its quasi-chivalrous rules is echoed in a 'low-rent' environment, but in both situations the inconclusive and not-yet serious foreshadows the catastrophic dénouement.

The deaths of Sarpedon, Patroklos, and Hektor

The essence of heroic narrative is starkly expressed in Jesus' words to Peter: 'Put up again thy sword into his place: for all they that take the sword shall perish with the sword' (Matthew 26:52). The basic narrative pattern is that of a chain of revenge triangles in which the killer is killed. In the *Iliad* that chain leads from Sarpedon through Patroklos and Hektor to Achilles. We are on safe grounds in affirming the traditional nature of this motif. On the other hand, the Iliadic elaboration of that chain involves low-frequency phrases that may be rooted in traditional verse-making but were composed and put in their different places for a particular purpose.

The deaths of Patroklos and Hektor are marked in an identical passage of 3.5 lines (16.855-8 = 22.361-4):

> *hôs ara min eiponta telos thanatoio kalupse:*
> *psuchê d' ek rhetheôn ptamenê Aïdosde bebêkei*
> *hon potmon goôsa lipous' androtêta kai hêbên.*
> *ton kai tethnêôta prosêuda*

> He spoke, and as he spoke the end of death closed in upon him,
> and the soul fluttering free of his limbs went down into Death's house
> mourning her destiny, leaving youth and manhood behind her.
> Now though he was a dead man (glorious Hektor | brilliant Achilles) spoke to him

The first line recurs in the death of Sarpedon, Patroklos' most important victim. Fragments of the second and third line occur in the *Odyssey*, but the striking phrases *psuchê d' ek rhetheôn ptamenê* and *lipous' androtêta kai hêbên* are unique. Should we treat this as independent occurrences of a 'death of the hero' pattern, or should we say that a narrative purpose governs the choice of representing these deaths in the same manner? Janko in his commentary on *Iliad* 16 writes that 'Homer or a recent predecessor reserved 855 for the deaths of his greatest heroes; its repetition stresses the uniquely important link between the deaths of Sarpedon, Patroklos, and Hektor'(Kirk 1985, 3: 420). This is a fine observation, but do we need 'or a recent predecessor'? Is the probability of a traditional 'death of greatest hero line' greater than the probability of a poet, using traditional techniques, crafting a unique line for a specific purpose?

If you opt for the latter and look for other evidence of shared and specific features between these death scenes, you discover ten additional doublets that establish a tight cluster of repetitions linking the deaths of Patroklos and Hektor with each other and with that of Sarpedon. As Sarpedon and Patroklos move towards their fateful encounter, Zeus is tempted to save his son, but Hera protests (16.441-3):

> Do you wish to bring back a man who is mortal, one long since
> doomed by his destiny, from ill-sounding death and release him?

1. Introduction

Do it, then; but not all the rest of us gods shall approve you.

When Zeus expresses pity at Hektor's fate and wonders whether to save him, Athene protests in the same words (22.179-81). Zeus expresses his pity in a phrase that is also used by Hera when she tells Zeus to satisfy his pity by giving Sarpedon a special funeral (*olophuretai êtor*, 16.450, 22.169).

The dying Sarpedon urges his companion Glaukos to rescue his body (16.492-3):

> Now the need comes
> hardest upon you to be a spearman and a bold warrior.

The same words are used by Achilles before he throws his first spear at Hektor. The separate components of this phrase are only found in locations that are also related to this context. The only other occurrence of 'Now the need comes' is spoken by Deiphobos (13.463), whose disguise Athene has assumed in her deception of Hektor. The second part of the phrase is found once within 30 lines of Sarpedon's first appearance (5.602).

There are two cases where a spoken phrase may be a deliberate echo. After inflicting a mortal wound on Patroklos, Hektor says 'You **did** say to take my city (*pou ephêsta*, 16.830), and later Achilles says to Hektor: 'You **did** say to be safe after killing Patroklos' (*pou ephês*, 22.331). The combination of the function word *pou* with a form of *phêmi* looks common enough, but is not found elsewhere. Similarly, after the death of Patroklos Hektor says 'Who knows whether Achilles will escape me?' (*tis d' oid' ei k' Achilleus*, 16.860), and Athene as Deiphobos ends her speech by saying 'let us fight so that we know whether Achilles … might be defeated by your spear (*eidomen ei ken Achilleus*, 22.244). 'Who knows whether' also looks like an unremarkable phrase. But in its only other occurrence (11.692-3) Nestor urges Patroklos to plead with Achilles:

> Who knows if, with God helping, you might trouble his spirit
> by entreaty, since the persuasion of a friend is a strong thing.

The doublets discussed above lend themselves to interpretation as purposeful allusions or reminiscences. It is harder to make a similar case for three other passages, which are semantically inert but in their aggregate corroborate the conclusion that the deaths of Patroklos and Hektor are specifically interdependent compositions:

1. Patroklos keeps the Trojans from returning to the city (*oude polêos eia hiemenous*, 16.396), while Achilles keeps the Achaeans from attacking Hektor (*oud' ea hiemenai*, 22.206).
2. The sequence *Patroklos. tou d' ouk* (16.480 and 22.397) is theoretically part of a broader pattern that goes 'verse-initial name phrase terminating a sentence, followed by an anaphoric pronoun'. But this pattern occurs only in one other location (5.18).
3. *Es diphron d' ana*bas (16.657 = 22.399) is another inconspicuous phrase. You find other combinations of *diphros+bainô*, and *es diphron d'* occurs verse-initially in other combinations. But this phrase occurs only twice. The first time it shows

Hektor in flight, the second time it describes Achilles as he prepares to drag the dead Hektor in his chariot. The image of a humiliated Hektor associates the two locations.

I have reserved for the end of this discussion a repeated phrase that with its minimal variation epitomises the thematic purpose that underlies the web of allusive links between the death scenes of Sarpedon, Patroklos, and Hektor. The narrator marks the imminent death of Patroklos by addressing him directly (16.693-4):

> Then who was it you slaughtered first, who was the last one,
> Patroklos, as the gods called you to your death?
> (*hote dê se theoi thanatond' ekalessan;*)

When Hektor recognises that Athene in the disguise of Deiphobos had tricked him, he says about himself what the narrator had said about Patroklos (22.297):

> No use. Here at last the gods have summoned me deathward.
> *ô popoi, ê mala dê me theoi thanatond' ekalessan:*

The shift from 'you' to 'me' is deliberate and colossal. It condenses into a difference of a single letter the theme of knowledge and delusion that is worked out in the careers and deaths of Sarpedon, Patroklos, Hektor, and finally Achilles himself, who after the death of Patroklos lives with a consciousness of his own death that is given to the other characters only in their last moments.

Beyond phrasal repetition

Homeric poetry is constructed from building blocks of poetic idioms that in their tolerance of repetition differ markedly from other texts that readers of Homer normally encounter. Coming to terms with that difference is a fundamental task in learning how to read Homer. Part of that task involves relating the distinctive fabric of Homeric verse to other levels of discursive organisation. Considered as a human utterance, a Homeric passage obeys rules of language that operate at different levels and with different degrees of flexibility. Phonetic and morphological rules are quite rigid: if somebody pronounces 'tomato' in one way you may predict with virtual certainty how he will pronounce 'dance' or 'horse'. A few syntactic rules belong to the realm of 'must', but many belong to the realm of 'should' or 'may'. Discursive rules, which govern the composition of larger textual structures, are more flexible still; indeed 'rules of discourse' are so sensitive to social and generic contexts as well as to individual preference that they can hardly be formulated at all except with the proviso 'unless the situation demands otherwise'.

The artificial epic language of Homer has an unusual number of dialectal phonetic or morphological variants, which create flexibility at the prosodic level. The combination of syntactic and metrical rules yields a phrasal repertoire that in its typical deployment and tolerance to repetition appears to be relatively predictable. Can you extrapolate from the verbal fabric of Homeric poetry to larger patterns and isolate narrative or thematic 'idioms' that operate with a similar degree of regularity?

1. Introduction

The answer is probably 'no'. Once you move beyond the level of sentence/verse, narrative or thematic conventions become increasingly variable. The distinction between 'oral' and 'literate', which has considerable explanatory force at the level of the individual verse, loses much of its power at higher levels of organisation You are better off with a broader category of the 'literary', which despite its etymological roots embraces the spoken and the written word, whether 'read' or 'performed'.

Consider the rhetorical strategies used to achieve variety in two passages of catalogue poetry. The first passage occurs in Wallace Stevens's *Sunday Morning*:

> Divinity must live within herself:
> Passions of rain, or moods in falling snow;
> Grievings in loneliness, or unsubdued
> Elations when the forest blooms; gusty
> Emotions on wet roads on autumn nights;
> All pleasures and all pains, remembering
> The bough of summer and the winter branch.

This catalogue balances a number of items: 'passions' against 'moods', 'grievings' against 'elations', 'pleasures' against 'pains', the 'bough' against the 'branch'. Variety enters through the avoidance of precise symmetry. 'Passions of rain, or moods in falling snow' does not divide right in the middle, and the qualifying phrases are attached to the governing nouns in slightly different ways ('of', 'in'). The second pair in the catalogue ('Grievings … blooms') is almost twice as long; the metrical imbalance, emphasised by the strong enjambment, is more pronounced, and the syntactical differentiation of the balancing clauses is greater as well. In the next item ('gusty … nights') balance is abandoned, as the structure of the phrase mirrors its wind-tossed content, but the return to virtual symmetry becomes the source of special effect in the following item ('All pleasures and all pains'). This phrase, however, does not occupy the entire line, and in the final item variety returns with the subtle differentiation of the 'bough of summer' and the 'winter branch'.

Nobody would quarrel with this description of the rhetorical tricks employed by an exceptionally artful twentieth-century poet. But now look at the following passage from the *Iliad* (14.511-22):

> *Aias rha prôtos Telamônios Hurtion outa*
> *Gurtiadên Musôn hêgêtora karterothumôn:*
> *Phalkên d' Antilochos kai Mermeron exenarixe:*
> *Mêrionês de Morun te kai Hippotiôna katekta,*
> *Teukros de Prothoôna t' enêrato kai Periphêtên:*
> *Atreïdês d' ar' epeith' Huperênora poimena laôn*
> *outase kal laparên, dia d' entera chalkos aphusse*
> *dêiôsas: psuchê de kat' outamenên ôteilên*
> *essut' epeigomenê, ton de skotos osse kalupse.*
> *pleistous d' Aias heilen Oïlêos tachus huios:*
> *ou gar hoi tis homoios epispesthai posin êen*
> *andrôn tressantôn, hote te Zeus en phobon ôrsen.*

> First Telamonian Aias cut down Hyrtios, he who
> was son to Gyrtios, and lord over the strong-hearted Mysians.

31

Antilochos slaughtered Phalkes and Mermeros. Morys
and Hippotion were killed by Meriones. Teukros cut down
Periphetes and Prothoön. Next the son of Atreus,
Menelaos, stabbed Hyperenor, shepherd of the people,
in the flank, so the bronze head let gush out the entrails
through the torn side. His life came out through the wound of the spearstab
in beating haste, and a mist of darkness closed over both eyes.
But Aias the fast-footed son of Oïleus caught and killed most,
since there was none like him in the speed of his feet to go after
men who ran, once Zeus had driven the terror upon them.

Just like Stevens's catalogue, the passage uses a number of devices to avoid rigid symmetry. A two-line account of the victim of the greater Aias is followed by three one-line killings in each of which an Achaean kills two Trojans. The word for 'killed' is different each time (*exenarixe, katekta, enêrato*) and the word order differs in the arrangement of subject, verb and the two objects (OSOV, SOOV, SOVO so that in the three lines no part of speech appears more than twice in the same position in the sentence. The three short killings are followed by four lines describing Menelaos' victory over Hyperenor. The lesser Aias brings up the rear and is responsible for an indefinite number of killings. The passage begins with one Aias and ends with another.

There is no significant difference between the rhetorical devices employed by the two passages, and you need very much the same analytical tools to read or describe them. This is not to say that you should read Stevens and Homer the same way. Every text needs to be read with proper attention to its own way of being in the world. But the tool kit is the same.

There are of course some ways in which the rootedness of Homeric art in oral verse-making shows up at higher levels of organisation. Every reader of Homer remembers recurring typical scenes. Walter Arend classified and compared them in a very fine monograph, roughly contemporary with Parry's work on the formula. He begins with scenes of arrival by visitors, messengers and dreams. There is a chapter on sacrifices and meals, another on journeys by land and sea. Arming and dressing receive special attention, as do sleep, deliberation, assemblies, oaths and baths. What emerges from the survey confirms the reader's sense that Homeric narrative displays rather than conceals its conventional elements. Stock situation requires no disguise to gain admission into epic narrative, which delights in repetition. In this regard the *Iliad* is much more like comedy than like later epics. Recurring scenes and narrative motifs are cousins of phrasal repetition. Both reinforce our sense that tolerance of repetition is a defining feature of Homeric style. It is also clear that the availability of stock themes is helpful to an oral composer and that one can hardly imagine oral narrative without it. But Homer's reliance on such conventions is no proof that his narrative is formulaic in a special sense that is radically different from, say, a rhetorician's use of topoi or the use of narrative conventions by such writers as Dickens or P.G. Wodehouse, both of whom revelled in the stock character of their situations.

Two general points can be made about Homeric narrative conventions. First, the most obvious ones are rather like name phrases. They occur in restricted contexts and set up a framework of stability. The highly stereotyped meal descriptions, for instance, resemble each other much more closely than the business that is transacted after them.

Second, and more important, the poet of the *Iliad* does not show his individuality by transforming individual conventions; instead he reveals his mastery through their deployment. It is not very difficult to dismantle the *Iliad* and classify a high percentage of its parts under a limited number of standardised modular components. The catalogue of parts, then, may suggest that the *Iliad* is the product of its conventions. But what literary critic would confuse a poem with a dictionary of its words? And yet whole branches of Homeric scholarship have flourished by turning this error into scientific procedure.

The critical question about Iliadic conventions is whether their deployment or relative degree of elaboration is governed by a narrative purpose. Take the example of Menelaos in Book 17. He is on the scene when Patroklos dies and protects his body, but when Hektor approaches he considers his choices and after much deliberation abandons the body. This is one of four such scenes in the *Iliad*, and one may construct from them a quite fixed pattern that begins with self-address, proceeds through a consideration of alternatives, marks the turning-point of the debate, and states the choice (Fenik, 1978). Each version stays quite close to the pattern so that it seems fair to say that a deliberation topos is part of the poet's inherited repertoire. But the topos is reserved for special occasions: not every retreat is preceded by elaboration. It is in the placement of the topos rather than in the elaboration of the scene that we catch the poet's special purpose. Why is Menelaos given the dubious privilege of being the only warrior in the *Iliad* to persuade himself that retreat is honourable? And why does he show this uniquely explicit concern for self-preservation on the occasion of the death of Patroklos, which will shortly motivate Achilles to return to battle despite his full knowledge that he will lose his life? The example provides some rules of thumb on how to 'read' Homer, keeping in mind the generic meaning of the word that covers both reading and listening in their specific senses. First, one must be aware of the existence of a convention, in this case the scene of deliberation in the face of the enemy. Second, one must be aware of its distribution in the poem, and one must relate its differentiation to the contexts of its occurrences. With the boastful Hektor, his resolution to stand up to the enemy ignominiously collapses at the sight of Achilles. Odysseus, in the tradition the most reluctant warrior to join the Achaean expedition, expresses the code of heroic resistance most fully and lives up to it even in the face of overwhelming odds. Menelaos persuades himself that preserving his own life comes before guarding the body of Patroklos. Each variation is unique in the poem and singularly appropriate to the poet's portrayal of the insecurity of Hektor, the rational courage of Odysseus, and the well-meaning inadequacy of Menelaos.

Third, one must attend to the meanings created by the silent juxtaposition of related scenes. That Paris is found by Hektor in Helen's bedroom is appropriate and not surprising. That Andromache in her anxiety for Hektor has rushed to the battlements is also not unexpected. That Hektor and Andromache meet away from home against the background of Paris and Helen at home is a specifically Iliadic effect. In short, the reader of the *Iliad* must be constantly alert to the narrative strategy that controls the use of particular conventions, which in their individual elaboration may not show unusual features but gain their meaning and effect through their deployment in a particular context and through their implicit relationship to each other.

The following chapters, in which I interpret the plot of the *Iliad* and survey various narrative and thematic aspects, owe whatever merit they have to my success in applying these rules of reading. I doubt the wisdom of deriving from the status of the *Iliad* as an oral composition special rules about how – or, rather, how not – to 'read' the text. On the contrary, the interpretability of the *Iliad* according to established literary canons strikes me as a cardinal fact about the poem that must govern our understanding of its origins.

Ben Jonson said of Shakespeare that he was for all time, thereby pointing to a defining feature of a class of works that travel well and can speak to successive and widely different ages with a peculiar ease and authority. This is as true of Dante and Shakespeare as it is of Bach and Mozart. To the authority of such works corresponds a plurality of responses. There is no right way of playing Bach (though there are some wrong ones). The *Iliad* and *Odyssey* are very prominent members of this class of works. This does not make Homer 'our contemporary', and we must pay proper attention to those aspects of the Homeric poems that require historical explanation. But in the current state of Homeric criticism the proper understanding of the *Iliad* is more hampered by excessive historicism than by naive identification. To be guided by Homer and Nature in Pope's sense is more likely to direct our attention to those aspects of the *Iliad* that account for our continuing interest in it.

The fact that in looking at the *Iliad* and its modern reader I emphasise continuities in human nature has as its corollary that I also play down the differences between Homer and classical Greece, following such scholars as Lesky and Lloyd-Jones rather than Fränkel, Snell and Dodds. I have not hesitated to interpret the action of the *Iliad* in tragic terms and to use concepts that derive in one form or another from Aristotle's *Poetics*. There are clearly contexts in which it is essential to articulate sharply the differences that divide Homer and Greek tragedy. For my purposes it has been more important to emphasise a perspective that derives its authority from Plato, who called Homer the 'first teacher and master of tragedy' (*Republic* 595c).

The Plot of the Iliad

Achilles, Hektor and the Fall of Troy

Homer's narrative is not particularly allusive or cryptic – it differs in this regard from an epic like *Beowulf* – but it assumes on the part of its readers a general knowledge of a set of stories no longer current in our culture. It is useful to begin with a summary of the 'Trojan Cycle', as one might call this set of stories, which intertwines two narrative strands, both of which lead back to a sexual adventure by Zeus. Some of these stories are explicitly referred to in the *Iliad*; others are known directly only from later sources. We cannot decide with certainty whether Homer did not know or did not choose to refer to elements of the narrative tradition known to us only from post-Homeric sources. The situation is further complicated by the fact that virtually all stories include many and often significant variants. I shall assume here, without further argument, that Homer and his audience were familiar with substantially the same stories about Troy that were current in fifth-century Athens.

The first narrative strand leads back to Peleus and Thetis. Zeus took an interest in the latter but, learning of a prophecy that she would bear a son greater than his father, married her off to the mortal Peleus, to whom she bore Achilles. The wedding of Peleus and Thetis was celebrated with great pomp, and all the gods were invited, except for Eris (Quarrel). She took revenge by tossing into the company an apple with the inscription 'To the fairest'. Aphrodite, Athene and Hera each claimed possession of the apple, and it was decided to make Paris the arbiter of the dispute. The three goddesses presented themselves to Paris, then a shepherd on Mount Ida, and each sought to bribe him by a promise. Athene promised wisdom, Hera wealth and power, and Aphrodite the most beautiful woman. Paris chose Aphrodite.

At this point the story connects with the other strand, which leads back to Zeus' adventure with Leda, whom he visited in the shape of a swan. As a result of their union she laid an egg from which were hatched Helen and the twin brothers Kastor and Pollux. Because Helen grew up to be the most beautiful woman in the world, all Greek heroes became her suitors. Her human father Tyndareus extracted from them an oath that they would protect her marriage regardless of her choice. She married Menelaos, king of Sparta, but later Paris with the help of Aphrodite abducted Helen, while a guest at the court of Menelaos. Sworn to vengeance, the Greeks assembled at Aulis for a retaliatory expedition against Troy under the leadership of Agamemnon, the king of Mycenae and brother of Menelaos. At Aulis the fleet was becalmed, because Artemis was angered at Agamemnon's shooting of a hind in her sanctuary, and the prophet Kalchas revealed that only the sacrifice of Agamemnon's daughter Iphigenia would appease the goddess. In some versions of the story Iphigenia is sacrificed, in others the sacrifice is averted at the last minute when Artemis spirits her away to Tauris and substitutes a hind on the altar. Homer's silence on this event, which provides the major motif for Klytaemnestra's murder of Agamemnon in the *Oresteia*, is very striking and is more likely the result of repression than of ignorance. Indeed, a veiled allusion to the events at Aulis may occur in the introduction of Kalchas (1.71), where he is described as having guided the ships of the Achaeans towards Troy through his prophetic powers. Agamemnon's hostility towards Kalchas may also be referred to that story.

The siege of Troy dragged on for ten years until, after the deaths of Hektor and Achilles, the city fell. But the Trojan Cycle does not come to an end with the conquest of Troy. On their return home, the victors suffered fates as lamentable as those of the defeated. Menelaos indeed returned home safely, and we meet him in Book 4 of the *Odyssey*, leading an affluent life spiced by reminiscence. Odysseus also made it home, although only after much hardship. But Agamemnon returned to a humiliating death at the hands of his wife. Other warriors, like the lesser Aias, incurred the wrath of the gods and were shipwrecked. If we add to the sufferings of the victors the misfortunes of those who lost their lives before Troy was taken, the tradition presents us with a picture in which the concept of victory loses most of its meaning. The ambiguity of victory and defeat is echoed in the association of excellence and disaster that appears in the figures of Helen and Achilles, 'causes' of the beginning and end of the Trojan War. The wedding of Peleus and Thetis links them even prior to the birth of Achilles, and this narrative link is the source of the peculiar twilight in which these two semi-divine stars appear in the *Iliad*: *kakomêchanos eris* ('disaster-causing quarrel', 9.257), presides over both their fates.

The Iliad is in no sense a chronicle of the Trojan Cycle outlined above. Aristotle laid great stress on this point when he argued that Homer alone of the epic poets had a proper understanding of plot and concentrated on a single and unified action as opposed to a mere sequence of events (*Poetics* 17.1455b16). Horace echoes the insight when he praises the author of the *Iliad* for 'plunging the reader in the midst of things' rather than beginning with the egg laid by Leda (*Ars Poetica* 145-9). An innocent reader approaching the text without a knowledge of its title would not long remain in doubt about the limited scope of the narrative, since the first seven lines tell him to expect a poem about the cause and consequences of Achilles' anger but say nothing about the beginning of the war, the progress of the ten-year-long siege, or the fall of Troy. Why did the Greeks call this poem about Achilles the *Iliad* even though Troy is not even mentioned in the poet's announcement of his theme? The traditional title points to the dual nature of the poem, which is indeed an account of the anger of Achilles, but moves beyond its own limits to include the larger event of which it is a part. The specific greatness of the *Iliad* resides in those principles of organisation that make the poem about Achilles a poem about Troy.

In composing an 'Achilleid' that later ages would justly call the *Iliad* the poet's fundamental decision was to make the war hinge on the fate of Hektor, the 'holder' of Troy, as his name indicates. Troy stands or falls with Hektor, whose power the Trojans celebrated by calling his son Astyanax, 'city-guardian', for 'Hektor alone protected Ilion' (6.403).

The association of Hektor's death with the fall of Troy is strongly marked in the *Iliad*. The famous prophecy about Troy's fall is put in Hektor's mouth when he meets Andromache on the battlements (6.450-9):

For I know this thing well in my heart, and my mind knows it:
there will come a day when sacred Ilion shall perish,
and Priam, and the people of Priam of the strong ash spear.

Siege imagery occurs repeatedly with Achilles' re-entry into battle, and when Hektor is killed the Trojans respond as if the city itself were burning and in ruins (below, p. 105).

This identification of the death of Hektor with the fall of Troy is the reason why the *Iliad* avoids any references to the particular circumstances of the city's end. Odysseus, still incognito among the Phaiakians, tests the extent of his reputation and establishes a setting for the revelation of his identity by asking Demodokos to sing about the fall of Troy. Demodokos sings how the Greeks pretended to abandon the siege, leaving behind a giant wooden horse as a gesture of propitiation, and how Odysseus, leading a contingent of warriors hidden in the horse, brought about the ruin of the city (*Odyssey* 8.499). That is appropriate to a poem starring Odysseus but it destroys the premise of the *Iliad*: if the Achaeans could not take Troy without the ruse of the Wooden Horse, Hektor was not after all the 'holder' of the city. Accordingly, the Wooden Horse is never mentioned in the *Iliad*, except for a veiled prophecy by Zeus that Troy will fall 'through the wiles of Athene' (15.71). Similarly, there is a tradition that Philoktetes is essential to the conquest of Troy: the archery of Paris must be balanced by archery on the Achaean side. That tradition is incompatible with both the *Iliad* and the *Odyssey* and is consequently ignored, except for a brief reference in the Catalogue of Ships (2.724).

The death of Hektor not only seals the fall of Troy; it also completes the destiny of Achilles, for according to his mother's prophecy 'it is decreed your death must come soon after Hektor's' (18.96). Achilles has a choice between a long and inglorious and a short and glorious life. The motif translates into the narrative of an individual life the condition of the warrior's existence: he cannot acquire glory without the risk of his life. The risk increases with the degree of excellence, and at the highest level the certainty of great fame is balanced by the certainty of early death.

A good story requires turning-points at which events could go in one direction or another. *The Iliad* is organised in such a way as to exclude turning-points beyond the death of Hektor. Achilles will die, and Troy will fall: there is no need for the poet to detail the circumstances by which events will take their course towards these inevitable outcomes. From the decision to hinge the outcome of the war on the death of Hektor arises the need to turn the duel of Hektor and Achilles into an encounter that both warriors must seek or cannot avoid. In the beginning Hektor and Achilles have individual reasons for avoiding one another. Hektor knows that he is the weaker fighter, and Achilles knows that he will not long survive an encounter with Hektor. The story therefore requires a motive that will urge Achilles towards Hektor even at the cost of his life and will make Hektor stand up to him even in the face of certain death.

Achilles in Book 1

The initial position of Achilles is ambiguous and frustrating. He is 'a man of short life' (*minunthiados*, 1.352), as he says in his prayer to his mother. He is aware of his choice but sees the promise of glory eluding his grasp. In the *Odyssey* the shade of Achilles regrets the choice made in life: 'Better, I say, to break sod as a farmhand for some poor country man, on iron rations, than lord it over all the exhausted dead' (*Od.* 11.489-91). That is a parody of the choice in the *Iliad*, where the alternative to heroism is hardly the life of a serf but the prosperous existence of a Thessalian landowner (9.395-400):

> There are many Achaian girls in the land of Hellas and Phthia,
> daughters of great men who hold strong places in guard. And of these
> any one that I please I might make my beloved lady.
> And the great desire in my heart drives me rather in that place
> to take a wedded wife in marriage, the bride of my fancy,
> to enjoy with her the possessions won by aged Peleus.

The Iliad does not represent the enactment of Achilles' choice. He has already made it when the heroic world first beckons to him in the form of Nestor and Odysseus on a recruiting mission and he literally jumps at the opportunity (11.776-9):

> we came
> and stood in the forecourt, and Achilleus sprang up wondering
> and took us by the hand and led us in, and told us to sit down,
> and set hospitality properly before us, as is the stranger's right.

But Achilles flirts with unmaking his choice, and the intensity of that flirtation is a measure of his frustration. Ten years have gone by without the great event that would justify his choice. Then suddenly a plague strikes the Achaean camp and threatens to put an ignominious end both to the war and to his career. His first words give expression to his fear and implicitly tell us why the assembly was called by him rather than by an older warrior with more experience in council (1.59-61):

> Son of Atreus, I believe now that straggling backwards
> we must make our way home if we can even escape death,
> if fighting now must crush the Achaians and the plague likewise.

The seer Kalchas reveals the cause of the plague. Agamemnon erred in not honouring the request by the priest Chryses to ransom his daughter. Apollo sent the plague in response to the prayers of the injured father and will not relent until Agamemnon returns Chryseis with damages. Agamemnon yields but demands that the army make up his losses. When Achilles suggests that this compensation be deferred until after the fall of Troy, Agamemnon refuses and goes on the offensive: unless he is reimbursed now he will take someone else's concubine, perhaps Achilles'. And he suggests that Achilles might be put in charge of returning the daughter of Chryses – leaving Agamemnon in a strong position to seize Briseis during his absence (1.146).

At this point Achilles explodes into the anger that will not cease until Hektor is ransomed. Like the motif of choice, the anger of Achilles is an idiosyncratic feature only to the degree that it reflects the warrior's condition with unmatched purity and intensity. The warrior's life is governed by two forms of competition. He competes with his enemy for victory and with his peers for honour. The paternal advice 'always excel' means 'always excel among your peers by defeating your enemies' (11.784). The warrior takes part in a dual distribution of rewards. In the competition with the enemy he seizes what he can take by force. His success supports his claim in a second distribution, where he receives what his peers are willing to allot him as his honour or *timê*: literally, an assessment of his worth expressed in material goods. This second distribution determines his standing among his peers, and it is essential that this allotment be given to, rather than taken by, him. Thus the society of warriors is motivated by intense peer rivalry and faced with the task of distributive justice. This inherently unstable situation is the breeding ground for *cholos* or *mênis*, the uncontrollable anger of which Achilles is the most spectacular example.

Anger is a necessary condition of the warrior's success in battle. The rhetoric of battle, with its speeches of reproach, encouragement and exultation, aims at unleashing it. More effective than such rhetoric is the death of the friend or kinsman, which impels the warrior to fierce revenge (below, p. 95). These episodes of revenge in particular make clear how much the warrior's success depends on the speed with which he can be angered into violent action. To condition the warrior to an instant release of angry violence is one thing; to ensure that the target is chosen with discretion is another. Here the dual competition for honour reveals its paradoxical side. Peer rivalry creates frustrations that are as conducive to the release of anger as the encounter with the enemy, but in coping with these frustrations the warrior must be patient – a task to which he is the less fitted the more he excels in his métier. Anger is the dangerous passion that creates and destroys the warrior. Anger is to heroic what sex is to Victorian morality, and it is the favourite topic of parental advice, as in the words of Peleus that Odysseus recalls to Achilles (9.254-8):

> My child, for the matter of strength, Athene and Hera will give it
> if it be their will, but be it yours to hold fast in your bosom
> the anger of the proud heart, for consideration is better.
> Keep from the bad complication of quarrel, and all the more for this
> the Argives will honour you, both their younger men and their elders.

Once Achilles explodes into anger, his quarrel with Agamemnon soon leaves behind its immediate cause. Achilles does not blame Agamemnon for his treatment of Chryses or for ignoring the advice of the army. The particular grievance triggers an outburst that shows him despairing of his promised hour of greatness. When he asks 'Why am I here?' or 'What have the Trojans done to me?' he speaks out of anxiety about the choice he made when he leapt up at the sight of Odysseus and Nestor. That is why at the end of the speech Achilles flirts with the possibility of revoking that choice (1.169-71):

> Now I am returning to Phthia, since it is much better
> to go home again with my curved ships, and I am minded no longer
> to stay here dishonoured and pile up your wealth and your luxury.

Agamemnon responds to this flirtation by branding Achilles a traitor, and by announcing that he will personally seize Briseis. These two insults put Achilles beside himself with rage, and he is on the verge of killing Agamemnon, thereby forfeiting glory for ever. In the space of less than a hundred lines the protagonist's quest for glory and the poet's quest for motivating his final event are threatened with a premature catastrophe of ignominious violence. This is the first instance in the *Iliad* of what Karl Reinhardt (1961, 48) has called the 'epic almost', the poet's penchant for momentarily twisting the action towards a resolution that would frustrate his own and his characters' ends. These moments of false resolution serve an important function since they articulate major changes of direction. The narrative that returns from its absurd escapade does so with a firmer sense of its true course. Thus, after the abortive duel of Paris and Menelaos, Zeus proposes to settle the war peacefully, but the indignant response of Hera results in Athene's mission to persuade Pandaros to break the truce. Similarly, Achilles almost suffers the unheroic fate of drowning (21.240), but his escape from the river is the last course correction in a narrative that rushes towards its climax with resistless force.

The change of direction usually involves the intervention of a god. In Book 1 it is Athene, appealing to Achilles' reason, while his sword is already drawn (1.194) – a vivid image of the extremity of the situation. Athene persuades him to refrain from violence and promises rich rewards in the future for putting up with Agamemnon's insults. Achilles substitutes invective for the sword and 'together with the son of Menoitios' (1.307) returns to his tent, where he will nurse his anger until the death of Patroklos will call him to battle again. The casual mention of Patroklos points forward to that moment and is a reminder of the poet's strategic use of detail.

Achilles' calling of the assembly, motivated by the desire to clear the path for decisive action, has the unintended consequence of putting up new and more impenetrable barriers. Whereas previously it was the external fact of the plague that stood in the way of triumph, now it is his own sense of injured honour. He summons his mother from the sea, rehearses the story of his outrage, asks her to intercede with Zeus on his behalf, and concludes with the extraordinary request (1.407-12):

> Sit beside him and take his knees and remind him of these things
> now, if perhaps he might be willing to help the Trojans,
> and pin the Achaians back against the ships and the water,
> dying, so that thus they may all have profit of their own king,
> that Atreus' son wide-ruling Agamemnon may recognize
> his madness, that he did no honour to the best of the Achaians.

It is a commonplace that Homeric warriors have a weakly developed sense of group loyalty. Allegiance to a common cause runs a poor third to the quest for individual honour and the commitment to an immediate kinsman or companion in arms. Even in this hierarchy of values Achilles' request amounts to treason, and, as events will show, it is a *hamartia* in Aristotle's sense, a disastrous error of judgement the mortal consequences of which will rebound upon Achilles himself.

The request originates with Achilles. Nothing that Athene had told him would prompt or justify so desperate a step. 'Wait and you will be recompensed', Athene had said – not unlike the witches' words: 'All hail, Macbeth, that shalt be king hereafter.' Both times the human recipient of the prophecy goes beyond its terms, and in acting to ensure its success fatally taints the manner of its fulfilment. In strict narrative terms the request is redundant. What Achilles asks for is no more than what will happen as the consequence of his withdrawal: without his presence Hektor will take the offensive and wreak havoc among the Achaeans. But, while the request does not affect the sequence of events, it radically changes their significance. Without the request, Agamemnon bears the blame for the consequences of their quarrel. That is the view held by the characters in the poem, all of whom are ignorant of Achilles' dealings with Zeus and Thetis. Agamemnon himself admits that he is at fault well before the consequences of his mistake are apparent (2.378). But for the reader the request changes the allocation of responsibility. The suffering of the Achaeans no longer appears as the regrettable consequence of a position into which Achilles was forced. Not a quarrel started by Agamemnon, but the vindictive despair of Achilles becomes the *archê* of the tragedy; the causal chain leads back to an action by Achilles rather than, as Redfield has argued, to his reaction to the arrogance of Agamemnon (Redfield 1975, 107, 122).

Achilles' request for the destruction of the Achaeans, so redundant on the narrative level, is the poet's chief device for establishing a problematic relationship between self and action and for concatenating his plot in a tragic manner. Fragment 231 from Aeschylus' lost Achilles trilogy cites the fable of the eagle who recognises as his own the feathers guiding the arrow that mortally wounded him. The passage is perhaps the most striking expression of the paradox of that relationship in Attic tragedy (Schadewaldt, 1970). The plot turns on a disaster that overwhelms the protagonist from without and yet is intimately tied to his own being. The fable of the eagle focuses on the moment of recognition. The correlate of such recognition is ignorance. In Attic tragedy the beginning of ignorance usually lies outside the action itself, since it prefers the crisis of disillusionment to the progressive entanglement in delusion. Because the epic narrative has time for both, the exposition of the *Iliad* gives emphatic attention to the initial moment of blindness. Patroklos will be the most prominent of the Achaeans whose death Achilles so ardently desires at this point. If Achilles knew this, he would never utter his wish; that he can do so is a measure of his blindness.

Hektor during the absence of Achilles

The opening book of the *Iliad* creates the conditions for the fulfilment of Achilles' destiny, but from Achilles' perspective the possibility of heroic achievement has receded. The restless activity that brought disaster to so many cities around Troy, if not to Troy itself, has come to an indefinite halt. The change in the situation of Achilles produces a similarly ironic change in his antagonist. Hektor is at heart a defensive warrior, but the absence of Achilles tempts him beyond the walls into a new and more aggressive role. When he is about to set fire to the ship and victory seems in his grasp he imagines that the world outside the walls is his true home (15.718-23):

> Bring fire, and give single voice to the clamour of battle.
> Now Zeus has given us a day worth all the rest of them:
> the ships' capture, the ships that came here in spite of the gods' will
> and have visited much pain on us, by our counsellors' cowardice
> who would not let me fight by the grounded ships, though I wanted to,
> but held me back in restraint, and curbed in our fighters.

Hektor's confidence rests on a misunderstanding but, as with Achilles, the misunderstanding is essential to his achievement of heroic fame.

Homer takes great pains to establish that Hektor's natural place is inside the city. While Hektor appears sporadically in the first few books, his full introduction is delayed until Book 6, where he appears in a setting that emphasises social integration. The poet even takes some narrative risks to achieve the setting. At a moment of danger Hektor returns to Troy and tells his mother to offer a sacrifice to Athene. It would make more strategic sense to entrust such an errand to a herald, but Homer wants Hektor inside Troy for reasons that become apparent with the description of his arrival (6.237-41):

> Now as Hektor had come to the Skaian gates and the oak tree,
> all the wives of the Trojans and their daughters came running about him
> to ask after their sons, after their brothers and neighbours,
> their husbands; and he told them to pray to the immortals,
> all, in turn; but there were sorrows in store for many.

This brilliant vignette establishes sympathetic identification as the basis of our response to Hektor, as Milton saw well when he used the scene to shape his account of the angels' reaction to the news of the fall of man (*Paradise Lost* 10.21). Hektor is 'like us' in the Aristotelian sense (*Poetic*, 13.1453a5) that transcends the difference between the seventh-century listener and the reader today. Like us, and unlike Achilles, he is defined by a web of communal relations rather than by an identity that realises itself in solitude and defiance of all social norms.

Hektor's visit to Troy unfolds as a sequence of three encounters with his mother, his brother and sister-in-law, and finally his wife and son. Three times Hektor refuses an invitation to stay. Although the visit is a reprieve from the furious pace of fighting, the narrative does not come to a rest. Hektor's sense of being in a hurry moves it along and introduces the disturbance of war into a world still untouched by it.

After giving instructions to his mother Hektor proceeds to the house of Paris, whom the reader had last encountered in his bedroom, where Aphrodite had taken him after his near-defeat at the hands of Menelaos. There, far from any sense of guilt or shame, he had made love to Helen, declaring that never before had he felt a similar passion for her (3.442). The narrative of Hektor in Troy does not allude to Paris' defeat in Book 3, but it endows Paris with the same languor to serve as a foil for Hektor's restless obsession with duty. As Hektor enters the house of Paris, the poet develops the contrast through the setting (6.318-24):

> There entered Hektor beloved of Zeus, in his hand holding
> the eleven-cubit-long spear, whose shaft was tipped with a shining
> bronze spearhead, and a ring of gold was hooped to hold it.
> He found the man in his chamber busy with his splendid armour,
> the corselet and the shield, and turning in his hands the curved bow,
> while Helen of Argos was sitting among her attendant women
> directing the magnificent work done by her handmaidens.

The spear in the hand is the sign of battle-readiness; it is the last piece of equipment taken by the warrior in the conventional arming scene. When Achilles seizes his spear, he is ready for battle (19.387); similarly, the failure of Patroklos to pick up the spear of Achilles points to his ruin (16.140). The spear is the first weapon of which the warrior disburdens himself. Thus Telemachos takes the spear of the disguised Athene and puts it in a rack with the spears of Odysseus, a sign of his competence as host and a reminder of the revenge that takes its beginning with this divine visit (*Od.* 1.127). Hektor holds on to his spear even inside the house of Paris, a visible reproof to his laggard brother who is busying himself about his 'splendid armour', but shows no particular signs of putting it on.

The scene moves quickly from Paris to Helen, who is no more successful than Hekabe in detaining Hektor: he has no time and must return to the Trojans in the field who miss him. But perhaps she could hurry up her husband, who might even catch up with him (6.365-8):

> For I am going first to my own house, so I can visit
> my own people, my beloved wife and my son, who is little,
> since I do not know if ever again I shall come back this way,
> or whether the gods will strike me down at the hands of the Achaians.

In this manner Homer introduces one of the most celebrated scenes in Western literature. The mise-en-scène is profoundly ironic, since the irresponsible brother's tardiness clears the time for the encounter of the dutiful husband with his faithful wife. Having twice refused the luxury of sitting down, Hektor finds time to visit his wife while Paris puts on his armour. Indeed, the arming of Paris frames the scene: Hektor on his way from Andromache meets with Paris prancing towards battle, and Paris in a bantering and apologetic mood asks whether he did hold up Hektor after all (6.518).

Similar ironies surround the place of the meeting. Unlike Hekabe and Paris, Andromache is not at home; husband and wife miss one another out of an identity of motives. He goes home because it might be the last time; she has madly rushed to the battlements because she fears for his life in the Achaean onslaught. And Hektor, deprived of the chance of sitting down at home, must rush off again to meet her as she comes running back from the battlements (6.390-4):

> So the housekeeper spoke, and Hektor hastened from his home
> backward by the way he had come through the well-laid streets. So
> as he had come to the gates on his way through the great city,
> the Skaian gates, whereby he would issue into the plain, there
> at last his own generous wife came running to meet him.

And so they meet, not at the appointed place and time, as one might expect from the orderly narrative of the grand epic when it brings together the prince and his consort, but somehow somewhere sometime as their paths cross and for a brief space their breathless confusion comes to a halt. If this sounds fanciful, compare the absence of ceremony with the formality of the encounters with Hekabe (242) and Paris (313). One might even think of the elaborately described bed of Odysseus and Penelope as a narrative possibility that the poet forgoes at this point (*Od.* 23.184).

The setting anticipates their conversation, which turns on the paradox that Hektor cannot stay at home precisely because he treasures its values so highly. Like Hekabe and Helen, Andromache seeks to detain Hektor, but her temptation is more radical, for she wants to keep Hektor in Troy altogether, fighting the enemy from the security of the towers (6.431). Andromache's temptation gains poignancy from her special circumstances. Hektor is all she has: her father and her brothers are dead, killed by Achilles when he sacked the city of Thebe; her mother, captive but ransomed, died shortly afterwards (6.429-30):

> Hektor, thus you are father to me, and my honoured mother,
> you are my brother, and you it is who are my young husband.

The history of Andromache sets up the expectation that Achilles, who deprived her of everything else, will also deprive her of Hektor. This expectation is both weakened and strengthened by the link of Andromache's history with the main plot. Through a stroke of economy pregnant with narrative implications Homer has identified the expedition against Thebe with the expedition during which Chryseis was captured. The link is stressed in the opening of Achilles' narrative to his mother: 'We went against Thebe, the sacred city of Eetion' (1.366). Inasmuch as the withdrawal of Achilles results from this expedition, the fears of Andromache are, for the moment, groundless. But inasmuch as this withdrawal leads to the death of Patroklos and to a re-entry into battle directed exclusively against Hektor her anxiety is only too well founded. And the poet looks forward not only to the time of Hektor's death but also to the savagery of its circumstances. What else could be the point of portraying an Achilles who in the Theban expedition scrupulously respected the rights of the dead, except to measure his transformation after the death of Patroklos (6.416-20):

> He killed Eëtion
> but did not strip his armour, for his heart respected the dead man,
> but burned the body in all its elaborate war-gear
> and piled a grave mound over it, and the nymphs of the mountains,
> daughters of Zeus of the aegis, planted elm trees about it.

Hektor's response, far from allaying her fears, confirms them. She had not dared to look beyond the possibility of Hektor's death, but his reply is grounded in the certainty of Troy's fall 6.447-9. But even so he must fight, not only to avoid the reproaches of the Trojans but also in order to live up to the commands of his self (6.444-6):

> since I have learned to be valiant
> and to fight always among the foremost ranks of the Trojans,
> winning for my own self great glory, and for my father.

Heroic clairvoyance may destroy human feeling. It threatens to do so in the case of Achilles, separated from his friend by death, from his father by distance, and from his mother by her divinity. The clairvoyance of Hektor, on the other hand, co-exists with intense feeling and regret, which manifests itself in the vision of the enslaved Andromache that closes his speech. From the horror of this vision Hektor turns to the present and indulges in the wish-fulfilment of an imagined future for his son. The relationship of father and son is central to the warrior code, and nothing expresses more fully the poet's sympathy with and ironic distance from that code than his subtlety in the treatment of that relationship. All Iliadic instances are in one form or another fractured. Nestor relates at length how he showed himself worthy of his father Neleus (11.683), but it is hard to imagine Nestor young, and when he appears in the

Iliad with his son Antilochos there is more than a touch of Polonius in him (23.301). Tydeus is twice held up as a heroic example to Diomedes, but he is long since dead (4.372, 5.800). Peleus must endure the afflictions of age while his son has gone never to return. With Priam and Hektor the poet had the opportunity to show the relationship with both father and son in their prime, embodying between them the continuity of succession and the fullness of the heroic ideal of courage and wisdom. But Hektor and Priam never appear together in the *Iliad*. When the *Iliad* brings together a father and a son both in their prime, it will be in the meeting of Achilles and Priam, the most violently broken and the most profound version of the relationship.

In Book 6 the father-son relationship appears in the form of the domestic idyll and becomes the crowning instance of the clash between the heroic and the domestic that pervades the entire book. As in the earlier Paris scene, a piece of armour provides the prop on which the scene turns. Hektor's most distinctive epithet is *koruthaiolos* ('helm-shimmering'). Others may recognise Hektor by the splendour of his helmet, but for Astyanax it blocks recognition, and in the typical gesture of a baby 'making strange' he seeks refuge in the familiar bosom of his nurse (6.466). The incident joins husband and wife in laughter and dispels for a moment the grim vision of a future in which Hektor is dead and Andromache captive. But the scene is no less prophetic than those visions: Astyanax turning away from his father's helmet anticipates in that gesture the denial of the heroic role his father wishes for him. No less meaningful is the gesture with which Hektor takes off his helmet a disarming and abandonment of heroic identity that looks forward to Patroklos' loss of his helmet (16.793) or the analogous loss by Andromache of her headgear when she faints on seeing the body of her husband dragged around the city (22.466). The no-longer-heroic father speaks to his never-to-be-heroic son, but out of this situation comes the most conventional prayer for heroic succession (6.476-81):

> Zeus, and you other immortals, grant that this boy, who is my son,
> may be as I am, pre-eminent among the Trojans,
> great in strength, as am I, and rule strongly over Ilion;
> and some day let them say of him: 'He is better by far than his father',
> as he comes in from the fighting; and let him kill his enemy
> and bring home the blooded spoils, and delight the heart of his mother.

The poet does not bother to register the response of Zeus to this so obviously deluded prayer. Instead he focuses on Andromache's response as she receives the child back in her arms, *dakruoen gelasasa* ('laughing amidst tears', 6.484). Is it permissible to think of Chekhov, where we find the same genius for establishing a coherent effect from a mosaic of contradictory emotions and utterances?

As he turns to his wife, Hektor changes moods again. In words designed to comfort Andromache he neither predicts doom nor indulges in dreams but retreats to a pragmatic fatalism: Who knows what is to come? In the meantime you do your work, and I will do mine (6.486). The end of the scene returns to its beginning. Andromache goes home, not to her weaving, as Hektor had told her, but to mourn him with her maids while he is still alive (6.500). The lines echo Hektor's earlier statement that he will visit Andromache because he might not return from battle (6.367).

The Hektor who leaves Andromache enters into a new role created by the absence of Achilles. It is a false role for him, and he does not become himself again until his death is imminent. Throughout the course of his seeming triumph, which takes him across the Achaean wall to the ship of Protesilaos, the poet consistently shows him as a man not fully in control of himself. The new Hektor is given to 'hectoring', as in the following speech early on the second day of fighting (8.173-83):

> Trojans, Lykians and Dardanians who fight at close quarters,
> be men now, dear friends, remember your furious valour.
> I see that the son of Kronos has bowed his head and assented
> to my high glory and success, but granted the Danaans
> disaster: fools, who designed with care these fortifications,
> flimsy things, not worth a thought, which will not beat my strength
> back, but lightly my horses will leap the ditch they have dug them.
> But after I have come beside their hollow ships, let there
> be some who will remember to bring me ravening fire,
> so that I can set their ships on fire, and cut down
> the very Argives mazed in the smoke at the side of their vessels.

The new Hektor shows a misplaced confidence in divine support and holds out the prospect of victories that never quite materialise. But he comes very close to his goals. Twice he pins the Achaeans back on the ships. The first time Hera inspires a counter-rally (8.217); the second time only nightfall saves the Achaeans from total disaster (8.348, 485).

Encouraged by the events of the day, the Trojans camp outside the city for the first time. Flaring fires express their new confidence, and in an exuberant speech Hektor promises to defeat Diomedes (8.532). Reality gives the lie to his hyperbolic boast: on the following day Diomedes easily has the upper hand; his spear, while failing to pierce Hektor's helmet, stuns him (11.354-6):

> But Hektor sprang far away back and merged among his own people,
> and dropping to one knee stayed leaning on the ground with his heavy
> hand, and a covering of black night came over both eyes.

This discrepancy between promise and performance is repeated in the long-delayed encounter of Hektor and Aias on the third day of fighting. At the end of Book 13 the warriors meet, and Hektor replies to a taunting speech by Aias with words that echo his presumption of divine support on the previous night (13.824-8; cf. 8.539-41):

> Aias, you inarticulate ox, what is this you have spoken?
> If I could only be called son to Zeus of the aegis
> all the days of my life, and the lady Hera my mother,
> and I be honoured, as Apollo and Athene are honoured,
> so surely as this is a day that brings evil to the Argives.

The expected clash of the warriors does not happen immediately, but when it takes place Aias is clearly victorious: only the assistance of his companions saves Hektor from certain death on this occasion, and it takes the healing skills of Apollo to restore him to battle (14.402, 15.239).

The two incidents in part derive from the Achaean bias of the narrative. The plot requires that Hektor be second only to Achilles, but the poet is also subject to constraints that prevent him from crediting Hektor with a clear-cut victory over an Achaean of the first rank. The constraint in Homer's hands becomes a potent tool of characterisation and serves to underscore the imbalance of word and action that defines the changed Hektor. There are other expressions of this lack of balance. A fairly common convention associates the warrior at the height of battle with personifications of terror. The persistent use of this motif with Hektor suggests that the withdrawal of Achilles has put him in some sense beside himself. In his pursuit of the Achaeans he appears 'wearing the stark eyes of a Gorgon, or murderous Ares' (8.349). Odysseus portrays him to Achilles as seized by *lussa*, a word for madness also used of rabid dogs (9.239, 305). In his attack on the gates Hektor is dark as night with fiery eyes (12.462). There may be a kind of sublimity in that image, but the degraded violence of a rabid animal comes more readily to mind in the description of Hektor's final assault on the ships (15.607-9):

> A slaver came out around his mouth, and under the lowering
> brows his eyes were glittering, the helm on his temples
> was shaken and thundered horribly to the fighting of Hektor.

Hektor's instability is further underscored through a change in flanking characters. The sense of social obligation that is so much part of his nature had been conveyed through the contrast of Hektor and Paris. But the poet drops the contrast of the unequal brothers after Book 6 and shows Hektor in the company of his cousin Poulydamas, a sober counsellor whose advice he rejects at critical moments. Completely untouched by the *lussa* that has taken hold of his greater cousin, Poulydamas points to delusion as the central theme in the career of Hektor. It is a telling detail that on the one occasion on which Hektor upbraids Paris during the third day of fighting he is wrong and Paris tells him so in words that clearly contrast with the meek and apologetic spirit in which he previously accepted his brother's remonstrations (13.775; cf. 3.59, 6.333).

Poulydamas and Hektor first clash when the Trojan attack on the wall stalls, partly because of Achaean resistance and partly because of a bird omen that terrifies the Trojans. Poulydamas offers what turns out to be the correct interpretation of the omen: the Trojans will not sustain their attack but will suffer losses and eventual defeat just as the eagle in the omen was unable to hold on to the snake it had caught. On the basis of this interpretation Poulydamas counsels retreat (12.216), but Hektor indignantly rejects this advice and pits his earlier assurances from Zeus (11.192) against the augur's professional competence. This is the speech that contains the famous line 'one bird sign is best: to fight in defence of our country' (12.243). The line is often quoted out of context to demonstrate the noble patriotism of Hektor. So it does, but it also marks a state of delusion that invests his sentiments with a peculiar pathos. This is the one opportunity for Hektor to retreat without loss of face from his exposed situation. He misses it because he does not know the ambiguity of Zeus' promise. The perspective from which the contradiction of divine utterance is resolved, and which is always available to the reader, becomes apparent to the character only through a catastrophic denouement. There is a strong parallelism between Hektor and Achilles in this regard: just as Hektor rejects sensible advice out of a misplaced confidence in Zeus, so

Achilles rejects the offer of Agamemnon out of the conviction that he enjoys the special protection of Zeus (below, p. 51)

The rejection of Poulydamas' advice marks the midpoint in Hektor's career and is followed shortly by his first great achievement, the storming of the gates. In the counter-offensive brought about by the intervention of Poseidon, Hektor plays a marginal role as the poet keeps him in reserve for his triumphant appearance in the battle of the ships. Where the poet focuses on Hektor in this part of the work he dwells on the vulnerability of his strength and judgement: here we find his unjustified attack on Paris and his ignominious defeat at the hands of Aias.

The triumph of Hektor begins with his restoration by Apollo. Once more he rushes into battle, and with the god's support his progress is irresistible. Apollo levels ditch and wall with the ease of a child trampling a sandcastle (15.360), and the Trojans flood across the opening and towards the ships. Hektor's offensive threatens to undo nine years of war as the narrative returns to its point of departure. In the second book the first marshalling of the Achaeans on the plain, probably an echo of their first arrival, had been compared to a gathering of migrating birds in the Caystrian plain. The same birds recur here, 'feeding alongside a river', but now they are attacked by the eagle Hektor (2.460 =15.692). The same return to the beginning underlies the poet's choice of the ship to which Hektor sets fire. It is the ship of Protesilaos, of whom the catalogue tells us that he was the first warrior to land and to be killed on Trojan soil (2.698). For Hektor, of course, this return to the beginning is the desired end; little does he know that the narrative will recoil from this 'almost' only to move more fiercely towards its eventual goal.

The Embassy

The encounter of Achilles and Hektor depends upon the withdrawal of the former, which tempts Hektor beyond the safety of the walls. The withdrawal is the beginning of the plot, the duel its end. The protagonist is absent in the middle. That absence is a fact of great and continuing significance. But its representation poses a narrative problem. So does the difficulty of developing in adequate detail the character of the protagonist if the design of the plot severely limits the places of his appearance.

The Embassy is Homer's answer to both problems. A delegation of Achaeans implores Achilles to give up his anger, accept enormous damages from Agamemnon and rejoin the fighting. The attempt must fail since the absence of Achilles must continue, but the failure turns into a magnificent occasion for impressing his absent presence on the reader's mind. Moreover, the Embassy does for Achilles what the encounter with Andromache did for Hektor: it provides a setting in which he can speak freely and passionately about the conditions of his existence.

The decision to approach Achilles is made in a council of Achaean leaders. Nestor diplomatically but firmly points to the link between the desperate situation of the army and Agamemnon's treatment of Achilles. He urges Agamemnon to reconcile Achilles 'with splendid gifts and gentle words' (9.113). Agamemnon readily concedes his mistake (114), states his willingness to make amends and lists a long catalogue of gifts that are indeed splendid. He concludes with words that are deficient in gentleness but may be no more than an attempt to save a little face in a humiliating situation (9.160-1):

And let him yield place to me, inasmuch as I am the kinglier
and inasmuch as I can call myself born the elder.

Nestor is full of praise: 'nobody could blame your gifts', he says, but then takes care
to ensure that the proper words will be spoken as well. He picks the delegation to offer
the settlement to Achilles, consisting of Phoinix, the former tutor of Achilles, Aias,
the leading soldier after Achilles, and Odysseus, the shrewdest counsellor. Although
Agamemnon's offer as he stated it was incomplete, what Achilles receives is a proper
offer of 'splendid gifts and gentle words'. The delegation is as high-ranking as
Homeric protocol can imagine. It is out of the question that Agamemnon should go
himself. The bitterness of their quarrel makes mediation imperative and socially
acceptable. When Achilles later says 'He wouldn't dare come here himself' (9.373),
the words cannot be taken as the poet's criticism of Agamemnon but reflect Achilles'
disastrous refusal to acknowledge the change in circumstances. That Priam will in
person reconcile an even more implacable Achilles serves not to call into question the
propriety of the earlier occasion but to emphasise the unheard-of nature of Priam's
visit. The propriety of the offer is also a major argument in Phoinix's speech (9.518).

The arrival of the ambassadors marks one of those Homeric epiphanies in which
the poet looks back and forth to comprehend the entire action in one setting
(9.185-91):

Now they came beside the shelters and ships of the Myrmidons
and they found Achilleus delighting his heart in a lyre, clear-sounding,
splendid and carefully wrought, with a bridge of silver upon it,
which he won out of the spoils when he ruined Eëtion's city.
With this he was pleasuring his heart, and singing of men's fame,
as Patroklos was sitting over against him, alone, in silence,
watching Aiakides and the time he would leave off singing.

The lyre points back to the quarrel and forward to the fate of Andromache, Eëtion's
daughter. Achilles is inactive, but his unquenchable thirst for glory finds temporary
satisfaction in heroic poetry; his listener is Patroklos, the instrument and victim of his
ultimate triumph.

As the delegates approach, Achilles leaps up with the same impulsiveness that will
govern his response to Odysseus' speech; he does not even take the time to put aside
his lyre (9.194). His strong and cordial welcome is in character: the first book had
made a point of his courtesy in his treatment of the heralds who had come on the
unpleasant task of claiming Briseis (1.334). But the emphasis on courtesy also
establishes a background for the violence of the subsequent eruption. After the
customary meal Odysseus turns to business. At the centre of his speech stands the
verbatim repetition of Agamemnon's offer, minus the concluding insistence on his
superiority. The arguments that frame it are from the speaker's perspective the most
persuasive he can think of, but as the poet's words they are composed with a
knowledge of the future and look forward to the consequences of Achilles' refusal.
Odysseus describes in lurid detail how Hektor has become a threat to the Achaeans
and how Achilles' prophecy in the first assembly has come true. The words are meant
to gratify Achilles, but Odysseus attaches a warning, and the poet looks forward to the
Patrokleia (9.247-51):

> Up, then! if you are minded, late though it be, to rescue
> the afflicted sons of the Achaians from the Trojan onslaught.
> It will be an affliction to you hereafter, there will be no remedy
> found to heal the evil thing when it has been done. No, beforehand
> take thought to beat the evil day aside from the Danaans.

Encouraged by the courteous reception, Odysseus then strikes a tone of camaraderie (*ô pepon*, 9.252) and puts himself in the position of an older mentor, reminding him of his father's advice to control his temper in order to gain glory among the Achaians. This memory provides the link to the repetition of Agamemnon's lavish offer. At the end of his speech he returns to the theme of the raging Hektor. If Agamemnon is hateful to you, he says, think of the other Achaeans and the glory they will bestow on you (9.304-6):

> For now you might kill Hektor, since he would come very close to you
> with the wicked fury upon him, since he thinks there is not his equal
> among the rest of the Danaans the ships carried hither.

The words project a non-tragic resolution and set the stage for Achilles' violent refusal through which such a resolution is ruled out for ever. Achilles' refusal is not, as Eichholz argued in an influential essay, a just response to an inadequate offer but an intensified repetition of his behaviour in Book 1. The Embassy continues the theme of vindictive intransigence that began with his prayer to Zeus and represents the repeated 'no' of Achilles as a decision for whose consequences he bears the responsibility.

Whereas Odysseus had dwelt emphatically on the change in the circumstances of the Achaeans, Achilles pretends that nothing has changed. His speech is a passionate repetition and extravagant elaboration of his earlier grievances about Agamemnon's rapacity. The six lines of the original complaint (1.163) are magnified as Achilles sees himself as a mother bird ceaselessly working on behalf of her young while Agamemnon sits back, dividing the spoils and keeping the lion's share. The iterative verb forms, lost in the translation, add colour to his language. His whole life is based on the premise of distinction, but the war has proved a great leveller: 'we are all held in a single honour, the brave with the weaklings' (9.319). He has gained nothing from always risking his life (9.322). Why should he fight for other men's wives (9.339)? The rehearsal of grievances leads, as in the assembly, to a flirtation with the alternative of an unheroic life, also greatly intensified (9.356-63):

> But, now I am unwilling to fight against brilliant Hektor,
> tomorrow, when I have sacrificed to Zeus and to all gods,
> and loaded well my ships, and rowed out on to the salt water,
> you will see, if you have a mind to it and if it concerns you,
> my ships in the dawn at sea on the Hellespont where the fish swarm
> and my men manning them with good will to row. If the glorious
> shaker of the earth should grant us a favouring passage
> on the third day thereafter we might raise generous Phthia.

There is in the *Iliad* a rhetoric of the unreal, that is to say, a tendency to elaborate through special flights of language departures from reality as the poet and his reader know it. The suspicion aroused by such rhetoric is usually confirmed if we compare what the character says with what actually happens. Diomedes and Aias give the lie to Hektor's boasts (above, p. 46). The gifts of Agamemnon are described in such lavish detail because they will be rejected. Achilles' elaboration of his plan to go home is similarly deflated by reality. When Achilles speaks of arriving in Phthia on the third day (or the day after tomorrow, as we would say) that prediction contrasts with the reality of the duel of Hektor and Achilles, which will take place on that day. It is a further ironic effect that Achilles' outburst occurs in the same night in which Hektor makes his decision to stay outside the walls (8.497).

Achilles' rejection of Agamemnon's gifts exceeds their description in its extravagance. He will have nothing to do with them even if they outnumber the sand on the beach, nor will he marry the daughters of Agamemnon even if they combine the beauty of Aphrodite with the skills of Athene. When in this context Achilles claims that Agamemnon will not persuade him 'until he had made good to me all this heart-rending insolence' (9.387) the words cannot be taken as referring to some inadequacy in Agamemnon's offer. Rather, they show that there is no conceivable settlement that Achilles would accept. Unreality also pervades Achilles' portrayal of the quiet life that awaits him on his return to Phthia, but the height of absurdity is reached when Achilles, the paragon of the risk-taking man, exalts survival as the highest value and argues that not even the treasures of Troy should lead a man to risk his life (9.400). At this point the motif of the choice appears in its explicit form (9.410-16):

> For my mother Thetis the goddess of the silver feet tells me
> I carry two sorts of destiny toward the day of my death. Either,
> if I stay here and fight beside the city of the Trojans,
> my return home is gone, but my glory shall be everlasting;
> but if I return home to the beloved land of my fathers,
> the excellence of my glory is gone, but there will be a long life
> left for me, and my end in death will not come to me quickly.

Here is another Homeric 'almost'; what will bring about the fulfilment of the original choice is precisely the mode in which Achilles seeks to cancel it.

Whereas Odysseus had dwelt on the opportunities for glory, Phoinix in the second plea turns to the consequences of intransigence. He ends with a warning: if you do not give up your anger now when you can cash it in for the reward of glory, you may have to give it up when you will get nothing for it. Achilles in his response dwells on the sufficient honour he is receiving from Zeus (9.608), without recognising that this honour will be purchased at the price of Patroklos' life. His misplaced confidence is the structural equivalent of Hektor's when he rejects the advice of Poulydamas (above, p. 47). Yet there is an important tension between the beginning and the end of Achilles' response to Phoinix. While his confidence in Zeus is a sign of his continuing intransigence, the conclusion of his speech yields a little. To Odysseus he had said: 'Tomorrow I will sail.' To Phoinix he says: 'Tomorrow we will deliberate whether to go home or stay.' This partial yielding will happen again in the response to Aias (9.650) and at the opening of the Patrokleia (16.60), with results far worse than either a complete turn or continued intransigence.

Aias does not initially address Achilles at all but comments to Odysseus on the failure of the mission (9.624). The words of the plain soldier are particularly valuable because they show how much Achilles' behaviour breaks established norms. Men have been known to settle disputes over the death of a kinsman, he says, but you – and here he suddenly turns to Achilles – persist in a quarrel over nothing more than a girl (the emphatic enjambment *heineka koures/ oiês* makes his point very well, 9.637-8). Gradually the speech of Aias turns into a final appeal that recalls Achilles' welcoming words in which he had greeted the delegates as the dearest of the Achaeans (9.639-42):

> Now make gracious the spirit within you.
> Respect your own house; see, we are under the same roof with you,
> from the multitude of the Danaans, we who desire beyond all
> others to have your honour and love, out of all the Achaians.

If the words of Aias show his incomprehension of Achilles' behaviour, it seems that Achilles himself is puzzled by the resistance of his passion to conventional forms of treatment, for his response to the blunt Aias is unexpectedly conciliatory (9.644). He yields a little more. Gone is the flirtation with going home and, while he still refuses to fight, the future he now envisages is dominated by Hektor (9.650-5):

> that I shall not think again of the bloody fighting
> until such time as the son of wise Priam, Hektor the brilliant,
> comes all the way to the ships of the Myrmidons, and their shelters,
> slaughtering the Argives, and shall darken with fire our vessels.
> But around my own shelter, I think, and beside my black ship
> Hektor will be held, though he be very hungry for battle.

The progress of the Embassy repeats that of the first assembly. An original decision to go home is replaced by a decision to wait while Hektor inflicts damage. The moment of crisis, however, is more sharply defined: whereas in the assembly Achilles foresaw in general terms the savage work of Hektor, now he envisages more clearly the battle near the ships, and he states the point beyond which he will not allow Hektor to go. What changes the situation from the first book is the fact that the attitude of Achilles persists in the light of a serious attempt, fully adequate to the norms of the warrior code, to offer a just settlement. Achilles' refusal to accept the offer changes the mode of conflict resolution from negotiation to violence and greatly increases the cost to himself. Thus the Embassy does to the story of Achilles what the abortive duel of Menelaos and Paris and the broken truce do to the story of the war.

The Patrokleia

The plot of the *Iliad* is made possible by the blindness of the protagonists. Hektor and Achilles become mortal enemies through a sequence of errors. The first and most pregnant of these errors is Achilles' prayer to Zeus after his withdrawal from battle. It leads to Hektor's false security, and it sets Achilles on the path of blind intransigence. In the Embassy, Achilles compounds the initial error by rejecting an opportunity that would more than redress his grievance. But the Embassy also puts an end to the flirtation with the pleasures of the quiet life. When we next see Achilles he has become an active observer. As the battle rages and even Aias is forced to retreat, he stands in the bow of his ship 'looking out over the sheer war work and the sorrowful onrush' (11.600) and, we may confidently add, waiting for Hektor. Nestor drives by, carrying on his chariot the wounded Machaon, whom Achilles does not quite recognise. He summons Patroklos to find out (11.602-4):

> At once he spoke to his own companion in arms, Patroklos,
> calling from the ship, and he heard it from inside the shelter, and came out
> like the war god, and this was the beginning of his evil.

Here is another instance of the poet's tracing of a causal chain to an act of Achilles. Whereas in the previous scenes Patroklos was present, now he is summoned to his fate. The poet honours him with the epithet *isos Arêi*; 'like the war god', but he dwells on his passive role as respondent. The beginning of his tragedy points forward to the circumstances of his death in which his status as victim finds its most pitiful expression.

Patroklos dutifully goes to Nestor's tent, where he sees Machaon. His task is done; it only remains for him to return to Achilles and tell him. Anxious to leave, he does not enter the tent nor does he accept an invitation to sit down, but Nestor detains him anyhow with a litany of Achaean woes that soon turns into an account of his first triumph as a young warrior. The rambling narrative implicitly contrasts the eagerness of the young Nestor with the reluctance of Achilles. In the final part of his speech Nestor's reminiscences turn to Achilles directly. We learn about the recruiting mission of Odysseus and Nestor, about Peleus' warnings about the consequences of yielding to anger, and about the counselling role Patroklos as the older friend is supposed to play. Returning to the present, Nestor suggests a compromise: if you cannot persuade him to fight, perhaps he will let you fight in his armour. Stirred by Nestor's words Patroklos hurries to Achilles' tent, no longer to confirm the identity of Machaon, but to try his skill at persuasion. This new intention is both blocked and advanced by yet another obstacle that prevents the speedy execution of his mission. On his way back he encounters Eurypylos (11.811-13):

> there Eurypylos, who had been wounded in the thigh with an arrow,
> met him, the illustrious son of Euaimon, limping
> away from the battle, and the watery sweat was running
> down his shoulders and face, and from the sore wound dark blood
> continued to drip, and yet the will stayed steady within him.

Like Machaon, Eurypylos is the victim of Paris' archery. The characters are doublets: the former motivates Patroklos' visit to Nestor, the latter delays his return until the fighting has taken an even more desperate turn. The narrative motivation has a thematic colouring. Despite his loyalty to Achilles, Patroklos does not hate the Achaeans. Nestor's words had moved him; in the figure of Eurypylos the suffering of the Achaeans confronts him in concrete form. Patroklos speaks to him in pity, and Eurypylos asks him to conduct him to his tent and look after his wounds. The request puts Patroklos in a bind: is not his goal to return to Achilles and act on Nestor's advice? But the immediacy of Eurypylos' suffering brooks no delay, and he goes with him.

The loyal companion of Achilles has become the helper of the Achaeans and in the process has revealed much of his generous and cooperative nature.

When, after many delays, Patroklos reaches Achilles' tent and makes his plea, his friend yields, thereby setting in motion the chain of events that lead to the death of Patroklos and settle the fate not only of Hektor and Troy, but of Achilles as well. The yielding shows Achilles at the deepest point of delusion, and the poet takes care to portray his decision not as a change of heart but as a further development of the state of mind that had first manifested itself in the prayer to Zeus.

Patroklos' plea to Achilles is based on solidarity with the Achaeans, but Achilles responds to his friend's gentle nature rather than to his cause. The response appears in the affectionate banter with which he compares the tears of Patroklos to those of a little girl wanting to be picked up by her mother (16.7). But the woes of the Achaeans leave him untouched, as we learn from the lone of harsh self-righteousness with which he guesses the cause of his friend's tears (16.17) and from the hyperbolic wish that concludes his answer to Patroklos (16.97-100):

> Father Zeus, Athene and Apollo, if only
> not one of all the Trojans could escape destruction, not one
> of the Argives, but you and I could emerge from the slaughter
> so that we two alone could break Troy's hallowed coronal.

If we hold this conclusion against the image of the crying girl, we see that Achilles is swayed by two powerful emotions – the love of Patroklos and the hatred of the Achaeans – without any awareness of their contradiction. Under the sway of these emotions Achilles projects a vision of the future no less unreal than his flirtation with the pleasures of the unheroic choice. Patroklos is to join the fighting, but he is to stay within certain limits, so as not to threaten the supremacy of Achilles and to ensure his own safety as well. As a consequence the Achaeans will return Briseis and give many other presents besides. The vision concludes with the bizarre image of Patroklos and himself as sole survivors and conquerors of Troy. Reality will refute this vision at every point: Patroklos will not be circumscribed by the role Achilles assigns to him, Achilles will take no pleasure in gifts, and neither Achilles nor Patroklos will be present when Troy is taken.

The continuity of Achilles' behaviour at this point with his previous actions is the explicit subject of one of the most moving scenes in the *Iliad*. When Patroklos has left for battle, Achilles prays for his safe return. Elaborate preparations mark the solemnity of the occasion. From the bottom of a treasure chest given him by Thetis, Achilles fetches a goblet from which only he drinks, and only when sacrificing to Zeus. He cleans the goblet with sulphur and water, washes his hands, and begins his prayer with an invocation as unique as the circumstantiality of the preparatory narrative (16.233-5):

> High Zeus, lord of Dodona, Pelasgian, living afar off,
> brooding over wintry Dodona, your prophets about you
> living, the Selloi who sleep on the ground with feet unwashed. Hear me.

The prayer itself begins with an acknowledgement to Zeus of his previous support and seeks support for the future as well (16.236-8):

As one time before when I prayed to you, you listened
and did me honour, and smote strongly the host of the Achaians,
so one more time bring to pass the wish that I pray for.

Specifically, Achilles prays that Patroklos may win glory and a safe return (16.241-8):

Let glory, Zeus of the wide brows, go forth with him.
Make brave the heart inside his breast, so that even Hektor
will find out whether our henchman knows how to fight his battles
by himself, or whether his hands rage invincible only
those times when I myself go into the grind of the war god.
But when he has beaten back from the ships their clamorous onset,
then let him come back to me and the running ships, unwounded,
with all his armour and with the companions who fight close beside him.

Zeus 'granted him one prayer, and denied him the other' (16.250). This supreme moment of Iliadic irony derives its power not merely from the tension between the symmetry of the phrasing and the inequality of what is granted and denied, but from its critical function in the central plot. The Zeus who denies half of Achilles' prayer is the same Zeus who granted the former request, but now he exacts its price. Through the death of Patroklos, Achilles will learn what it means to pray for the destruction of the Achaeans and what it means for such a prayer to be heard.

The blindness of Achilles comes to an abrupt end with the news of Patroklos' death, which is the turning-point of the epic. But, despite his significance, Patroklos does not achieve a fate of his own: rather, his role is to fail in the role of Achilles – a failure foreshadowed by the spear of Achilles, which alone of all of his friend's arms he does not carry into battle (16.140). The life and death of Patroklos are primarily events in the life of Achilles. The poet's constant observance of this perspective accounts for the manner in which he represents the circumstances of his death.

In the famous scene in which Antilochos brings the news of Patroklos' death Achilles is represented as having anticipated the event already in his imagination (18.12). If we return from that scene to our last sight of Achilles, we find him putting the goblet back into its chest and following his friend with his eyes (16.253-6):

When Achilleus had poured the wine and prayed to Zeus father
he went back into the shelter, stowed the cup in the chest, and came out
to stand in front of the door, with the desire in his heart still
to watch the grim encounter of Achaians and Trojans.

The lines are a discreet reminder of Achilles' anxiety; they also guide the perspective of the reader, who follows Patroklos where Achilles leaves off. The peculiar horror and pathos of Patroklos' death are in good measure a result of the manipulation of the reader's response so that he stands in for Achilles and becomes the witness of the friend's death. From the pursuing glances to the moment of foreboding, Patroklos is never out of the eyes of the reader/Achilles.

In donning the arms of Achilles, Patroklos for a while assumes his invincible strength. He drives the Trojans away from the ships of Protesilaos, cuts off their escape to the city, and wreaks havoc among them. But after his victory over Sarpedon he disregards the explicit advice of Achilles, goes on the offensive, and in the subsequent attack on Troy loses his life.

Patroklos' death is at one level a version of the death of Achilles. The *Iliad* presupposes and repeatedly alludes to the tradition according to which Achilles during an attempt to storm Troy suffered death at the hands of Paris and Apollo, the human and divine archers. The *Iliad* mirrors that tradition when Diomedes, the replacement for Achilles, suffers a non-lethal wound in the heel at the hands of Paris (11.377). Patroklos' death at the hands of Apollo and the brother of Paris is a more serious version of that tradition, a vicarious anticipation of the death of Achilles that permits the poet to incorporate into his epic an event that lies beyond its narrative scope. This procedure underscores the pivotal nature of Patroklos' death: he dies like Achilles because Achilles dies with him. Inseparable in life, their ashes united in a common urn (23.91), their virtual identity also manifests itself in the manner of their death.

While the death of Patroklos anticipates that of Achilles, it also has distinct features of its own, designed to impress on Achilles that Patroklos is the victim of his revenge on the Achaeans. The helpless agony of his last moments is a fitting and horrible conclusion to a heroic career that, despite its temporary glamour, lacks independence. The passive nature of Patroklos, which appeared in his silent listening (9.190) and in his response to Achilles' summons (11.604), manifests itself also in his final glory. The poet could have shown a warrior who in the exultation of victory wilfully and explicitly disregards advice and ventures into a more aggressive role. But Homer represents this transgression as a being drawn; and Patroklos' moment of exultation triggers a reflection on human impotence (16.684-93):

> But Patroklos, with a shout to Automedon and his horses,
> went after Trojans and Lykians in a huge blind fury.
> Besotted: had he only kept the command of Peleiades
> he might have got clear away from the evil spirit of black death.
> But always the mind of Zeus is a stronger thing than a man's mind.
> He terrifies even the warlike man, he takes away victory
> lightly, when he himself has driven a man into battle
> as now he drove on the fury in the heart of Patroklos.
> Then who was it you slaughtered first, who was the last one,
> Patroklos, as the gods called you to your death?

In his final assault Patroklos threatens the city itself, which would fall but for the intervention of Apollo. The god rebuffs his attack with words that both differentiate him from and identify him with his greater friend (16.707-9):

> Give way, illustrious Patroklos: it is not destined
> that the city of the proud Trojans shall fall before your spear
> nor even at the hand of Achilleus, who is far better than you are.

From this rebuff the battle moves towards an encounter of Patroklos and Hektor. The former scores an initial success by killing Hektor's charioteer Kebriones, and a fierce battle ensues over the body of the fallen warrior. At the climactic point of this fight the narrative takes an unexpected turn from what had been a fairly conventional account of battle. Instead of making the defeat of Patroklos depend on an aggressive act by Hektor, the poet makes Apollo intervene directly. He strikes Patroklos from behind with his flat hand and stuns him (16.793-805):

> Apollo now struck away from his head the helmet
> four-horned and hollow-eyed, and under the feet of the horses
> it rolled clattering, and the plumes above it were defiled
> by blood and dust. Before this time it had not been permitted
> to defile in the dust this great helmet crested in horse-hair;
> rather it guarded the head and the gracious brow of a godlike
> man, Achilleus; but now Zeus gave it over to Hektor
> to wear on his head, Hektor whose own death was close to him.
> And in his hands was splintered all the huge, great, heavy,
> iron-shod, far-shadowing spear, and away from his shoulders
> dropped to the ground the shield with its shield sling and its tassels.
> The lord Apollo, son of Zeus, broke the corselet upon him.
> Disaster caught his wits, and his shining body went nerveless.

The helpless terror of the stricken warrior has its only parallel in the *Iliad* in the much briefer account of the panic of Alkathoös, who becomes the victim of Poseidon and Idomeneus (13.436; below, p. 57). But in the case of Patroklos it is not Hektor who, like Idomeneus, takes advantage of the opportunity created by the god. Homer introduces a new character, the young Euphorbos, who wounds Patroklos and then is so terrified even by the naked Patroklos that he immediately retreats to the safety of his comrades. Struck by the god and by Euphorbos, Patroklos finally becomes an easy prey for Hektor (16.818).

The incomprehension and helplessness of Patroklos at the point of death contrast sharply and deliberately with the death of his noblest victim. The function of Sarpedon in the *Iliad* is to provide the career of Patroklos with a suitably climactic achievement. To that purpose he is introduced earlier in the poem as an adversary whose nobility is manifest both in words and deeds. He anticipates Hektor's success in breaching the wall (12.397), and Homer gives to him the most celebrated and complete statement of the warrior's creed (12.310). Sarpedon is a textbook hero, and as such he is also a paradigm of heroic friendship. When he first appears, he kills Tlepolemos but is seriously injured in turn. Immediately his friends surround him; Hektor holds the Achaeans at bay while his friends carry him to an oak-tree where he faints and then recovers (5.663). His famous speech is addressed to his friend Glaukos, who is far more than a convenient addressee and turns out to be no less essential to the death than to the life of the hero.

Sarpedon attacks Patroklos and is mortally wounded by him. His fall is an important event, marked by two similes and a speech. Apart from Hektor and Patroklos, Sarpedon is the only character to whom the poet gives the power of speech at the moment of death. The most remarkable quality of Sarpedon's final words is their matter-of-factness. He does not express surprise or regret at his fate. He had acknowledged the risk of death in the conclusion of his creed (12.326-8):

> But now, seeing that the spirits of death stand close about us
> in their thousands, no man can turn aside nor escape them,
> let us go on and win glory for ourselves, or yield it to others.

When death comes he is ready for it. His final words encourage his friend Glaukos to
do what the warrior's code requires on such an occasion: rescue the body (16.492).
Having said his piece, he dies, as he lived, by the book, but – and this is the crucial
point – protected both in life and in death by his confidence in the presence and help
of his friends. That Glaukos will follow the command of his friend goes without
saying, but the poet none the less makes a fuss about his compliance. It turns out that
Glaukos cannot help Sarpedon because he is still suffering from a hand-wound
received earlier in the day. In his despair Glaukos turns to Apollo, who listens to his
prayer and instantly heals his wound (16.508). It is not the poet's usual manner to
worry about loose ends. Thus the serious thigh-wound of Sarpedon suffered in Book
5 is entirely forgotten in Book 12. Why twenty lines to draw attention to an inconsis-
tency nobody would notice? The answer is surely that the episode serves to foreground
the theme of heroic fellowship: if one has to die in battle, then it is best to die like
Sarpedon in the company of a friend. The death of Sarpedon underscores the pathos
of the death of Patroklos, who dies alone and unexpectedly, confronted with an
experience of overwhelming terror. When Achilles blames himself later for not having
been at the side of his friend (18.98), the poignancy of that self-accusation is greatly
increased by the reader's experience of the contrasting deaths of Sarpedon and
Patroklos.

   With the death of Patroklos the careers of Hektor and Achilles reach their point of
maximum delusion. To Achilles' attempt to prescribe the limits of Patroklos' action
corresponds Hektor's boastful triumph over his dying victim (16.837-42):

> Wretch! Achilleus, great as he was, could do nothing to help you.
> When he stayed behind, and you went, he must have said much to you:
> 'Patroklos, lord of horses, see that you do not come back to me
> and the hollow ships, until you have torn in blood the tunic
> of manslaughtering Hektor about his chest.' In some such
> manner he spoke to you, and persuaded the fool's heart in you.

Like Achilles before him, Hektor is wrong on every single point. Patroklos, who
in his death regains his mental composure, points this out and predicts Hektor's
death at the hands of Achilles (16.844). The words have a chastening effect on
Hektor. He does not (how could he?) accept their truth, but neither does he reject
them, answering instead with a question to which he pretends the answer is still
open (16.859-61):

> Patroklos, what is this prophecy of my headlong destruction?
> Who knows if even Achilleus, son of lovely-haired Thetis,
> might before this be struck by my spear, and his own life perish?

He cannot know that the poet has provided an answer in advance when he describes
the moment of Patroklos' death in three lines that he will later use for Hektor as well
(16.855-7 = 22.361-3).

   Although Achilles has anticipated the death of Patroklos in his imagination, the
violence of his response is in no way diminished. He is so wild in the expression of
his grief that his mother hears him in the depth of the sea. She comes to comfort him
and undertakes to ask Hephaistos for a new armour to replace the one lost by

Patroklos. This is the second visit she pays to Achilles. She will come a third time to bring the order of the gods that Hektor should be ransomed. The visits of Thetis articulate the turning-points of Achilles' career and establish relations between them. This is especially true of the second visit, in which Achilles recognises the death of his friend as the consequence of his prayer to Zeus. The theme of 'only connect', to borrow E.M. Forster's phrase in *Howard's End*, is sounded in Thetis' first words. Not only are her opening words the same as on the previous occasion (18.73-4 = 1.3623), but she also refers explicitly to the fulfilment of Achilles' request, echoing with slight changes the original wording (18.74-7):

> These things are brought to accomplishment
> through Zeus: in the way that you lifted your hands and prayed for,
> that all the sons of the Achaians be pinned on their grounded vessels
> by reason of your loss, and suffer things that are shameful.

As in the description of Zeus' response to Achilles' second prayer, formal identity points to substantive difference. But Achilles is no longer blind, and his response names the difference (18.79-82):

> My mother, all these things the Olympian brought to accomplishment.
> But what pleasure is this to me, since my dear companion has perished,
> Patroklos, whom I loved beyond all other companions,
> as well as my own life. I have lost him, and Hektor, who killed him,

From the fact of Patroklos' death arises the need to avenge him even at the cost of his own life. For the first time, Achilles has a vision of his complete destiny, moving back in time to the wedding of his parents when the gods gave Peleus the arms that his greater son would bear (18.83), and looking forward to his death, which he accepts as the consequence of his revenge on Hektor (18.98-104):

> I must die soon, then; since I was not to stand by my companion
> when he was killed. And now, far away from the land of his fathers,
> he has perished, and lacked my fighting strength to defend him.
> Now, since I am not going back to the beloved land of my fathers,
> since I was no light of safety to Patroklos, nor to my other
> companions, who in their numbers went down before glorious Hektor,
> but sit here beside my ships, a useless weight on the good land ...

Here the poet reaps the reward of his strategy of emphasising the gentleness of Patroklos and the helpless terror of his death: Achilles' words would not resonate so strongly if we did not remember Patroklos tending to the injured Eurypylos and later naked and bewildered by the stroke of the god. The two images lend weight to the moment when Achilles recognises the implications of having asked for the suffering of the Achaeans, whom in retrospect he identifies, together with Patroklos, as his 'companions'.

The death of Patroklos turns the blind into a seeing Achilles. For the rest of his brief life he will act in a state of clairvoyance that is given to other characters only at the point of death. The gain of this clairvoyance is the ultimate reason for the strategy of deferring the death of Achilles beyond the end of the narrative and refracting it in the death of Patroklos. Heroic action gains its value from the risk of death. But death stands in a paradoxical relation to experience. What we call human experience in the fullest sense requires two conditions: the event must be given immediately to its subject, and the subject must be capable of continuing reflection on it. The experience of death does not meet both conditions. One's own death puts an end to reflection, and that of another lacks immediacy. The literary convention of the death speech is clearly an attempt to bridge the gap between reflection and immediate sensation. The words of a dying character have a special authority because we pretend that they are spoken out of the immediate experience of death. But the convention has intrinsic limits. The death speech cannot be long, or its duration will undermine the fiction that makes the convention possible.

Homer uses the convention of the death speech for Sarpedon, Patroklos and Hektor. But for his protagonist he resorted to a fiction that provided him with richer opportunities to express the consciousness of death. Achilles witnesses and reflects on the death of Patroklos-as-Achilles. He experiences his own death as if it were that of another. The fiction depends on the reader's belief in the identity of Achilles and Patroklos. Once established, the fiction allows for a much wider range of representational devices, for it creates a hero who can be treated as if he were dead not only in his dying moments.

The death of Achilles begins with the news of Patroklos' death. One of the most attractive speculations about narrative sources of the *Iliad* holds that Achilles' initial response and Thetis' subsequent visit are modelled on an account of Achilles' death (Kakridis, 67-70). When Achilles hears the words of Antilochos he is prostrate with grief: *autos d'en konieisi megas megalôsti tanustheis/ keito* ('and he himself, mightily in his might, in the dust lay at length', 18.26-7). A slight rearrangement of that phrase, *keito megas megalôsti* ('he lay mightily in his might') occurs in the Patrokleia (16.776), where it refers to the body of Kebriones, and in the second underworld scene of the *Odyssey*, where it refers to the dead Achilles (24.40). When Thetis arrives she cradles her son's head in her hands in a gesture reminiscent of ritual mourning (18.71). Add to this Antilochos' fear that Achilles will kill himself (18.34), and you have fairly suggestive evidence that the scene in which Achilles learns about the death of his friend is modelled on a scene in which he is treated as a corpse.

Because Achilles has 'already died', prophecies do not disturb him. When his horses at Hera's command foretell his death he replies with weary indignation that he need not be told what he already knows (19.420). He foresees his own death in the Lykaon scene, and when the dying Hektor gives the most precise account of his imminent death at the hands of Paris and Apollo (22.359) he replies: So be it. Finally, Achilles always thinks of the funeral for Patroklos as a funeral for himself as well (23.141, 243).

As a result of Patroklos' death the heroic energy of Achilles is no longer turned inward against his own comrades as a *mênis oulomenê*, but turns against Hektor, his destined enemy. The return is more than a restoration. Achilles' anger grew as it swerved from its proper object, and in its return it burns with even greater intensity. When Thetis brings the weapons of Hephaistos, their glare frightens the Myrmidons, who do not dare look at them (19.15-17):

2. The Plot of the Iliad

> Only Achilleus
> looked, and as he looked the anger came harder upon him
> and his eyes glittered terribly under his lids, like sunflare.

He has found an answer to the question first asked in Book 1 and repeated in Book 9: What have the Trojans done to me? The war has acquired a cause that concerns him and only him. Yeats, who often used Greece as a metaphor for Ireland, said in 'Easter 1916': 'A terrible beauty is born.' The oxymoron is singularly appropriate to the status of Achilles once he re-enters battle. He stands in the shadow of death, and the poet surrounds him with an aura that marks him off from all others. But, although no human adversary can resist or escape Achilles, even his course of victory is not without obstacles, and it is precisely at the point at which he rages with an elemental force that he meets the most radical threat to his heroic destiny. In the most daring 'almost' of the poem he is confronted with the indignity of death by water.

The threat occurs at a morally significant point. Achilles has pursued the Trojans into the river that is reddened by the blood of his victims. There is no comparable image of carnage in the *Iliad*, but the slaughter is not the ultimate expression of Achilles' violence. He takes twelve prisoners alive to be sacrificed at the grave of Patroklos (21.26). More than even the most violent form of battle death, the stylised ritual of that sacrifice expresses the extremity to which Achilles has been driven by his grief. The very formlessness of death by water may be a response to that stylisation. The river pursues Achilles and undercuts his very being. He who is 'swift of foot' not only must use his feet in flight rather than pursuit, but the river attacks the source of his strength and makes him lose the ground under his feet (21.269). Never before has Achilles suffered such helplessness, and in his appeal to Zeus he envisages an unheroic end far worse than his fantasies about returning to Phthia (21.281-3):

> But now this is a dismal death I am doomed to be caught in,
> trapped in a big river as if I were a boy and a swineherd
> swept away by a torrent when he tries to cross in a rainstorm.

At this point the poem touches for a moment on the mythical and supernatural sphere. Achilles is not a monsterslayer like *Beowulf*. Heroes of that type are familiar to the *Iliad*, but they belong to a past from which the epic distances itself. Achilles' return to battle, however, involves a deliberate straining of natural limits. The hero's arms are made and brought to him by gods. His horses speak to him. And Achilles emanates a terror that is systematically associated with many forms of fire (below, p. 105). Because Achilles is a kind of fire he is threatened most radically by water, and aid comes to him from the god of fire himself, not in his guise as mastercraftsman but in his elemental shape. The river, though it comes close to extinguishing the fire of Achilles, is no match for the fire god himself and, as in the other instances of 'almost', the narrative rebounds from its false turn and moves towards its resolution with greater force. Will Hektor be a match for an Achilles whose fire has successfully defied the quenching power of water?

61

Hektor after the death of Patroklos

Whereas through much of the *Iliad* the courses of Achilles and Hektor converge on paths of error, Achilles' recognition changes the pattern of convergence. Hektor's confidence at the end of Book 8 corresponds to Achilles' rejection of Agamemnon's offer. Achilles' vision of himself and Patroklos as sole conquerors of Troy is mirrored in Hektor's deluded words to the dying Patroklos. But Hektor's recognition lags behind that of Achilles, which produces for a while the contrast between a seeing Achilles and a blind Hektor. The contrast appears most fully in the second assembly of the Trojans.

Night has fallen, and once more the Trojans assemble outside the walls of the city. But everything has changed. The mere appearance of Achilles has routed the Trojans and has caused them to abandon the body of Patroklos. No fires flare to express their confidence; instead we learn that they are too frightened to sit down (18.246). Poulydamas gives sound advice, as he had done in Book 12, and counsels retreat under the cover of night. Once again Hektor contemptuously rejects his cousin's advice, showing an intransigence in the face of changed circumstances very similar to Achilles' behaviour in the Embassy. If Achilles had indeed returned to battle – as if any doubt were possible about the apparition that routed them (18.306-9):

> the worse for him if he tries it, since I for my part
> will not run from him out of the sorrowful battle, but rather
> stand fast, to see if he wins the great glory, or if I can win it.
> The war god is impartial. Before now he has killed the killer.

This is less of a prediction of victory than his previous boast that he would kill Diomedes, but it is just as discrepant with the reality that gives the lie to it.

When the rout of the Trojans is complete, Hektor alone does not return to the safety of the city (22.5-6):

> But his deadly fate held Hektor shackled, so that he stood fast
> in front of Ilion and the Skaian gates.

This is exactly the same place where, according to Achilles' words to Odysseus, he had once before braved Achilles – and had barely escaped (9.354). Whereas on that occasion the Skaian gates had marked the farthest point of Hektor's courage, now they mark the closest point to safety and measure no longer his daring but his retreat from the open field of battle that in the exuberance of victory he had claimed as his true home (15.720). On the borderline between the security of the walls and the danger of the open field, Hektor must make a choice. His parents beg him in the strongest terms to return to the city and to think of his obligation as the protector of Troy (22.37). But he is unmoved. His subsequent soliloquy, the longest such speech in the *Iliad*, expresses the reasons why he cannot return to his former role (22.99-130). He does not at any point deal with the arguments raised by his parents, and his deafness to them may itself be a telling index of the degree to which he is trapped by his previous choices, which he now recognises as mistakes blocking his return. We may remember the Trojan women thronging Hektor upon his return to Troy asking anxiously about the fate of their sons, brothers and husbands. What is he to tell them now? Better to face Achilles in honourable defeat (110) than to live with the reproaches of his inferiors: 'Hektor believed in his own strength and ruined his people' (107). But Hektor's resolution is not very firm. Odysseus in a similar situation had considered flight only to reject it by reminding himself of the warrior code (11.407-10):

> Yet still, why does the heart within me debate on these things?
> Since I know that it is the cowards who walk out of the fighting,
> but if one is to win honour in battle, he must by all means
> stand his ground strongly, whether he be struck or strike down another.

Hektor, on the other hand, looks for ways out. It is only the impossibility of finding such a way that makes him stand. Thus his first decision to face Achilles (109) gives way to an imagined negotiation: should he take off his arms, promise to return Helen, and share the treasures of Troy with the Achaeans? To imagine the solution is to discover its impossibility (22.123-5):

> I might go up to him, and he take no pity upon me
> nor respect my position, but kill me naked so, as if I were
> a woman, once I stripped my armour from me.

It is striking that Hektor does not refer to Patroklos at this point, although it is Patroklos rather than Helen who has become the *casus belli* for Achilles. But the poet may remember Patroklos: had not Hektor killed him naked and helpless (16.815)? For a second time Hektor resolves to confront Achilles, but in the face of his approach his resolution buckles and he runs away.

James Redfield (p. 128) has interpreted Hektor's decision to await Achilles as his third and final error: having first decided to go on the offensive (Book 8), and having decided not to retreat after the death of Patroklos, Hektor now fails to return to the safety of the city. Redfield writes with great insight of the disjunction between heroic identity and social obligation that defeat creates for the warrior: while his defeat has proved him 'not to be what he claimed to be' (p. 154), his protective function still remains necessary to his community. But for some heroes, as for Hektor, the balancing act of weighing present loss against future usefulness becomes impossible. Redfield sees Hektor's decision to face Achilles as a sign of Hektor's inability to take the longer view of things that springs from greater self-assurance. But what obsesses Hektor's consciousness is less the fact of defeat than the recognition that defeat is the consequence of his folly. Not unlike Achilles, who discovers the connection between his anger and the death of Patroklos, he sees himself as the prisoner of his previous decisions. In both cases the acknowledgement of past error leads to the discovery of the single remaining path of action. Thus it does not seem right to speak of Hektor's choice as a new and additional error. He correctly recognises that his past actions have blocked his return to the city. The fact that this recognition takes place immediately outside the gate is deeply ironic. But the open gate does not, like the advice of Poulydamas, point to a road Hektor should have taken. For that it is too late. Hektor's disillusionment, unlike that of Achilles, does not occur in a single moment of radical insight; it is a process that for a while even breeds new delusions. His recognition of past errors and their consequences does show him the only way that remains open, but his ability to go that way depends on the continuing delusion that he might be equal to Achilles. The two moments of resolution in his speech (22.109, 130) leave the outcome of their encounter in doubt, and this hope, rather than the decision to stay, represents Hektor's continuing error.

Hektor's flight, like that of Achilles from the river, tests the limits of the hero's existence. Achilles learns about a world of natural forces to which human heroism is irrelevant. Hektor's lesson is more obviously a moral one: in his flight he recognises the false premisses of the new role that he had claimed for himself outside the walls of Troy. Hektor does not justify his flight (as Menelaos justifies his retreat from the body of Patroklos). It overcomes him, and it is in a peculiar sense his first honest act. For this reason the poet's restoration of Hektor begins with what is on the surface an act of shameful cowardice. Homer does not blame Hektor for running away. Instead he transforms what might be an abject spectacle into a noble competition in which one competitor is worthy (*esthlos*), but the other far better (*meg' ameinôn*), and in which the trophy is far more valuable than the usual bull's hide or ritual beast, for it is the life of Hektor (22.158). The prestige of the competition is enhanced by the fact that the gods themselves – all of them – act as spectators 22.166.

The transition from race to fight recapitulates the delusion to which Hektor had been prone and lays the foundation for the final moment of recognition. In the terror of his isolation Hektor hears the voice of Deiphobos – the disguise Athene has adopted to carry out the resolution of the gods that Hektor should die. Deiphobos/Athene promises help in standing up to Achilles (22.229). It is a common tactic for one warrior to come to the help of another in confronting a superior enemy. Thus, Aeneas and Pandaros fight Diomedes (5.166), Diomedes and Nestor fight Hektor (8.99), Menelaos and Antilochos fight Aeneas (5.561). What makes this scene so special (and Athene's appeal so treacherous) is the fact that the offer of heroic fellowship comes to a warrior who has experienced the terror of isolation in its most excruciating form. When Deiphobos/Athene tells Hektor that he has ventured outside the walls despite the pleas of Priam and Hekabe, the words cannot fail to impress Hektor, who has just rejected similar pleas.

Athene's cruel lie makes the courage of Hektor possible and his death inevitable. Readers have often found difficulty with her role in the death of Hektor since it goes beyond the assistance that gods give to their favourites. There are, however, good reasons for Athene's extraordinary intervention. First, the fact that Hektor's final courage rests on a false premise echoes and crystallises the condition of Hektor's career throughout the poem. This is an instance of the poetic justice that establishes a significant relationship between a character's life and the mode of his death. Second, the deluded courage of Hektor yields to true courage in the end. When his spear has failed to pierce Achilles' armour, Hektor asks Deiphobos for another spear. But he is gone. Now the poet could have plunged Hektor into a new panic, but instead he endows him with a knowledge that is instantaneous, comprehensive, and leads to a resolution that no longer requires the treacherous support of hope (22.297-305):

> No use. Here at last the gods have summoned me deathward.
> I thought Deïphobos the hero was here close beside me,
> but he is behind the wall and it was Athene cheating me,

and now evil death is close to me, and no longer far away,
and there is no way out. So it must long since have been pleasing
to Zeus, and Zeus' son who strikes from afar, this way; though before this
they defended me gladly. But now my death is upon me.
Let me at least not die without a struggle, inglorious,
but do some big thing first, that men to come shall know of it.

The words receive additional depth from a powerful verbal correspondence with the Patrokleia. When Homer introduces its last act he asks (16.692-3):

Then who was it you slaughtered first, who was the last one,
Patroklos, as the gods called you to your death?

What Homer says about Patroklos, Hektor says about himself. The simple change of pronoun distinguishes the pathos of Patroklos' end from the heroic defeat of Hektor. At this moment, and only at this moment, Hektor is equal to Achilles, and superior to all other Iliadic characters, in the depth and intensity of his consciousness of life as limited and valorised by the fact of death.

The death of Hektor and the structure of the *Iliad*

The death of Hektor requires an interpretation at three levels. First, it is the end to his individual career. Since the poet marked the beginning of that career in the encounter with Andromache, he returns to that beginning at the point of death. Andromache's reaction to her husband's death brings to a close the initial mourning for Hektor and does so in a manner that recalls their encounter in Book 6. Second, the death of Hektor stands for the end of the war. This aspect is represented through an elaborate set of correspondences that relate the duel of Achilles and Hektor to a montage of the beginning of the war represented in Books 2-5. At the third level, the death of Hektor generates a new action that has to do with the maltreatment of his body, his ransom and his funeral. This action, through an elaborate set of formal correspondences, reaches back to the events of the first book and establishes an ultimate frame of anger and reconciliation. The story of Hektor, Patroklos and Achilles thus has a triple frame, which defines the story, expands it and gives to it both the narrative and thematic comprehensiveness that turn it into a poem deserving of the title 'Iliad'.

One may see in this frame a monumental application of 'ring composition', a device that consists of marking the end of a passage by a repetition of its beginning: A B C D A. The device is common in Homeric speeches and often takes more complicated forms, as when the poet approaches a central passage in one order and leads away from it in reverse order: A B C D C B A. The centre of such a passage is like the turning-post in an ancient chariot race, and Lohmann (p. 15) points out that the most elaborate example of ring composition in a Homeric speech occurs in Nestor's advice to Antilochos on how to win a chariot race, with the centre taken up by a description of the turning-post (23.306). Cedric Whitman has seen the entire *Iliad* as an application of this design, which he relates to the geometric art of the eighth century. Whether one speaks of ring composition or geometric structure, it is important to recognise that the design has a dramatic function: the balance of correspondences points inward towards a pivot, whether it is the turning-point of the racecourse, or, as in the entire *Iliad*, the death of Patroklos.

Hektor and Andromache

Andromache frames the individual career of Hektor that stretches from his departure from Troy to his encounter with Achilles. Her response to her husband's death is ironically related to her anxieties on the earlier occasion. There she had feared for his life, and like a madwoman (*mainomenêi eïkuia*) had rushed to the towers (6.389). After returning home, she had mourned Hektor as if he were already dead. But now she is lost in the peace of domestic work: she is weaving while water is heating on a tripod for a bath on his return (22.445-6):

> poor innocent, nor knew how, far from waters for bathing,
> Pallas Athene had cut him down at the hands of Achilleus.

The noise of the mourners, among which she distinguishes the voice of Hekabe, brings the idyll to an abrupt end. Once more she rushes to the towers 'like a raving woman with a pulsing heart' (*mainadi isê/ pallomenê kradiên*, 22.460-1), and she arrives in time to see Hektor's body being dragged towards the ships (22.466-72):

> The darkness of night misted over the eyes of Andromache.
> She fell backward, and gasped the life breath from her, and far off
> threw from her head the shining gear that ordered her headdress,
> the diadem and the cap, and the holding-band woven together,
> and the circlet, which Aphrodite the golden once had given her
> on that day when Hektor of the shining helmet led her forth
> from the house of Eëtion, and gave numberless gifts to win her.

The description of her reaction is among the most poignant instances of the Homeric technique of evoking the beginning at the end, and it derives much of its power from Andromache's words in Book 6, where she had seen herself as the sole survivor of a family destroyed by Achilles. The logic of her words then finds its fulfilment now when she sees that Achilles has taken the one, Hektor, who remained to her. When she regains consciousness, her own words confirm the fatal links between Thebe and Troy (22.477-81):

> Hektor, I grieve for you. You and I were born to a single
> destiny, you in Troy in the house of Priam, and I
> in Thebe, underneath the timbered mountain of Plakos
> in the house of Eëtion, who cared for me when I was little,
> ill-fated he, I ill-starred. I wish he had never begotten me.

The Trojan War: beginning and end

The immensely moving story of individual death and bereavement is embedded in a wider frame that articulates the collective fate of Troy and explores the relationship between the cause and consequences of the war. As a proleptic image of the fall of

Troy the death of Hektor contrasts systematically with a montage of the beginning of the war that is found in the duel of Paris and Menelaos and in the breaking of the truce.

Instead of telling the story of the Trojan war in chronological order, the *Iliad* focuses on a decisive event in the final phase of the war. But, since the withdrawal of Achilles in Book 1 creates a narrative gap, the poet fills that gap with events that stand for the beginning of the war, thus creating the illusion that his narrative, in tracing the events from the anger of Achilles to the death of Hektor, also traces the course of the entire war from beginning to end. This peculiar sleight of hand begins with the marshalling and roll-call of the army in the second book. As the Achaean and Trojan armies move towards one another, Paris proposes to decide the war by means of a duel. Menelaos accepts the offer as a rational way of settling their conflict without bringing additional sufferings on others (3.98). While the preparations for the duel are under way Helen appears on the walls and answers Priam's questions about the identity of various heroes. After the Achaeans and Trojans have sworn solemn oaths to respect the outcome of the duel, the fighting begins. Menelaos has the upper hand but Aphrodite snatches Paris from the battlefield before he is injured and takes him to his bedroom. Then she compels Helen to return to Paris. While the two make love and re-enact the original offence, Agamemnon claims victory and demands Helen's extradition.

The events of this exposition fit the first year of the war much better than the tenth. Priam asking Helen about the identity of Agamemnon is only the most obvious anachronism; the entire idea of restricting the conflict to those with a direct interest is also more appropriate to an early phase of the war. Narrative convenience has a part in the poet's decision to equate the beginning of his narrative with the beginning of the story, but his purpose goes beyond clarity of exposition. We get a glimpse of this purpose if we follow the order of events beyond the inconclusive duel and analyse correspondences between them and the death of Hektor.

The impasse produced by Aphrodite's capricious rescue of Paris is broken by Athene and Zeus in a manner that looks forward to their role in the death of Hektor. When the gods witness the race of Achilles and Hektor, Zeus remembers the piety of the latter and wonders whether the gods should save him. But he yields to Athene's protests and dispatches her to bring about Hektor's death. In the opening scene of Book 4 a similar sequence is developed in fuller detail. Zeus 'teases' Hera and Athene, who have done so much less than the unwarlike Aphrodite to help their protege Menelaos. He asks whether Troy should be saved – a question that produces a bitter outburst from Hera (4.25). Once again Zeus yields, but not without regret at the fate of a Troy that has been, like Hektor, punctilious in its sacrifices to him (4.48). He sends Athene down to the field to break the truce. As in the death of Hektor, Athene uses deception to carry out her task. She persuades the foolish archer Pandaros to take a shot at Menelaos in the hope of gaining glory among the Trojans – a deluded enterprise given the express hatred of the Trojans for Paris (3.320). Athene deflects the arrow from Menelaos so that he receives only a minor injury. Agamemnon solemnly declares the truce broken and predicts the fall of Troy. Pandaros does not long survive his treacherous act. Diomedes kills him with a spear guided by Athene (5.290).

Pandaros is a composite character, combining elements of Paris and Hektor. Like Paris he is an archer. His injury to Menelaos causes the war to begin again. His death resembles that of Hektor, for he falls at the hands of the Achilles substitute and with the assistance of Athene. The fate of Pandaros is a foreshortened image of the war as a whole, linking its beginning to its end. It also points to a crucial theme of the *Iliad* in its linkage of Paris and Hektor: the war is not decided by, nor its suffering restricted to, those who caused it. *The Iliad* sees war as a phenomenon that spreads beyond its cause; indeed, the poet goes farther and holds that war does not come into its own until its 'original' cause is lost.

The duel of Paris and Menelaos, instead of settling the war, leads to a re-enactment of the original offence. Paris makes love to Helen, while his substitute injures Menelaos on the battlefield. But the war that begins with the broken truce is fiercer than the war that preceded it. The bow-shot of Pandaros marks the beginning of a new era and is analogous to the death of Patroklos, which marks the beginning of the war for Achilles. The poet emphasises the relationship between these two pivotal events through the peculiar role that Menelaos plays in the rescue of the body of Patroklos. Menelaos is the first Achaean to arrive at the body of Patroklos. He stands over the body 'as over a first-born calf the mother cow stands lowing, she who has known no children before this' (17.4). The image is profoundly ironic. Patroklos is indeed the first child of war, the first victim whose death really matters, and Menelaos has given birth to it. The poet seems to honour Menelaos by making him be on the spot and protect his fallen friend against the attack of Euphorbos. But is not the dead Patroklos a rebuke to the living Menelaos? The irony deepens when Menelaos falters at the approach of Hektor and considers his choices. He recognises that Patroklos died for his cause (17.92), but persuades himself that the odds justify his retreat. There is no parallel to such calculating prudence in the *Iliad*, and it contrasts both with the reckless enthusiasm that drove Patroklos towards his death and with the absolute commitment of Achilles to risk certain death in avenging his friend.

The poet is not particularly interested in blackening the reputation of Menelaos. He shows him as well-meaning and valiant (up to a point), but inadequate to the events unleashed by his marriage with Helen. Even his reminder that Patroklos died for his cause is out of place: he does not understand that with the death of Patroklos the war ceases to be about Helen. The poet gives his measure of Menelaos by giving him prominence in a context most likely to reveal his limitations.

Achilles and Priam

Contrary to romantic clichés about heroism, the Homeric warrior is not the opposite of the haggling shopkeeper. Exchange, negotiation of disputes, and settlements are honourable transactions in the Homeric world, to be carried both with a keen calculation of material advantage and with a deep sense of ceremony. What characterises the action of the *Iliad*, however, is the progressive collapse of established procedures for resolving conflicts. This collapse begins with the Chryses episode in Book 1, continues with the broken truce and the failure of the Embassy, and leads, beyond the confines of the narrative, to the ruin of Troy, which the tradition viewed as a catastrophe for the conquerors no less than for the vanquished. Within the narrative, the ultimate point of this collapse is Achilles' maltreatment of Hektor's body. But the *Iliad* recoils from this extremity and concludes with a transaction that arrests, if only temporarily, the progress towards chaos: Achilles accepts ransom from Priam in exchange for the body of Hektor. The ransoming of Hektor mirrors and elaborates the ransoming of Chryseis. Thus the violence and chaos of the action are enclosed by a narrative frame that moves from chaos to the order of ceremonious exchange. At this third and ultimate level of interpretation, the death of Hektor is not an end, but a beginning.

The collapse of a world based on rational exchange is the central theme of the speeches that frame the duel of Hektor and Achilles. Hektor offers a contrast with the gods as witness: the victor will strip the vanquished of his armour but should return the body itself. In view of the gods' failure to enforce the contract between Paris and Menelaos, the appeal to the gods (22.254) has an ironic ring, and Achilles will have none of it: 'Hektor, argue me no agreements. I cannot forgive you' (22.261). The word for 'agreement', *sunêmosunê*, which occurs only here in Homer and is very rare in later literature, is clearly a derivative of *suniêmi*, 'to understand'. The choice of the word may indicate that an 'understanding' in the sense of settlement is an innate aspect of human nature. Achilles' explanation of his refusal is highly significant (22.262-6):

> As there are no trustworthy oaths between men and lions,
> nor wolves and lambs have spirit that can be brought to agreement
> but forever these hold feelings of hate for each other,
> so there can be no love between you and me, nor shall there be
> oaths between us, but one or the other must fall before then

The words rest on the premise that the enmity of Hektor and Achilles has cancelled the species bond that makes contracts possible. The cancellation of that bond is more explicit when the mortally wounded Hektor returns to the same theme. He no longer offers a contract (how could he?), but instead supplicates Achilles to accept ransom for his body. The greater intensity of the request meets with an even harsher refusal (22.345-54):

> No more entreating of me, you dog, by knees or parents.
> I wish only that my spirit and fury would drive me
> to hack your meat away and eat it raw for the things that
> you have done to me. So there is no one who can hold the dogs off
> from your head, not if they bring here and set before me ten times
> and twenty times the ransom, and promise more in addition,
> not if Priam son of Dardanos should offer to weigh out
> your bulk in gold; not even so shall the lady your mother
> who herself bore you lay you on the death-bed and mourn you:
> no, but the dogs and the birds will have you all for their feasting.

Achilles goes beyond the animal comparisons of his previous speech and seeks to transform himself and Hektor into animals for whom implacable hostility is a natural condition. This is the second time in the poem that the motif of cannibalism appears, and on both occasions it serves as a counter-image to the world of covenants. In the deliberations about the truce Zeus had said that only by eating the raw flesh of Priam and his children could Hera quench her hatred of the Trojans (4.34). The motif will occur once more when Hekabe vainly seeks to dissuade Priam from his journey to Achilles and wishes she could eat his liver (24.212). The motif traces the progress of savagery from the broken truce through the death of Patroklos to the mutilation of Hektor's body. At the same time, in its second and third occurrences it marks a turning-point. Achilles may refuse to entertain the thought of accepting ransom for Hektor in language as hyperbolic as his rejection of Agamemnon's gifts, but through his words the poet looks forward to what will happen.

Achilles' rejection of Hektor's supplication and his subsequent maltreatment of the body lie outside the norms of the warrior code, but they are not unexpected. They are anticipated by the three suppliant episodes of Books 6, 11, 21. In the first of these, Menelaos captures Adrestos and is on the point of honouring his ransom offer when Agamemnon intervenes (6.55-60):

> Dear brother, o Menelaos, are you concerned so tenderly
> with these people? Did you in your house get the best of treatment
> from the Trojans? No, let not one of them go free of sudden
> death and our hands; not the young man child that the mother carries
> still in her body, not even he, but let all of Ilion's
> people perish, utterly blotted out and unmourned for.

The poet calls Agamemnon's words 'just', perhaps because of the blatant injustice the Trojans have committed in breaking the truce. In other circumstances, Menelaos' action would have been proper, but Agamemnon draws attention to the changed nature of the war. His savage threat against the unborn child is deliberately placed by the poet in a context that will soon see Hektor among the women of Troy. A repetition of this incident occurs in Book 11, where the sons of Antimachos, a prominent supporter of Paris, supplicate Agamemnon but meet with no success, since he remembers the special wrong their father has done to Menelaos (11.138).

The final and by far the most elaborate suppliant episode is the encounter of Lykaon and Achilles in Book 21. It differs from the others in that the rejection of the supplication turns on the death of Patroklos rather than on the offence to Menelaos. It also makes explicit the premise that a suppliant can normally expect a favourable response. The poet reports that Lykaon had once before been captured by Achilles, who had saved his life and sold him to Lemnos, where he had regained his freedom and via a curiously circuitous route had found his way back to Troy. The Achilles he now encounters is much changed and wonders with mock astonishment how it was possible for Lykaon to return across the hostile sea. Now he will send him on another voyage to find out (21.62-3)

> whether he will come back even from there, or the prospering
> earth will hold him, she who holds back even the strong man.

To this implacable and sardonic Achilles, Lykaon addresses a half-hearted supplication, of which he himself seems to recognise the futility and which culminates in a vain attempt to dissociate himself from his half-brother Hektor. But, like Agamemnon, Achilles refuses to make distinctions: all Trojans are the objects of his wrath, and in particular all the sons of Priam. He begins his rejection with an emphatic statement of the contrast between now and then. He did indeed spare the lives of his prisoners 'in the time before Patroklos came to the day of his destiny' (21.100), but now nobody will escape him. He dispatches Lykaon with a sword, throws his body into the river, and exults at the prospect of fish nibbling away at it.

2. The Plot of the Iliad

With its sharp division of the world into before and after the death of Patroklos, the Lykaon episode seems to express most fully the dynamic of events in the Trojan war. It looks back to a world in which norms of rational exchange prevailed even in war; it manifests the irrelevance of these norms to a world of savage and destructive anger. The Achilles who refuses to speak of covenants and will maltreat the body of Hektor is clearly the same Achilles who throws Lykaon to the fish. From this perspective, the mutilation of Hektor's corpse is the logical outcome of the plot of the triad, and one could imagine a poem that ends with a vision of destruction. The proemium does indeed foreshadow such an ending when it describes the denial of burial as the consequence of Achilles' anger. But the *Iliad* does not end this way; it ends, on the contrary, with a spectacular scene of reconciliation in which two men destined by their history to implacable enmity not only restore the possibility of rational exchange, but also discover a human solidarity through their respective status of bereaved father and doomed son.

The first inkling of this return occurs paradoxically in the Lykaon scene, where embedded in the scornful words and deeds of Achilles there is a moment of chilling serenity when he sees Lykaon, Patroklos and himself as united by a common fate (21.106-13):

> So, friend, you die also. Why all this clamour about it?
> Patroklos also is dead, who was better by far than you are.
> Do you not see what a man I am, how huge, how splendid
> and born of a great father, and the mother who bore me immortal?
> Yet even I have also my death and my strong destiny,
> and there shall be a dawn or an afternoon or a noontime
> when some man in the fighting will take the life from me also
> either with a spearcast or an arrow flown from the bowstring.

Unknown to Achilles, the startling address *philos*, 'friend', looks beyond his words to Hektor: *hôs ouk est' eme kai se philêmenai* ('since you and I cannot be *philoi*', 22.265). To be somebody's *philos* refers to kinship or equivalent ties that exist quite independently of feeling or love, although they are usually accompanied by it. In his encounter with Lykaon, Achilles discovers what he will momentarily and savagely deny in the encounter with Hektor: the common humanity of victor and vanquished. The Achilles of the Lykaon scene is already in some sense the Achilles of the Priam scene. The sublimity of the scene, which virtually every reader of the *Iliad* has acknowledged, arises from the extreme dissonance of cruel scorn and sympathetic understanding, a dissonance that the subsequent narrative will resolve in one direction.

The finale of the *Iliad* systematically reverses the events of the beginning (Table 4). The movement from disorder to order implicit in this narrative framework is anticipated in the first book, which closes with the reconciliation of the gods. Their quarrel is resolved by Hephaistos, and our final vision of the gods in Book 1 is dominated by divine laughter, the lyre of Apollo and the song of the Muses. The resolution of Book 1, however, does not resolve the quarrel of Agamemnon and Achilles, which comes to a formal end in Book 19, where Agamemnon apologises and Achilles accepts the gifts he had so violently rejected in the Embassy. But that

71

Table 4. The beginning and end of the *Iliad*

Agamemnon denies ransom request by Chryses. Apollo intervenes. Nine-day plague and burning of the dead. Assembly on tenth day. Quarrel of Agamemnon and Achilles. Removal of Briseis.
Achilles sends request to Zeus via Thetis.
Twelve-day interval (ceremonious return of Chryseis). Thetis secretly persuades Zeus. Hera accuses Zeus. Their quarrel reconciled by Hephaistos.

Achilles grants ransom request by Priam. Achilles reunited with Briseis. Nine-day preparation for Hektor's funeral. Burning of pyre on tenth day.
Zeus sends request to Achilles via Thetis.
Twelve-day maltreatment of Hector's corpse. Apollo intervenes. Hera's last protest overruled by Zeus. Thetis summoned and publicly welcomed by Hera and Athene.

resolution no longer matters, and it establishes no closure because, while bringing to an end one form of Achilles' anger, it only intensifies another. As the formal correspondences between the first and last books make clear, the quarrel of Agamemnon and Achilles does not find its true resolution until the dishonouring of Chryses by Agamemnon is balanced by the honour Achilles shows to Priam.

The nature of that resolution and its significance for the interpretation of the work as a whole are not easy to describe, and readings of the last book have run the gamut from seeing in it no more than a tagged-on ending to interpreting it as a profound revaluation of the warrior code. Assuming an integral function for the last book, a minimal reading would hold that the violation and restoration of order leave Achilles and Priam with a more explicit understanding of the values of their society. Such a view is compatible with the fact that the ransom transactions of the first and last books are in principle identical even though the characters differ in status and significance. But it is also possible to argue that the words of Priam and Achilles display an ethos in which the values of the warrior society are transcended. This view receives powerful support from the surprises and the reversals that inform the last encounter. No two men have more reason to hate one another, and yet Priam becomes a suppliant to Achilles. Undetected by mortal eyes, he suddenly appears in the tent of Achilles (24.477-84):

> came in unseen by the other men and stood close beside him
> and caught the knees of Achilleus in his arms, and kissed the hands
> that were dangerous and manslaughtering and had killed so many
> of his sons. As when dense disaster closes on one who has murdered
> a man in his own land, and he comes to the country of others,
> to a man of substance, and wonder seizes on those who behold him,
> so Achilleus wondered as he looked on Priam, a godlike
> man, and the rest of them wondered also, and looked at each other.

At the end of his supplication Priam stresses the uniqueness of his action (24.505-6):

2. The Plot of the Iliad

I have gone through what no other mortal on earth has gone through;
I put my lips to the hands of the man who has killed my children.

What makes the bridging of this enormous gap possible is the theme of fatherhood. Both at the beginning and towards the end of his speech Priam reminds Achilles of the aged Peleus, and Achilles yields because he sees Peleus in Priam (24.507-12):

So he spoke, and stirred in the other a passion of grieving
for his own father. He took the old man's hand and pushed him
gently away, and the two remembered, as Priam sat huddled
at the feet of Achilleus and wept close for manslaughtering Hektor
and Achilleus wept now for his own father, now again
for Patroklos. The sound of their mourning moved in the house.

From this perception arises the discovery of a shared humanity that transcends the opposition of Achaean and Trojan in which their hostility is rooted. Achilles formulates it in his answer to Priam. This, too, is a kind of reversal since wisdom is a privilege of age, but here a young man, not previously known for his counsel, becomes a spokesman of the final wisdom and expounds it to an old man who is his patient listener:

There are two urns that stand on the door-sill of Zeus. They are unlike
for the gifts they bestow: an urn of evils, an urn of blessings.
If Zeus who delights in thunder mingles these and bestows them
on man, he shifts, and moves now in evil, again in good fortune.
But when Zeus bestows from the urn of sorrows, he makes a failure
of man, and the evil hunger drives him over the shining
earth, and he wanders respected neither of gods nor mortals (24.527-33).

The generalisation returns to its point of departure when Achilles illustrates its truth through the careers of Peleus and Priam, paradigms not so much of mixed blessings, but of great blessings cursed in the end (24.534).

The speech of Achilles posits a human solidarity in the face of divine indifference and persecution, but it does not proclaim a new ethos. It states from the human perspective what the gods habitually assert from theirs: divisions among mortals become irrelevant in the light of the gulf that separates men and gods. The final wisdom of the *Iliad* also remains without effect on future action. In *Paradise Lost*, for instance, the estrangement and reconciliation of Adam and Eve lead to the explicit formulation of a new code of patience and obedience that will govern the conduct of Adam, if not of all his descendants (*Paradise Lost* 12.561). From the perspective of such radical change, the reconciliation of Achilles and Priam remains without consequences. None the less, if revaluation seems too strong a term for the last book of the *Iliad*, it is inadequate to see the narrative as merely returning to its beginning, even granting to the characters the gain of a disillusioned knowledge they did not possess at the beginning.

The change introduced in the last book is best seen by pursuing two distinct features of the Priam-Achilles encounter: its secrecy and its emphasis on contemplation. The encounter is not public but occurs in the middle of the night. Achilles

73

remarks at one point that if Agamemnon saw Priam the ransom would be delayed (24.654), and when Hermes appears to the sleeping Priam he makes a similar point to hurry his departure (24.686). But if Homer had wanted to make the ransoming of Hektor a public event he could have done so. There are no narrative constraints that forced the poet into the opposition between a public reconciliation of Agamemnon and Achilles in the open assembly and a private reconciliation of Achilles and Priam under cover of night. Beyond the privacy of the scene there is also the eerie ambience that is created by the intervention of Hermes, who acts not only as the god of wayfarers but also as the conveyor of the dead. Michael Nagler perhaps goes a little far when he interprets the scene as a *katabasis* or journey to the dead and sees in the curiously magnified camp gate the gate to the underworld (p. 184), but the setting of the encounter is unquestionably remote.

Proponents of revaluation can argue that this remoteness is an index of new values. The public and meaningless reconciliation of Achilles and Agamemnon yields to the private and deeply felt reconciliation of Priam and Achilles as father and son. But to locate truth and value on the second term of an outer-inner or public-private opposition seems more in line with novels like *Persuasion* or *Bleak House*, perhaps even plays like the *Philoctetes* or *Oedipus at Colonus*, than with the conventions of Homeric narrative, and it is important to remember that the encounter of Achilles and Priam constitutes only a temporary retreat to the private sphere. As Redfield has written: 'The ceremony of Book Twenty-four takes place outside the human world because the contradictions it reveals cannot be resolved within the human world' (Redfield 1975, 222). The ceremony does indeed involve reconciliation and something like forgiveness on the ethical level, but it culminates in an aesthetic gesture of mutual contemplation (24.628-32):

> But when they had put aside their desire for eating and drinking,
> Priam, son of Dardanos, gazed upon Achilleus, wondering
> at his size and beauty, for he seemed like an outright vision
> of gods. Achilleus in turn gazed on Dardanian Priam
> and wondered, as he saw his brave looks and listened to him talking.

The final wisdom of the *Iliad* is not the attainment of a new and more human order born out of the destruction of the warrior code, but the temporary and ordered vision of the suffering and contradictions of human life. We are not far from the Ovidian conceit of Orpheus, whose power of song in the underworld made even the wheel of Ixion stand still (*Metamorphoses* 10.42).

The view of the final book as an aesthetic resolution gains support from the wonderful way in which the poet first introduces Helen(3.125-8):

>   she was weaving a great web,
> a red folding robe, and working into it the numerous struggles
> of Trojans, breakers of horses, and bronze-armoured Achaians,
> struggles that they endured for her sake at the hands of the war god.

Powerless to affect the sufferings of which she is the cause, Helen is endowed with an awareness that finds expression in art. Song replaces tapestry in the words with which Helen invites Hektor to stay during his visit to Troy (6.345-8):

how I wish that on that day when my mother first bore me
the foul whirlwind of the storm had caught me away and swept me
to the mountain, or into the wash of the sea deep-thundering
where the waves would have swept me away before all these things had happened.

But above all it is the conclusion of the first book that supports this view of the last book. I argued above (p. 71) that the resolution of the divine quarrel at the end of Book 1 does not resolve the quarrel of Agamemnon and Achilles. Resolution occurs through a shift to the divine associated with music and laughter. I interpreted this shift as a deliberate suspension to be fully resolved in the reconciliation of Achilles and Priam. That view holds as long as we do not attribute to the poet the belief that his poems have achieved a lasting moral revolution. For the last book also involves a shift analogous to the move from human sorrow to divine laughter. The reconciliation of Priam and Achilles takes place under peculiar circumstances of 'removal'. Achilles and Priam will return to the scene of destruction, and Troy will fall. *The Iliad* remains.

3

Fighting in the *Iliad*

My purpose in this chapter is to survey the representation of battle in the *Iliad*, moving from the components that make up the individual encounter to the devices by which larger narrative units are created from such encounters. This goal requires a very different strategy from the one adopted in the previous chapter. There I was concerned with tracing the design of the central action, and I selected detail in the light of its bearing on the structure and unity of the poem. Here my chief aim is to classify phenomena and to convey a sense of their relative frequency. It is in the battle scenes that the modern reader is most likely to be wearied by the seemingly endless succession of virtually identical incidents and to experience the 'formulaic style' at its stereotyped worst. For this reason there is some virtue in sorting out the frequency of typical incidents and in establishing the degree of variation between closely related phenomena. As it turns out, the impression of endless repetition rests on a fairly small base, and many details of battle owe their 'typically Homeric' status not to repetition but to vividness of language, like the 'Homeric' laughter of the gods that arises only once in the *Iliad* (1.599).

There is no doubt that battle scenes, which amount to 5,500 lines or a good third of the *Iliad*, enjoy considerable autonomy in the poem. The poet and his audience like such scenes, and their periodic occurrence requires no greater motivation than barroom brawls in a Western. But although narrative control over the battle scenes is often relaxed, it is rarely absent, and it would be a great mistake to ignore specific narrative aims that guide the elaboration or deployment of particular motifs. Such questions as 'Why does this convention occur three times in this part of the poem?' often have an answer that points to the story of Achilles, Patroklos and Hektor. Often, but not always: a judicious reader must be alert to the function of detail without demanding the rigorous integration of every particular into the design of the poem. (In the following pages I am much indebted to Friedrich, 1956, and Fenik, 1968, whose books subsume much of the extensive literature on fighting in the *Iliad*.)

The ethos of Homeric fighting

Warfare in the *Iliad* depends entirely on the strength and courage of the individual fighter. There is no room for strategy or cunning. There is not even much interest in skill. It is assumed that the warrior knows how to throw a spear or wield a sword, but special dexterity in the use or avoidance of a weapon is not a significant feature of the narrative. This attitude is Iliadic rather than Homeric or heroic. Cunning is highly regarded in the *Odyssey*, and in the *Iliad* there are occasional references to it. The shield of Achilles shows men gathered in an ambush and increasing their strength through cunning (18.513). Idomeneus praises the sang-froid Meriones would display in an ambush (13.275). Nestor likes to give orders and advice of a strategic kind (2.362, 4.297); he also tells Antilochos how a good charioteer can use intelligence (*mêtis*) to compensate for inferior horses (23.313), and the dutiful son remembers the advice so well that he seeks to improve his position in the race by reckless cheating (23.402). On another occasion Nestor tells how in the old days Lykurgos killed Areithoös 'by guile rather than force' (7.142). But, while the *Iliad* is clearly familiar with a world in which the outcome of contests turns on the unscrupulous use of intelligence and the ruthless exploitation of the opponent's weakness, the poem banishes both from its arena and presents a spectacle of war at once brutal and innocent: no ambush, no stratagem, no diversionary or dilatory tactic qualifies the encounter of enemies in the field of battle. The bow is a marginal weapon in this world and does not become a major warrior. It is used by Pandaros, Paris and Teukros, but Odysseus, who gives a taste of his cunning in the wrestling match with Aias (23.725), left his bow at home when he sailed for Troy and like other major warriors fights with spear and sword. Only accident is allowed to qualify open force: some dozen warriors in the *Iliad* lose their lives because they stand in the path of a spear aimed at someone else. The trickery of the gods is a special case. The one part of the *Iliad* in which deception plays a major role, the Doloneia (Book 10), has been firmly established as a later addition to the epic (below, p. 186)

The ethos of fighting is perfectly embodied in the words that precede Hektor's attack on Aias in their duel in Book 7 (242-3):

> Yet great as you are I would not strike you by stealth, watching
> for my chance, but openly, so, if perhaps I might hit you.

Fighting in this spirit not only despises guile and cowardice; it is also constrained by an implicit notion of fairness. The actual fighting in the *Iliad* does not always live up fully to that ideal; indeed, it is Hektor himself who runs away from Achilles and takes ruthless advantage of Patroklos' injury. How typical are these striking violations of the code?

The question of fairness arises wherever a warrior is taken by surprise. Leaving aside the few bow-shots and the spear-casts that hit someone else, such surprise is not very common. In the fourth book, Elephenor bends over a slain warrior to strip him. As he does so, his ribs are exposed and Agenor hits him (4.463). Similarly, Koön takes Agamemnon by surprise as he removes the armour of Iphidamas (11.248). These incidents reflect on the victim's lack of caution. On two occasions in Book 13 a Trojan warrior unsuccessfully attacks an Achaean only to be caught unawares by Meriones on his retreat (13.567, 650). A more drastic instance of intervention by a third warrior occurs when Menelaos kills Dolops from behind as he is facing an attack by Meges (15.525). All three cases seem less than heroic and occur in a stretch of fighting distinguished by savagery of other kinds (below, p. 83) None of these incidents, however, matches the ruthlessness of Hektor's killing of Patroklos. On three occasions a warrior kills an enemy whom he has previously disabled (below, p. 79). But there is no other case of a warrior killing an enemy whom someone else has disabled.

If the death of Patroklos is the most serious violation of fairness, the duel of Hektor and Achilles provides the most glaring example of loss of courage. The Homeric warrior aims at inspiring in his opponent the uncontrollable fear that leads to flight (*phobos*). Instances of such panic are numerous, but they are typically a collective phenomenon. Individual flight is a much rarer and more qualified phenomenon. When Zeus turns the scales of battle in favour of the Trojans and the Achaeans run away, Diomedes is the only warrior to come to the help of the stranded Nestor. He calls on Odysseus as he runs past, but Odysseus does not hear him or does not listen (the text is ambiguous, 8.97). Odysseus, however, makes the fullest statement of the code of courage when, surrounded by Trojans, he refuses to yield in the face of overwhelming odds (11.401). Between these extremes, there are intermediate positions. Diomedes is afraid to yield lest Hektor accuse him of cowardice. It takes the advice of Nestor and three thunderbolts from Zeus to persuade him that retreat on this occasion is inevitable and not shameful (8.130). The hand of the god is generally a valid excuse for yielding. So Diomedes in Book 5 organises a retreat because Hektor is aided by a god (5.604). Zeus inspires Aias with fear 11.544, but even so his retreat is slow and reluctant. A warrior may without serious loss of face retreat from an enemy who is clearly superior. Thus Menelaos persuades himself that he may abandon the body of Patroklos when Hektor approaches (17.91), and Aeneas yields to Menelaos and Antilochos (5.571), but Diomedes scornfully rejects the advice to retreat before the joint attack of Aeneas and Pandaros, and events prove him right (5.251).

There are limits to Hektor's courage even before the encounter with Achilles. At the order of Zeus he avoids Agamemnon (11.187) just as at the order of Apollo he avoids Achilles (20.376), although he breaks that command when he witnesses the death of his brother Polydoros (20.419). He also avoids Aias on his own initiative (11.542). When Patroklos routs the Trojans, Hektor at first resists the attacks of Aias by his skill at evasive action – the only time in the *Iliad* this skill is made much of (16.359) – but then he, too, joins the rout (367). He teams up with Aeneas against Automedon in the hope of conquering the horses of Achilles, but he retreats in fear when the Aiantes come to the aid of Automedon (17.483). But neither his previous behaviour nor the other scenes of more or less honourable retreat are any precedent for his extraordinary loss of courage at the approach of Achilles. A warrior may persuade himself to stay (Odysseus) or to retreat (Menelaos), but only Hektor persuades himself to stay and fails to live up to his resolution. It is important to remember, however, that the poet sees Hektor's flight less as a failure of Hektor's courage than as a symptom of the overwhelming terror emanating from Achilles.

The individual encounter

The unit of fighting is the individual encounter. The most salient feature of this unit is its brevity. In other forms of heroic poetry warriors demonstrate their prowess in protracted struggles with one or more opponents. Hours or days and many lines may pass before the decisive stroke, and the victor may suffer as many wounds as the vanquished. Not so in the *Iliad*, where the first blow disables the opponent, occasionally through injury, but mostly through death, which is always instantaneous.

Except for two occasions, the injured warrior has no power to strike back. Agamemnon and Odysseus withdraw from battle after killing the men who injure them. The other injured warriors do not return to battle until a god heals or strengthens them as happens to Diomedes (5.111), Aeneas (5.305, 445, 512), Glaukos (12.387, 16.509) and Hektor (14.402, 15.239). The wounding of Menelaos by Pandaros does not occur in battle. Sometimes injuries are forgotten or trivial and healed by the surgeon. Sarpedon, who suffers a serious thigh-wound on the first day (5.660), fights on the third day as if nothing had happened to him. Similarly, Teukros suffers what appears to be a disabling shoulder injury on the second day of fighting (8.324), but is all there again on the following day. It is hard to tell whether these cases are due to heroic resilience or to a lapse of memory, but the three Achaean leaders wounded in Book 11 hobble to the assembly on the following day (19.47).

Out of some 140 specified encounters only twenty involve more than one blow, and except for the duel of Hektor and Aias no encounter goes beyond a second exchange of blows. On three occasions, the victim is only disabled by the first blow, and it requires a second blow to kill him (4.517, 527; 20.478). The death of Patroklos at the hands of Apollo, Euphorbos and Hektor is an elaboration of these cases.

On two occasions, the warriors let go of their missiles simultaneously (5.655, 13.584). On seven occasions, the aggressor misses the enemy or does not pierce his armour fatally and is killed or disabled in return. The victim is always a Trojan. We find this pattern with Pandaros and Diomedes (5.280), Ares and Diomedes/Athene (5.850), Euphorbos and Menelaos (17.43), Hektor and Aias (14.402). A slight variation occurs in the duel of Meges and Dolops. Meges is hit by Dolops, whose spear does not pierce. Meges, who has used his spear to kill another Trojan, hits Dolops with his sword. This stroke, however, is not fatal, and Dolops is killed by Menelaos, who comes up from behind and pierces his chest with his spear (15.525). Finally, in two closely related scenes, the Trojan aggressor injures an Achaean who retains enough strength to avenge himself on his aggressor but is then forced to leave the battle. This pattern is found in the wounding of Agamemnon and Odysseus in Book 11 by Koön and Sokos (11.248, 428). Agamemnon is injured less seriously than Odysseus but, while he continues to fight for a while after Koön's death, the poet does not attribute any named slayings to him.

Only eight encounters go beyond a first exchange of blows – a telling indication of the narrator's preoccupation with the decisive moment. The first exchange always involves spears and has a variety of outcomes. Peneleos and Lykon miss one another (16.335). So do Sarpedon and Patroklos, but each of them hits another victim, the latter the charioteer of Sarpedon, the former the trace horse of Patroklos (16.462). The outcome of the first exchange reflects the relative strengths of the combatants in the duels of Paris and Menelaos and Achilles and Aeneas (3.355, 20.259). On both occasions, the Trojan fails to pierce the Achaean's shield. The Achaean does pierce the armour of his opponent, who somehow 'ducks' the spear. On four occasions it is the victor who misses on the first throw. Thus Agamemnon misses Iphidamas (11.233), Menelaos Peisandros (13.605), Achilles Asteropaios (21.171) and Achilles Hektor (22.273-6). In each case the opponent hits but fails to pierce; the ambidextrous Asteropaios discharges two spears at once, one of which sticks in Achilles' shield whereas the other grazes his hand.

There is no standard procedure for the second exchange, although it usually involves a change from spear to sword. Menelaos attacks Paris with a sword, which breaks. He then pulls Paris by the strap of his helmet, but Aphrodite snaps the helmet strap. Agamemnon hits Iphidamas with his sword. The duels of Peisandros and Menelaos and Lykon and Peneleos are alike in that both involve a simultaneous exchange of blows in which the Trojan's blow fails. But Peisandros wields a battle-axe instead of a sword, the only warrior in the *Iliad* to do so. Sarpedon and Patroklos exchange spears in the second round. The former misses, the latter hits. Asteropaios, the man with two spears, has no sword. As he vainly tries to pull the spear of Achilles out of the ground, Achilles dispatches him with his sword. Achilles rushes at Aeneas with his sword, and Aeneas stands ready to throw a rock, but Poseidon puts an end to the encounter before the second exchange can take place. The most famous victim of Achilles can only be a victim of his spear: Hektor rushes at Achilles with his sword, but Achilles kills him with the spear that Athene returned to him after he missed on his first throw.

The longest fight in the *Iliad*, curiously enough, is the not entirely serious encounter of Hektor and Aias in Book 7. Their duel does not involve the characteristic change from spear to sword, but is based on the triple repetition of a throwing contest in which Aias comes out slightly ahead each time. When the warriors turn to their swords the heralds put an end to the fighting by pointing to the onset of night.

Injury and death

Battle narrative in the *Iliad* is dominated to the point of obsession by the decisive and disabling blow. Some 170 Trojan and 50 Achaean named warriors lose their lives in the *Iliad*; another dozen, evenly divided between the two sides, are injured. About 80 of these die in lists, two, three or four to a line, such as the following victims of Patroklos (16.694-6):

> Adrestos first, and after him Autonoös and Echeklos,
> Perimos, son of Megas, and Epistor, and Melanippos,
> and after these Elasos, and Moulios, and Pylartes.

The remaining 140, only two dozen of them Achaeans, attract more of the poet's attention at the point of their death. The degree of attention varies enormously and observes a delicately graded hierarchy: Hektor, Patroklos and Sarpedon, but also Euphorbos, Iphidamas and Sokos, stand out against the many warriors about whom the poet tells us no more than their name, patronymic, and the nature of their invariably fatal injury. What unites the greatest and the least warriors is the experience of sudden and violent death.

The poet goes out of his way to introduce variety into his grim litany. Take the narrative stretch that describes a rout of the Trojans and shows six Achaean leaders each killing an opponent (5.37-83). Hodios falls off his chariot hit by Agamemnon's spear between the shoulders. Idomeneus hits Phaistos on the right shoulder as he mounts his chariot. Menelaos, like his brother, hits the fleeing Skamandrios between the shoulders. Meriones' spear pierces the right buttock and bladder of Phereklos. Meges hits Pedaios in the back of the head, cutting through his teeth and tongue. Eurypylos rushes at Hypsenor with a sword and cuts off his arm. A similar stretch in the *Patrokleia* features wounds in the thigh, chest, hip, flank, shoulder, neck, shoulder, mouth, as well as a cut-off head (16.306-50).

Here are the victims of Achilles, the final list of slayings in the *Iliad* (20.381-489). Iphition is hit in the middle of the head, Demoleon on the temple. His helmet does not hold: the spear crashes through the bone and brain splatters on the inside of the helmet. Hippodamas is hit in the back, Polydoros in the navel: he falls holding his guts in his hands. The spear of Achilles hits Dryops in the neck and Demouchos in the knee. Laogonos and Dardanos are dispatched with spear and sword respectively, but their injuries are not specified. Tros vainly seeks to supplicate Achilles: a swordstroke makes his liver slip out. The spear drives in at one ear of Moulion and out at the other. The sword plunges deep into the neck of Echeklos and is heated by his blood. Deukalion is hit in the elbow; unable to move, his head is cut off and flung away with the helmet. Marrow jets out of his spine. Rhigmos is hit in the abdomen, Areithoös in the back.

This survey of some two dozen injuries from four killing scenes provides a fairly representative sample of injury and death in the *Iliad*. The upper body and the head are the most common targets for the spear, the neck and head for the sword. In any sequence of killings the poet will vary the injuries and the degree of detail. He may state the mere fact of death, or he may dwell in great detail on the circumstances of a particular slaying, but most commonly he will use a phrase that is specific without being very descriptive, such as 'on the right shoulder', 'through the chest', 'below the ear'. Against the background of ordinary killings some scenes stand out for their special precision, atrocity or extravagance. In our sample, the victims of Meriones and Meges in Book 5 as well as several of Achilles' victims fall in this category.

These special injuries require separate attention because they have an effect quite disproportionate to their scarcity. Mention the *Iliad* in a conversation, and someone is likely to point to some particularly grisly injury as a typical instance of Homeric narrative. But such injuries are not nearly so pervasive as casual readers assume. Out of 140 specified injuries only 30 are remarkable in one way or another, and their description takes up a bare hundred lines. Far from being instances of epic battle-lust, these descriptions are associated with particular characters or situations, and they owe their prominence as much to strategic placement as to vividness of detail.

First, a brief survey of the grisly scenes. A few injuries are remarkable less for their cruelty than for their attention to real or imagined anatomical detail. Thus Amphiklos is hit 'at the base of the leg where the muscle/ of a man grows thickest so that on the spear head the sinew/ was torn apart' (16.314-16). Ancient scholiasts wondered about this injury because it does not appear to be particularly lethal. Antilochos rushes at Thoön and 'shore away the entire vein/ which runs all the way up the back till it reaches the neck' (13.546-7). For all its precision, the description defies human anatomy. The third example of what Friedrich (p. 44) has called fake realism occurs in Book 14 where Archdochos is hit 'at the joining place of head and neck, at the last/ vertebra, and cut through both of the tendons' (14.465-6).

Much more important to the tone of the poem are scenes in which a head is either severed or smashed in a particularly brutal way. Three times, and in words that echo each other, the helmet shatters under the blow of a spear and is besplattered on the inside with brain (11.97, 12.183, 20.397). Idomeneus drives a spear through the mouth and into the brain of Erymas. The skull splits, teeth fall out, and the eye sockets fill with blood, which also wells up through nose and mouth (16.345). The helmet of Hippothoös cannot withstand the force of Aias' blow, 'and the brain ran from the wound along the spear by the eyehole, bleeding' (17.297-8). The spear of Diomedes drives through eye, nose and teeth of Pandaros before cutting off his tongue at the base (5.291). A whole line is given over to Pandaros' tongue, perhaps because he had been such a braggart in his life, but Pedaios (5.73) and Koiranos (17.617) suffer a similar fate. The realm of the probable is clearly left behind in two scenes where the violence of the blow forces the eyes out of their sockets so that they fall on the ground, the fate of Peisandros (13.616-17) and Kebriones (16.741-2).

Decapitation occurs half a dozen times, sometimes as a form of mutilation. Aias Oileus cuts off the head of the dead Imbrios and throws it at Hektor's feet (13.202). Agamemnon chops off Koon's head over the body of his brother Iphidamas (11.261). When he hews off the arms and head of Hippolochos, killing and mutilation are both present (11.145). The same is true of one of the most grotesque scenes in the *Iliad*. Ilioneus is speared in the eye; as he falls backward, Peneleos cuts off his head and triumphantly lifts his spear, with the head stuck on it 'like a poppy' (14.499). The same Peneleos later severs the head of Lykon so that it dangles from the body by a mere piece of skin (16.339).

Abdominal injuries are not uncommon, but are usually not specified beyond such phrases as *kata laparên* ('in the flank'), *mesên kata gastera* or *neiairêi d' en gastri* ('in the middle or lower belly'). Where the wound is elaborated, the poet dwells on the image of guts spilling out of the body. This happens to Peiros (4.525) and to three victims of Achilles (20.418, 470, 21.180). The most gruesome image, however, occurs in Book 17. On two occasions a spear misses and continues to quiver after it hits the ground (13.504, 16.614). This image is varied in the death of Aretos, whom Automedon, the charioteer of Patroklos, kills in revenge for his fallen comrade: the spear quivers in the entrails of the hapless victim (17.523).

Groin injuries occur four times. One of them is passed over in a phrase (4.492), the other three are remarkable for being the work of Meriones, a ruthless and somewhat sneaky warrior. The first injury is suffered by Phereklos, son of the man who built the ships for Paris' fateful voyage (5.59). An ancient scholiast interpreted the wound as poetic justice for the whoring of Paris. The other two occur in adjacent and similar passages in the aristeia of Idomeneus (below p. 92 for a discussion of the term): a Trojan fails to pierce the armour of an Achaean; as he retreats, Meriones hits him in the groin 'where beyond all places/ death in battle comes painfully to pitiful mortals' (13.568). The death spasms of the victims are compared to a twitching bull (13.571) and a wriggling worm (13.654) – unique images that make it clear that a sense of revulsion is intended and not the result of a more refined sensibility.

There remain three unique and bizarre scenes of death in the *Iliad*. Two of them involve charioteers. A straightforward version of a charioteer's death occurs after the death of Asios. His unnamed charioteer loses his wits, is hit in the stomach by Antilochos and falls off his chariot (13.394). In Book 5, Menelaos kills Pylaimenes, and once more it is Antilochos who kills the charioteer, but the motif of the fallen warrior is varied: his head is stuck in the deep sand, and the body remains standing for a while – an image that gains force from the contrast with typical closing phrases like 'he fell thunderously and his armour clattered about him'. In the other version, the motif of the charioteer's paralysis is varied. Patroklos kills the terrified Thestor by stabbing him in the jaw and then (16.406-10):

> hooked and dragged him with the spear over the rail, as a fisherman
> who sits out on the jut of a rock with line and glittering
> bronze hook drags a fish, who is thus doomed, out of the water.
> So he hauled him, mouth open to the bright spear, out of the chariot,
> and shoved him over on his face, and as he fell the life left him.

3. Fighting in the Iliad

Finally, perhaps the most bizarre death of all, a second variation on the theme of the spear quivering in the ground. Paralysed by Poseidon, Alkathoös stands immobile as Idomeneus pierces his armour and drives the spear through his heart (13.441-4):

> He cried out then, a great cry, broken, the spear in him,
> and fell, thunderously, and the spear in his heart was stuck fast
> but the heart was panting still and beating to shake the butt end
> of the spear. Then and there Ares the huge took his life away from him.

With the exception of Koiranos (17.617), the victims of gruesome injuries are always Trojans, a reflection of the bias of the poet's narrative sources. Some interesting conclusions emerge from looking at the distribution of these injuries and at the identity of the killers. Twenty-eight of 30 injuries occur in Books 5, 13-14, and in the aristeias of Achilles, Agamemnon and Patroklos (including the fight over his body). The killers are either minor warriors or major warriors in extreme situations. The reasons for this distribution are not hard to find. Minor warriors are both distinguished and placed by their association with fanciful and cruel injuries. Meriones is the specialist in groin injuries; Peneleos acquires similar notoriety through the brutality of head-wounds he inflicts. The cluster of unusual injuries in Books 13 and 14 has two reasons. We may distinguish in the *Iliad* between fights that sharply focus on a concrete object (the wall in Book 12, the ships in Book 15, the body of Patroklos in Book 17) and diffuse fighting scenes in which the general sense of battle yields to the individual encounter. Gruesome injuries are almost completely absent from the fighting scenes of the former type (except for the fighting over Patroklos), and they are clustered in the scenes of the latter type. The desire to make individual encounters more colourful and inevitably more brutal accounts for the frequency of unusual injuries in Book 5 and in Books 13 and 14, but it does not explain the much greater brutality of Books 13 and 14. Again the reason is not hard to find. The cruelty of Books 13 and 14 measures the changing nature of the war. The reminder of increasing brutality comes just before Patroklos re-enters the fighting. Patroklos, we recall, is singled out in the *Iliad* for his gentleness, and the brutality of his fate is a major theme of the poem. But, if Patroklos becomes a victim of war, he is also transformed by its rage: the fighting he leads is exceptionally bloody, and of the five unusual injuries it causes he himself is responsible for two.

It is hardly necessary to point out why cruel injuries are frequent in the aristeia of Achilles: his violence is a response to and further intensification of the brutality that has claimed Patroklos, but as with Patroklos it is at odds with his character: 'Achilles' unyielding harshness to both living and dead enemies is less the function of his nature than of his fate' (Friedrich, 60).

Agamemnon is a different case. His cruelty manifests itself in the first scene of the *Iliad* when he rebuffs Chryses, and his bloody aristeia seems quite in character. On the other hand, Agamemnon as the leader of the expedition has the strongest sense of the wrong done by the Trojans. His killing of the suppliants Adrestos and Hippolochos is motivated by his sense of outrage. Thus even the Iliadic Agamemnon may not be cruel by nature, but we discover in his portrayal the theme of the brutalising force of a moral mission, which Aeschylus was to develop with magnificent thoroughness.

... and his armour clattered about him

The preoccupation with the individual encounter and the decisive stroke of death appears in another Iliadic convention, the phrase, ranging in length from a half-line to three lines, by which the poet confirms the death of the victim. These poetic death certificates appear roughly a hundred times and exhibit considerable variety.

Death appears as the loosener of limbs in a set of phrases of which *luse de guia* (6x) is the commonest. Another set of phrases equates death with the literal fall of the warrior. *Doupêsen de pesôn*, 'he fell with a thud' (19x), occurs most frequently, its very sound echoing the fall of the warrior on the ground. Less onomatopoeic is a set of phrases that are derived from the verb *ereipein*, 'to fall', and specify the direction or origin of the fall, such as 'from the chariot', 'over his feet', or 'in the dust'. The phrases *keito tanustheis* (2x) and *keito tatheis* (2x), 'he lay stretched out', dwell on the result of the fall. After the death of Kebriones there is fighting over his body, and the poet returns to the body on the ground (16.775-6)

> *ho d' en strophalingi koniês*
> *keito megas megalôsti lelasmenos hipposunaôn*

> he lay in the whirling dust
> mightily in his might, his horsemanship all forgotten.

The falling phrases may stand by themselves but more commonly they are combined with others. The most famous of these combinations contrasts the thudding sound of the body with the clatter of its armour, imitating the contrast in its own phonetic structure: *doupêsen te peson, arabêse de teuche' ep' autôi*, 'he fell with a thud and his armour clattered about him' (6x). Another phrase for the accompanying noise of the armour *is amphi de hoi brache teuchea poikila chalkôi* (3x), 'his glittering armour clattered about him'. The sound can also be the death shout of the falling warrior, as in *gnux d' erip' oimôxas*, 'he fell backwards in the dust with a shout' (2x), and in the phrase that closes the falls of Asios and Sarpedon (13.392-3):

> *hôs ho prosth' hippôn kai diphrou keito tanustheis*
> *bebruchôs konios dedragmenos haimatoessês.*

> So he lay there felled in front of his horses and chariot,
> roaring, and clawed with his hands at the bloody dust.

A similar gesture of futility appears in the phrase *ho d'en koniêisi pesôn hele gaian agostôi*, 'falling in the dust he clutched the earth with his hand' (5x). Even more pathetic is the vision of the dying warrior stretching out his hands towards his comrades: *ho d'huptios en koniêisi/ kappesen amphô cheire philois hetaroisi petassas* 'he fell backward in the dust stretching out his hands towards his companions' (2x).

The contrast of death and fertility occurs in a line that closes catalogue killings: *pantas epassuterous pelase chthoni pouluboteirêi*, 'all these he felled to the bountiful earth in rapid succession' (3x). Perhaps a similar association informs the line *keito tatheis, ek d'haima melan rhee, deue de gaian*, 'he lay at length, and the black blood flowed, and the ground was soaked with it' (21.119).

The most impressive of these closing phrases transform the absence of life into a dark and threatening presence. *Ton de skotos osse kalupse* (11x) ('darkness covered his eyes') is the commonest version of a theme on which the poet likes to play sombre variations:

thanatos de min amphekalupse ('death covered him all around')
nephelê de min amphekalupse kuaneê ('a dark cloud covered him all around')
stugeros d' ara min skotos heilen (3x) ('hateful darkness took him')
ton de kat'osse'/ ellabe porphureos thanatos kai moira krataiê ('the red death and destiny the powerful took hold of both his eyes')
amphi de min thanatos chuto thumoraistês ('life-rending death was poured about him')
ton de kat'ophthalmôn erebennê nux ekalupse ('baleful night covered him from the eyes down')

In two cases, this possession appears as a grim exchange:

ôka de thumos/ ôchet' apo meleôn, stugeros d' ara min skotos heilen (2x) ('swiftly the spirit fled from the limbs but hateful darkness took him')
psuchê de kat' outamenên ôteilên/ essut' epeigomenê, ton de skotos osse kalupse ('life rushed from the wound, urged on, but darkness covered his eyes')

The collective impact of these phrases is very powerful and shapes the representation of death as a sudden and violent disaster. The frequency and elaboration of such phrases in different parts of the narrative is random. In this they differ from the unusual injuries, which are highly context-bound. It is clear, however, that the poet avoids the use of the same phrase in successive scenes. Such repetition occurs twice with relatively colourless phrases (7.12-16, 11.240, 260), and the arresting line *ho d'en koniêisi pesôn hele gaian agostôi*, 'falling in the dust he clutched the earth with his hands', occurs twice within the space of thirteen lines (13.508, 520), possibly to underscore the tit-for-tat of slaying and counterslaying. But a survey of scenes in which warriors are killed in quick succession shows the poet at pains to achieve variation. This is most apparent in the 50-line stretch in Book 5, where six Trojans die, each with a different closing statement:

He fell, thunderously, and his armour clattered upon him (5.42)
He dropped from the chariot, and the hateful darkness took hold of him (5.47)
He dropped forward on his face and his armour clattered upon him (5.58)
He dropped, screaming, to his knees, and death was a mist about him (5.68)
and he dropped in the dust gripping in his teeth the cold bronze (5.75)
and the red death and destiny the powerful took hold of both eyes (5.82-3)

The deaths of Patroklos and Hektor are so central to the poem and so deeply interrelated that the poet describes them in lines reserved for them (16.855-7 = 22.361-3):

He spoke, and as he spoke the end of death closed in upon him,
and the soul fluttering free of his limbs went down into Death's house
mourning her destiny, leaving youth and manhood behind her.
Now though he was a dead man (glorious Hektor | brilliant Achilles) spoke to him:

The first of these lines is also used of Sarpedon, Patroklos' noblest victim and the only other character to be honoured with a death speech.

Necrologues and gloating speeches

Of the victims in the *Iliad* only Sarpedon, Patroklos and Hektor, and to a lesser degree Asios, Pandaros and Euphorbos, play any role prior to their death. The rest appear and disappear at the moment of their death and occupy the poet's attention for the space of a few lines only. Most of these victims might as well be nameless, but in some thirty cases the poet gives a sketch of the warrior's background and history. These little necrologues, consisting typically of three or four lines, are, like the similes, a master-stroke of Iliadic art. Through them the poet not only introduces variety into his narrative, but also the collective effect of these miniatures is to create a powerful image of the suffering of war and to extend the narrator's sympathy to Trojans and Achaeans alike.

Evidently the narrative has a strong Achaean bias. Achaeans are killed rarely; even in scenes of Trojan victory, the Achaeans win most of the individual fights, and Achaeans are spared cruel and undignified injuries. Despite the premise that without Achilles the Achaeans are at the mercy of Hektor, no Achaean fighter of rank is defeated by Hektor, who in fact loses both to Aias and to Diomedes, does not confront Agamemnon, and is even denied the glory of killing Patroklos in open combat. It would have been possible for the poet to motivate this superiority of the Achaeans in moral terms and to attribute the defeat of the Trojans to a moral failing. Herodotus, who thought of his history as in some sense a continuation of the *Iliad*, interpreted the war of the Greeks and Persians as an East-West conflict, in which voluntary submission to law triumphs over the despotism of an oriental ruler. There are traces of such a conception in the *Iliad*. When the armies first clash, the order and silence of the Achaeans are contrasted with the noisy confusion of the Trojans and their allies (4.428). Such lack of control is easily related to great wealth and to the foolish passion of Paris that caused the war. Occasionally a Trojan death is seen as the consequence and punishment of wickedness. Thus Menelaos in a speech over the fallen Peisandros sees his victory as just retribution for Trojan licence (13.620). In two other cases the sketch of the victim's background sounds a similar theme. We hear of Phereklos that he was the son of Harmonides, who built the ships for Paris' fateful expedition (5.62). Peisandros and Hippolochos are the sons of Antimachos, who took bribes from Paris and prevented the return of Helen. Agamemnon, on listening to their supplication, remembers that their father proposed to kill Menelaos and Odysseus when they were on a diplomatic mission to Troy, and he proceeds to avenge the father's disgraceful deeds on the children (11.122).

Such moralising, however, is exceptional in the *Iliad*. The necrologue charac-teristically ignores the division of Achaean and Trojan and deals with the death of the warrior as a human event. Thus the pro-Achaean narrative bias of the poem generates its own counterpoint: the greater the successes of the Achaeans on the battlefield, the more the Trojan victims evoke the poet's sympathy. The poem's narrative bias leads to an unequal division of the poet's impartial sympathy: only seven victims with stories are Achaeans.

The narrator's impartial pity is established early and firmly. At the end of Book 4, Diorês, an Achaean ally, and the Thracian Peiros, a Trojan ally, have both been killed. The poet takes leave of this part of the battle by dwelling on the common fate that unites them in death (4.536-8):

> So in the dust these two lay sprawled beside one another,
> lords, the one of the Thracians, the other of the bronze-armoured
> Epeians; and many others beside were killed all about them.

The simplest necrologues add to the name of the father that of the mother and dwell on the circumstances of birth or conception. One is tempted to call the effect pastoral because it turns on the nostalgic evocation of a natural habitat from an unnatural perspective. On three occasions the mother is a water nymph whom the father encountered while tending his flocks or herds. Here is the story of Aisepos and Pedasos and their father Boukolion (the name means 'cowherd') (6.21-8):

> Aisepos and Pedasos, those whom the naiad
> nymph Abarbare had born to blameless Boukolion.
> Boukolion himself was the son of haughty Laomedon,
> eldest born, but his mother conceived him in darkness and secrecy.
> While shepherding his flocks he lay with the nymph and loved her,
> and she conceiving bore him twin boys. But now Mekistios'
> son unstrung the strength of these and the limbs in their glory,
> Euryalos, and stripped the armour away from their shoulders.

Similar stories are told about Satnios (14.444) and Iphition (20.383). The mother of Simoeisios was human, but not unlike a water nymph she gave birth to her son on the banks of Simoeis, while following the flocks of her parents (4.474). On other occasions the poet simply states the beauty of the mother (8.304) or the wealth and status of the father (5.77, 14.490, 16.595, 16.604, 17.575). Some of the biographical detail is anecdotal in character. Skamandrios, killed by Menelaos, was a favourite of Artemis, who taught him skill in hunting (5.53-4),

> Yet Artemis of the showering arrows could not now help him,
> no, nor the long spearcasts in which he had been pre-eminent,

Pedaios was the bastard son of Antenor, whose wife treated him like one of her own children to please her husband (5.70). The three Achaean victims Medon, Lykophron and Epeigeus are exiles who left their home after killing a man (15.334, 431, 16.571). This is of course the fate of Patroklos as well, and it may not be random that the three vignettes occur shortly before or during the Patrokleia. Periphetes, a victim of Hektor, is described as a better man than his father Kopreus ('Dung'), whom Eurystheus sent on errands to Herakles (15.639). This is one of two occasions when a necrologue refers to the body of legend outside the poem. The other and rather obscure passage refers to the father of Atymnios and Maris as the man who reared the *amaimaketê chimaira*, a monster of uncertain nature (16.328). In another case, the necrologue refers to an earlier event in the Trojan war: when Agamemnon slays Isos and Antiphos we learn that on a previous occasion Achilles captured them alive and freed them for ransom (11.104).

A motif that occurs three times in Book 13 and nowhere else involves a Trojan ally who is married to or a suitor of a Trojan princess. Imbrios married a bastard daughter of Priam and returned to Priam's house when war broke out (13.174). Othryoneus wooed Kassandra, the most beautiful of Priam's daughters, and boasted that he would drive off the Achaeans in return for her hand (13.363). Alkathoös was the son-in-law of Anchises (13.429-3)

> and had married the eldest of his daughters, Hippodameia,
> dear to the hearts of her father and the lady her mother
> in the great house, since she surpassed all the girls of her own age
> for beauty and accomplishments and wit; for which reason
> the man married her who was the best in the wide Troad.

It is quite common in the *Iliad* for brothers to suffer death at the hands of one warrior, and three passages in which the poet looks at brothers united in death are particularly affecting (5.541, 11.262, 16.326). But the most memorable of the necrologues dwell on the grief of the survivors, the parents – more specifically the father – and the wife. They echo and universalise the suffering of Andromache, Priam and Peleus, and in so doing they establish a powerful thematic link between the major and minor characters of the *Iliad*. Simoeisios, the first warrior to be singled out for a necrologue, 'did not return his parents' care for him' (4.477). If in this instance the grief of the survivors is only implicit, it is very explicit in the story of the father of Xanthos and Thoön (5.153-8):

> full grown both, but Phainops was stricken in sorrowful old age
> nor could breed another son to leave among his possessions.
> There he killed these two and took away the dear life from them
> both, leaving to their father lamentation and sorrowful
> affliction, since he was not to welcome them home from the fighting
> alive still; and remoter kinsmen shared his possessions.

Harpalion followed his father to war 'and did not come home again to the land of his fathers' (13.644); indeed, the grieving father walks behind the Paphlagonians who rescue the son's body (13.658). Ilioneus, we learn, is the only son of his wealthy father (14.492), Polydoros the youngest and favourite son of Priam, who vainly tried to keep him out of battle (20.408). In the case of Sokos, the figure of the grieving parents appears in Odysseus' speech of exultation (11.452). The motif also appears in the exchange of speeches between Euphorbos and Menelaos and is confirmed in the elaborate tree simile in which the dead Euphorbos is compared to a young tree, tended carefully by a man in a lonely place and suddenly torn up by a gust of wind (17.53).

Sometimes the father is a prophet. The soothsayer Merops vainly tried to prevent his sons from joining the war (11.329). Eurydamas, on the other hand, refused (or neglected) to interpret the dreams of his sons Abas and Polyides (5.149). Euchenor faces a dilemma not unlike that of Achilles: his father tells him that he must choose between a lingering sickness at home or death in battle. He chooses the latter and, curiously enough, dies at the hands of Paris, as Achilles later will (13.660).

The grieving wife appears in the story of Protesilaos, the first Achaean warrior to die at Troy, while his wife 'cheeks torn for grief, was left behind in Phylake/ and a marriage half completed' (2.700-1). The theme is implicit in the finest and most elaborate of all necrologues, the story of Iphidamas. Brought up by his maternal grandfather, he married his daughter and went from his wedding straight to the war, where he was killed by Agamemnon (11.241-5):

> So Iphidamas fell there and went into the brazen slumber,
> unhappy, who came to help his own people, and left his young wife
> a bride, and had known no delight from her yet, and given much for her.
> First he had given a hundred oxen, then promised a thousand
> head of goats and sheep, which were herded for him in abundance.

The impartial sympathy that the poet shows for the fallen warrior sharply contrasts with the savage partisanship the victors display on such occasions. But the gloating speeches are similar in function to the necrologues in that they keep the fallen warrior a little longer in the limelight. The distribution of gloating speeches relates them closely to grisly injuries. Of the sixteen instances, eight are found in Books 13 and 14, three in the Patrokleia, and four in the aristeia of Achilles. Only one such speech (11.450) is found outside this complex of scenes. On two other occasions, Pandaros (5.284) and Paris (11.380) exult prematurely at the prospect of triumph over Diomedes. But Pandaros misses his target and Paris does not inflict a fatal wound.

The gloating speeches share with the necrologues the motif of the grieving survivor, but they vary it to reflect the hostile perspective of the speaker. The triumphant warrior dedicates the corpse to animals and imagines the survivors' mourning deepened by the lack of the body to care for. The motif occurs in Achilles' speeches to Lykaon and Hektor (above, p. 70); words to the body of Sokos form an unusually sombre and restrained instance of the genre (11.450-5):

> Sokos, son of wise Hippasos the breaker of horses,
> death was too quick for you and ran you down, you could not
> avoid it. Wretch, since now your father and your honoured mother
> will not be able to close your eyes in death, but the tearing
> birds will get you, with their wings close-beating about you.
> If I die, the brilliant Achaians will bury me in honour.

The motif of burial is absent from the speech over the body of Ilioneus in which Peneleos contrasts two sets of survivors. The whole scene is worth quoting because it shows a single slaying elaborated by a grisly wound, a necrologue, a simile (short but striking) and a gloating speech, with the different components carefully interrelated. The death of Ilioneus brings to a close the string of brutal slayings in Books 13 and 14; its elaboration is in accordance with the climactic position it occupies (14.489-505):

He then stabbed with the spear Ilioneus
the son of Phorbas the rich in sheepflocks, whom beyond all men
of the Trojans Hermes loved, and gave him possessions.
Ilioneus was the only child his mother had borne him.
This man Peneleos caught underneath the brow, at the bases
of the eye, and pushed the eyeball out, and the spear went clean through
the eye-socket and tendon of the neck, so that he went down
backward, reaching out both hands, but Peneleos drawing
his sharp sword hewed at the neck in the middle, and so dashed downward
the head, with helm upon it, while still on the point of the big spear
the eyeball stuck. He, lifting it high like the head of a poppy,
displayed it to the Trojans and spoke vaunting over it:
'Trojans, tell haughty Ilioneus' beloved father
and mother, from me, that they can weep for him in their halls, since
neither shall the wife of Promachos, Alegenor's
son, take pride of delight in her dear lord's coming, on that day
when we sons of the Achaians come home from Troy in our vessels.'

On four prominent occasions the gloating speeches display coarse and savage irony. Thus Idomeneus addresses the body of Othryoneus, the boastful suitor of Kassandra, and offers him one of Agamemnon's daughters if he would join the Achaeans (13.374). After Idomeneus has killed Asios, Deiphobos kills Hypsenor in return and boasts that he has provided him with an escort on the way to Hades (13.413). Poulydamas goes one better on this conceit and boasts that his spear will serve his victim as a walking-stick (14.456). It is significant that the gentle Patroklos at the height of his triumph is tempted into such language. Here he is commenting on the fall of Kebriones from his chariot (16.745-50):

> See now, what a light man this is, how agile an acrobat.
> If only he were somewhere on the sea, where the fish swarm,
> he could fill the hunger of many men, by diving for oysters;
> he could go overboard from a boat even in rough weather
> the way he somersaults so light to the ground from his chariot
> now. So, to be sure, in Troy also they have their acrobats.

Twice the gloating speech turns into genealogical display (13.449, 21.184). More important to the structure of the poem is the preoccupation of several speeches with the theme of revenge. This theme links the speeches of Books 13 and 14 so that in each book they form a tight cluster. Thus, in Book 13, Deiphobos thinks of his killing of Hypsenor as revenge for the death of Asios (13.414), but Idomeneus retaliates by killing Alkathoös, and referring to his victories over Othryoneus, Asios and Alkathoös he replies: 'Deiphobos, are we then to call this a worthy bargain,/ three men killed for one?' (13.446-7). In Book 14, Aias kills Archelochos in return for the slaying of Prothoenor by Poulydamas, whose boast he answers thus (14.470-2):

> Think over this Poulydamas, and answer me truly.
> Is not this man's death against Prothoenor's a worthwhile
> exchange?

The Trojan Akamas thereupon kills Promachos and boasts that the Trojans are not alone in suffering pain and misery (14.479). This prompts Peneleos to kill Ilioneus and to compare the sufferings of his parents with those of Promachos' wife in the passage quoted above. The chain of retribution that is thematised in these exchanges clearly points forward to the major version of the revenge triangle in the story of Patroklos, Hektor and Achilles. The theme recurs in the speech of Automedon over the body of Aretos, whose death he sees as retribution, however inadequate, for the death of Patroklos (17.538). For the last time, it appears in Achilles' words to the dying Hektor (22.331-4):

> Hektor, surely you thought as you killed Patroklos you would be
> safe, and since I was far away you thought nothing of me,
> o fool, for an avenger was left, far greater than he was,
> behind him and away by the hollow ships.

Speeches of exultation form an important part of the aristeia of Achilles and culminate in the words just quoted. The first addressee is Iphition, for no other reason than that he is his first victim. The victim's fate is briefly summarised, but then Achilles lingers over the description of his home in a manner that recalls the rhetoric of the unreal with which he envisaged the life in Phthia to which he, likewise, will not return (20.389-92):

> Lie there, Otrynteus' son, most terrifying of all men.
> Here is your death, but your generation was by the lake waters
> of Gyge, where is the allotted land of your fathers
> by fish-swarming Hyllos and the whirling waters of Hermos.

The other speeches occur in the encounters with Lykaon, Asteropaios and Hektor. Of these only the Asteropaios scene stays within the convention of minor encounters. In both the Lykaon and Hektor scenes the speech of exultation is part of a more complex pattern.

Narrative patterns beyond the individual encounter

Homer has two procedures for weaving short individual encounters into larger narrative structures. The serial connection links the successive victims of one warrior (or group of warriors) without establishing a causal chain. In the reciprocal connection one slaying prompts a slaying by the other side and generates a chain of retribution.

Catalogues and aristeias

The simplest string of slayings is the catalogue of names that are listed as the victims of one warrior (e.g. 16.694-6, quoted above, p. 80). In a more complicated version of such a catalogue, the poet lists the successive victims of two or more Achaean or Trojan warriors. Thus the poet lists the victims of Diomedes and Odysseus (11.320), or those of Leontes and Polypoites (12.182). Book 6 begins with a catalogue of the victims of the Achaeans, while in Book 7 it is the Trojans' turn to have their victims listed (7.8). There is another Trojan catalogue in the battle of the ships (15.328). The catalogues of Books 5 and 16 differentiate elaborately between the victims and their wounds (above, p. 80); a somewhat less detailed version describes the rout of the Trojans at the end of Book 14 (above, p. 31).

By far the most important type of serial fight is the 'aristeia', in which a warrior becomes for a while the star of the show and displays his prowess. A very simple example of such an aristeia occurs when Teukros, protected by the shield of his half-brother Aias, kills eight Trojans in catalogue form and then takes three shots at Hektor (8.266-334). The first two miss Hektor and hit Gorgythion and Archeptolemos instead; he has no chance to get off the third shot because Hektor hits him with a stone that paralyses his arm.

The important aristeias are much more complex structures in which fighting comes to play a subordinate role. There are four major aristeias, and their respective heroes are Diomedes, Agamemnon, Patroklos and Achilles. Each of them leads to a turning-point in the narrative. The aristeias of Agamemnon, Patroklos and Achilles mark turning-points in Hektor's career: his course of victory is explicitly dated from the withdrawal of the injured Agamemnon, it culminates with the death of Patroklos, and comes to an end with his defeat by Achilles. The aristeia of Diomedes fits this pattern after a fashion, for it provides the background for the formal introduction of Hektor in Book 6.

The major aristeia begins with a scene of arming. The simplest version of this scene maintains the same order of elements that appears in the more elaborate forms. It occurs in the preparation for the duel between Paris and Menelaos, which is not, however, an aristeia (3.330-8):

> First he placed along his legs the fair greaves linked with
> silver fastenings to hold the greaves at the ankles.
> Afterwards he girt on about his chest the corselet
> of Lykaon his brother since this fitted him also.
> Across his shoulders he slung the sword with the nails of silver,
> a bronze sword, and above it the great shield, huge and heavy.
> Over his powerful head he set the well-fashioned helmet
> with the horse-hair crest, and the plumes nodded terribly above it.
> He took up a strong-shafted spear that fitted his hand's grip.

The other arming scenes maintain the same order but elaborate various elements in different ways. Thus the arming of Agamemnon (11.17) gives detailed descriptions of his corselet and shield, which are remarkable both for the skill of their metalwork and for the figures of terror inscribed on them. The arming is a prelude both to the aristeia of Agamemnon and to the third day of fighting: the emphasis on the terror emanating from Agamemnon's armour heralds the ferocity of the battle to come.

The greater achievement of Achilles is marked by an even more emphatic scene of arming. Indeed, the arms of Achilles are described in three separate scenes, as they are made, as Achilles first sees them, and as he puts them on. The making of the arms by Hephaistos at the request of Thetis is one of the most elaborate divine scenes in the *Iliad*. It fills half a book and culminates in a 130-line description of the shield of Achilles (18.478). The scene pre-empts a further description of the arms in the arming scene, which focuses on their effect. When Achilles first receives the arms, their brightness terrifies everybody but Achilles, whose eyes shine in a corresponding fire (19.13). When Achilles finally puts on his armour, the motif of brightness appears three different times (19.373). The gleam of armour is the typical finale to the arming scene; it is a harbinger of the destruction the warrior will cause. Its elaboration in the case of Achilles, in line with the fire motif that accompanies him throughout his aristeia, is a sign of his special destructiveness.

In the aristeia of Diomedes, where a complete arming scene would disrupt the narrative flow, the gleam of the armour synecdochically replaces such a scene (5.1-8):

> There to Tydeus' son Diomedes Pallas Athene
> granted strength and daring, that he might be conspicuous
> among all the Argives and win the glory of valour.
> She made weariless fire blaze from his shield and helmet
> like that star of the waning summer who beyond all stars
> rises bathed in the ocean stream to glitter in brilliance.
> Such was the fire she made blaze from his head and his shoulders
> and urged him into the middle fighting, where most were struggling.

In contrast to such emphatic brilliance, the arming of Patroklos is an impoverished account, remarkable for its negative qualities. No gleam emanates from his armour – any more than from that of Paris – signal of his eventual defeat. And the most elaborate detail in this arming scene concerns the spear of Achilles that Patroklos does not take (16.140).

The aristeia of Agamemnon is the shortest and simplest of the major aristeias. After the arming scene, there is an extended description of general preparation for battle and the first clash of armies (11.47-91), which is followed by the account of Agamemnon's victims. After an interlude about the absence of Hektor from this phase of the fighting (11.163-217), the poet returns to Agamemnon and describes in detail his victory over Iphidamas and the partial success of Koön, who pays with his life for his attempt to avenge his brother but wounds Agamemnon and forces him to leave the battle.

The aristeias of Diomedes and Patroklos are very similar to one another. After an initial killing by the hero, the poet continues with extended catalogues of slayings by Achaean warriors. In the Patrokleia, this leads to a rout of the Trojans and a catalogue of slayings by Patroklos. In the Diomedeia, the Achaean catalogue is followed by the first part of the Pandaros episode. Diomedes' re-entry into battle after his slight injury leads to a catalogue of his slayings. Thus both Diomedeia and Patrokleia observe the sequence (1) arming, (2) first slaying by the hero, (3) deeds of other Achaean warriors, (4) deeds of the hero. The third item is absent from the aristeias of Agamemnon and Achilles for obvious reasons. Agamemnon's aristeia is only a prelude to a day of battle that will introduce many heroes, and as his aristeia is also part of the successive wounding of Achaean warriors elaboration would obscure the proportions of the narrative. With Achilles, on the other hand, the single-minded concentration on his deeds reflects the theme that with the death of Patroklos the war has become his war alone. No other Achaean is mentioned once Achilles re-enters the battle – an exclusion that is made explicit in the pursuit of Hektor (22.205-7):

But brilliant Achilleus kept shaking his head at his own people
and would not let them throw their bitter projectiles at Hektor
for fear the thrower might win the glory, and himself come second.

As the aristeias of Patroklos and Diomedes continue, each develops its own shape to fit its narrative context, but there remain significant parallels and contrasts. The common element involves Apollo's hostility to the hero and the hero's victory over a Trojan opponent whose body becomes the special care of Apollo. In the Diomedeia that opponent is Aeneas, who is rescued from death and restored to health by the god. In the Patrokleia it is Sarpedon, whose body is rescued by Apollo and given to Sleep and Death to bury in his native Lykia. The victory over the Trojan leads on both occasions to a confrontation with Apollo in which the hero heeds the god's advice to retreat (5.433, 16.698). In the Patrokleia the god maintains his hostility and eventually strikes Patroklos; in the Diomedeia, the hero's respect for Apollo serves as the background for his successful attacks on the less dignified deities Ares and Aphrodite. It is probably a mistake to see in these common elements a conventional schema of heroic poetry; rather, the Diomedeia and Patrokleia are proleptic variations of the aristeia of Achilles, where the hostility of Apollo and his care for the Trojan opponent find their most significant expression.

The chain of retribution

Chain killings claim some sixty victims in the *Iliad* and occur typically in passages that link two to five deaths with more or less sharply drawn boundaries. There are fifteen to eighteen such chains in the *Iliad*, depending on how one draws the boundaries, and they are heavily concentrated in Books 13-17, with only seven scenes laying outside those books. The chains typically have 'scores' like 2:1, and they sandwich one, occasionally two, Trojan successes between Achaean victories. On a few occasions there is a draw; there is no chain in which Trojans outscore Achaeans.

The crucial importance of the chains consists in the fact that they exhibit the structure of retribution through which the destinies of the minor warriors are linked to those of the protagonists. Patroklos kills Sarpedon, Hektor's closest ally, and Kebriones, his charioteer. Hektor avenges their death by killing Patroklos, whereupon Achilles kills Hektor. Finally, Paris will take revenge on Achilles. In this strict form the pattern does not recur in the chain killings, if only because it consumes too many known characters. Only in one minor scene is the killer killed: the Trojan ally Peiros kills Diorês, whose companion Thoas kills Peiros in turn. The incident occurs at the very beginning of the fighting (4.517), and its exemplary nature is stressed by the fact that the poet dwells on the sight of the two enemies laying side by side on the battlefield, united in death. But this is the only encounter of two unknown, and therefore equally dispensable, warriors in the *Iliad*. The typical procedure is to pit an unknown against a known warrior, whom the poet cannot spare if he is not to run out of characters.

Narrative economy thus accounts for the fact that the motif of the slayer slain appears in variously displaced forms. On five occasions, injury displaces death in the act of retribution. Deiphobos and Helenos are both wounded after killing an Achaean warrior (13.527, 581). More interesting and elaborate are the injuries of the Achaean leaders. The Agamemnon and Odysseus scenes are very similar. The Achaean kills a Trojan whose brother injures him in return. The Achaean then kills the brother as well but is forced to leave the battlefield (11.221, 426). The pairs of Iphidamas-Koön and Charops-Sokos are unknown and dispensable. But this is not the case with Hektor and Paris, the opponents of Diomedes, neither of whom can be lost at this point of the narrative. Accordingly we find the following variation (11.338). Diomedes kills the unknown Agastrophos, whereupon Hektor attacks Diomedes but is stunned by Diomedes' spear. Diomedes proceeds to strip the body of Agastrophos, when Paris injures him with an arrow in the foot. Paris exults, but Diomedes taunts him in return, belittling the injury and threatening death for the future. Momentary fainting, a minor wound, the threat of death, and the death of an 'extra' replace the fatal injuries that would enchain slayer and slain in the pure version.

Displacement can also be achieved through substitution, which produces a narrative sequence in which a major warrior after killing a minor warrior is attacked by an opponent whose shot misses its intended target and hits another minor warrior. This happens half a dozen times in the *Iliad*. A good example occurs in the first fighting scene when Aias' victory over Simoeisios provokes an attack by Antiphos, who misses and hits a companion of Odysseus instead (4.489). The same scene includes another and unique device for 'saving' a well-known Achaean: Antilochos kills Echepolos but, instead of Antilochos, another Achaean, Elephenor, seeks to strip the fallen warrior and is killed by Agenor (4.457). Substitute slayings and other narrative restrictions abound in the opposition of Hektor and Aias, which on the one hand dominates much of the fighting during Achilles' absence but on the other hand must not produce an event of significance. On the part of Hektor we find avoidance of the enemy (11.542); on the part of Aias there is failure to pierce Hektor's armour (13.191, 16.358) or temporary injury (14.402). Substitute deaths occur on several occasions (13.183, 15.419, 17.304). The doubling of Patroklos' slayers permits the death of Euphorbos to function as a proleptic substitute for the death of Hektor.

Chain deaths are often motivated by the poet in terms of special ties of kinship or friendship that link warriors to one another. Sometimes retribution depends solely on the solidarity that warriors feel for anyone fighting on their side (4.473, 13.170, 15.518, 17.293). But on some two dozen occasions the poet provides an explicit motive for the act of retribution. He may point to the pity felt by one warrior at the side of a fallen warrior on the same side (5.561, 610). The simple statement of a relationship can also serve as a motive: Agamemnon kills a companion of Aeneas, whereupon Aeneas kills Krethon and Orsilochos (5.533). The two motivations appear together when Aeneas kills Leiokritos, 'the good companion of Lykomedes'. Lykomedes 'pities' his fall and kills the companion of Asteropaios, whose death moves Asteropaios to an unsuccessful attack (17.344).

Grief and anger are more common than pity. The subject of these emotions is usually an individual, but they may seize all Trojans (14.475) or Achaeans (16.599); they may also seize the Achaeans and one of them in particular, as with Antilochos (13.417), Aias (14.459) and Peneleos (14.484). The emotion is deepened by the closeness of the relationship between the fallen warrior and his avenger. Thus Odysseus feels 'fierce anger' at the death of his companion Leukos, and because his slayer had been a son of Priam he takes revenge on another son of Priam (4.491; cf. 8.124, 316, 12.392). Koön's reaction to the death of his brother is given in particular detail (11.248-50):

> When Koön, conspicuous among the fighters, perceived him,
> he who was Antenor's eldest born, the strong sorrow
> misted about his eyes for the sake of his fallen brother.

There are other occasions when the death of a kinsman is a spur to action. Sokos and Euphorbos say so explicitly in their attacks on Odysseus and Menelaos (11.430, 17.34). When Hektor's 'cousin' Kaletor is killed by Aias in the battle of the ships, Hektor kills Lykophron, of whom Aias says (15.437-9; cf. 13.463, 554):

> See, dear Teukros, our true companion, the son of Mastor,
> is killed, who came to us from Kythera and in our household
> was one we honoured as we honoured our beloved parents.

The death of Sarpedon provokes feelings commensurate with his greatness. The grief of his friend Glaukos is heightened by the fact that the injury he suffered earlier in the day keeps him from avenging his death or rescuing his body. After Apollo miraculously heals him he scolds Hektor for not coming to Sarpedon's aid, and collective grief strikes the Trojans (16.548), who are then led by Hektor, 'angered at the death of Sarpedon' (16.553). From this elaboration of the motif it is only a step to Achilles' reaction to the death of Patroklos – the wildest and most extravagant version of a familiar response (18.23-7):

> In both hands he caught up the grimy dust, and poured it
> over his head and face, and fouled his handsome countenance,
> and the black ashes were scattered over his immortal tunic.
> And he himself, mightily in his might, in the dust lay
> at length, and took and tore at his hair with his hands, and defiled it.

The close relationship of chain killings to the story of Achilles and Patroklos is also borne out by their distribution. They are most common in the fighting that precedes Patroklos' entry into battle, where they pursue the grim logic of retribution in multiple detail. They dominate Books 13 and 14. The centrepiece of Book 13 is the aristeia of Idomeneus and his companion Meriones, which differs from the other aristeias in that it contains no catalogues but is an elaborate chain of reciprocal deaths. This narrative stretch comes to a close with the killing of Euchenor by Paris, which is motivated by his anger at the death of his guest friend Harpalion. The death of Euchenor, who chooses between sickness and death in battle, has reminded some critics of the fate of Achilles. If they are correct, the placement of this episode at the end of a succession of retributive deaths may not be arbitrary. The fighting in Book 14 is dominated by a chain of five reciprocal slayings, all but the first followed by gloating speeches dwelling on the tit-for-tat of battle.

The progress of battle

An account of individual fights and their concatenation covers much but not all there is to be said about battle in the *Iliad*. Mass scenes are common, and in some stretches of narrative the contest for a particular objective takes precedence over individual encounters. There is a narrative rhythm that alternates general battle with individual encounters and fighting for strategic objectives with pure displays of individual prowess. To trace this rhythm is to describe the progress of battle as it unfolds in the *Iliad*.

The first major segment of battle narrative stretches from the initial clash of the armies after the broken truce to the beginning of the aristeia of Diomedes. Only a hundred lines long, this section is a prelude both to the Diomedeia and to the war at large. It is an astonishingly rich piece and, like an overture, sounds virtually every theme that will become important in the fighting. It begins with a majestic account of the clashing armies emphasised by an unusual river image (4.446-56):

> Now as these advancing came to one place and encountered,
> they dashed their shields together and their spears, and the strength
> of armoured men in bronze, and the shields massive in the middle
> clashed against each other, and the sound grew huge of the fighting.
> There the screaming and the shouts of triumph rose up together
> of men killing and men killed, and the ground ran blood.
> As when rivers in winter spate running down from the mountains
> throw together at the meeting of streams the weight of their water
> out of the great springs behind in the hollow stream-bed,
> and far away in the mountains the shepherd hears their thunder;
> such, from the coming together of men, was the shock and the shouting.

The narrative then turns to a chain of five reciprocal slayings (457-504). It moves back to a broader perspective when it shows a Trojan retreat and the intervention of Apollo on the Trojan and Athene on the Achaean side, each encouraging the troops to attack (506-16). Once again the poet focuses on an individual encounter: Peiros slays Diorês only to be slain in turn by Thoas. With the pathetic image of the two fallen warriors laying side by side on the battlefield (above, p. 94), the poet returns to a broader perspective, where he rests emphatically before proceeding to the aristeia of Diomedes (4.539-44):

> There no more could a man who was in that work make light of it,
> one who still unhit and still unstabbed by the sharp bronze
> spun in the midst of that fighting, with Pallas Athene's hold on
> his hand guiding him, driving back the volleying spears thrown.
> For on that day many men of the Achaians and Trojans
> lay sprawled in the dust face downward beside one another.

The Diomedeia is dominated throughout by individual encounters. While digressing to include the deeds of other warriors, both Achaean and Trojan, it pursues the hero's career from his victories over Pandaros and Aeneas to his attacks on Aphrodite and finally the god of war himself. Except for the curiously chivalric duel between Aias and Hektor in Book 7 there is not much fighting for the remainder of the first day.

Battle resumes in earnest on the following day. The events of that day are described in Book 8, which the ancients dubbed the 'curtailed battle' (*kolos machê*) because night falls before a decision is reached and perhaps also because the summary and truncated form in which an entire day of fighting is crammed into 300 lines (8.53-349) contrasts sharply with the lavish detail that characterises the battle descriptions of the first and third days.

After a general account of indecisive fighting, the turning-point in the second day's battle comes when Zeus intervenes on the side of the Trojans. In the Achaean rout the poet focuses on the rescue of Nestor by Diomedes and their counter-attack on Hektor. Threatened by the thunderbolts of Zeus, Diomedes retreats, and Hektor in a few lines pushes the Achaeans back on their ships that are now threatened with fire (a situation that it takes all of Book 15 to bring about on the following day). Inspired by Hera, the Achaeans stave off defeat temporarily, and in the description of their rally the poet focuses on Teukros. But when Teukros fails to hit Hektor and is injured by him the Trojans can no longer be stopped: once more they push the Achaeans back to their ships, where only nightfall saves them.

The battle scenes of the third day (11.1-18.242) can be divided into three phases of two movements each. The first phase, consisting of Books 11 and 12, narrates the wounding of the Achaean leaders and the battle of the wall. As in each of the three phases, the first movement is dominated by individual encounters. The aristeia of Agamemnon concludes with his injury, which is varied in the injury scenes of Diomedes and Odysseus. The narrative then focuses on the reluctant retreat of Aias and on the wounding of Machaon and Eurypylos by Paris. The second movement of this phase has as its subject the fight over the wall. The Trojan attack proceeds in three waves. A first attack by Asios is rebuffed by Polypoites and Leontes and ends with a brief aristeia of the two brothers (12.108-94). A second attack by Sarpedon and his Lykians leads to a first breaching of the wall but is beaten back by Aias (12.290-436). The third attack by Hektor is decisive and meets with no resistance. There is a clear crescendo in the three waves of attack. The first two conclude with the comparison of thrown stones to a blizzard, an image that is much elaborated in its second occurrence (12.156, 278). The climactic event, however, is individual. The hail of stones provides the background for Hektor's decisive attack, the elaborate description of which reflects its weighty position in the narrative (12.445-66):

> Meanwhile Hektor snatched up a stone that stood before the gates
> and carried it along; it was blunt-massed at the base, but the upper
> end was sharp; two men, the best in all a community,
> could not easily hoist it up from the ground to a wagon,
> of men such as men are now, but he alone lifted and shook it
> as the son of devious-devising Kronos made it light for him.
> As when a shepherd easily carries the fleece of a wether,
> picking it up with one hand, and little is the burden weighting him,
> so Hektor lifting the stone carried it straight for the door leaves
> which filled the gateway ponderously close-fitted together.
> These were high and twofold, and double door-bars on the inside
> overlapping each other closed it, and a single pin-bolt secured them.
> He came and stood very close and taking a strong wide stance threw
> at the middle, leaning into the throw, that the cast might not lack
> force, and smashed the hinges at either side, and the stone crashed
> ponderously in, and the gates groaned deep, and the door-bars
> could not hold, but the leaves were smashed to a wreckage of splinters
> under the stone's impact. Then glorious Hektor burst in

with dark face like sudden night, but he shone with the ghastly
glitter of bronze that girded his skin, and carried two spears
in his hands. No one could have stood up against him, and stopped him,
except the gods, when he burst in the gates; and his eyes flashed fire.

At this moment it seems as if nothing could stand between Hektor and the ships. But new obstacles arise suddenly and create the second phase of fighting, where again we may distinguish between a first movement dominated by individual fights (Books 13 and 14) and a second movement that portrays the attack on a strategic objective, in this case the ships (Book 15). The advance of the Trojans is stopped by the intervention of Poseidon. The elaborate accounts of his arrival (13.10) and departure (15.157) mark off the first movement of the second phase. The fighting of this movement intertwines two narrative strands. Less prominent, but of greater significance to the progress of the plot, is the strand that follows the fortunes of Hektor and develops his opposition to Aias, which will dominate the battle of the ships. This strand appears at the beginning and end of Book 13 (136-205, 674-837), as well as in Book 14, where it comes to a temporary halt with the defeat and injury of Hektor by Aias (14.402-32). The other, and in the immediate context more prominent, strand consists of the aristeia of Idomeneus and the related chain killings, which illustrate the growing intensity and ferocity of the war.

The second movement of this phase brings Hektor's successful attack on the ships. Once more the intervention of a god marks the articulation of battle. Poseidon had stopped the progress of the Trojans beyond the wall; now Apollo completes it. At the end of Book 12 we saw Hektor smashing the gates of the wall; when he resumes his course of victory in Book 15 he does so under the guidance of Apollo, who levels wall and ditch with childish ease and creates a broad and level passageway to the ships (15.343).

While the ensuing battle is dominated by Hektor and Aias, they appear mainly as leaders of their contingents rather than as individual warriors. In Book 13 and 14 the warriors had revelled in gloating speeches. These are entirely absent from Book 15, where by contrast there are four occasions on which Hektor and Aias each rally their troops (15.425, 486, 553, 718). The frequency and placement of these two types of speech in Books 13-15 has no parallel in the poem and is clear evidence that the poet used them as a structural device to characterise the opposition of the two movements of fighting in this phase.

In the battle of the ships we can again observe a triple articulation, although the dividing lines are not as clear as in the wounding of the Achaean leaders or in the attack on the wall. A first attempt to set fire to a ship fails as Aias kills Kaletor, who had come close to a ship with a torch (15.416). This event introduces two chains of reciprocal slayings, in which the Achaeans as usual have the upper hand. The second attempt produces a fierce battle over the ship of Protesilaos in which the poet goes out of his way to stress the closeness of the fighting (15.707-15):

It was around his ship that now Achaians and Trojans
cut each other down at close quarters, nor any longer
had patience for the volleys exchanged from bows and javelins
but stood up close against each other, matching their fury,
and fought their battle with sharp hatchets and axes, with great

swords and with leaf-headed pikes, and many magnificent
swords were scattered along the ground, black-thonged, heavy-hilted,
sometimes dropping from the hands, some glancing from shoulders
of men as they fought, so the ground ran black with blood.

Hektor's call for fire and Aias' retreat leave the outcome in suspense, and the poet turns to Patroklos and Achilles to prepare for the next movement. The second phase closes with the decisive attack: fire is set to the ship of Protesilaos (16.112). But this event is also the beginning of the third phase as Patroklos kills Pyraichmes ('Firelance') at the ship and drives the Trojans back to their citadel (16.284).

The third phase of the fighting consists of the aristeia of Patroklos and of the fight over his body. The first movement reverses the advances of the Trojans: the battle moves from the ships all the way back to the walls of Troy, and it takes the intervention of Apollo to prevent Patroklos from conquering Troy. Catalogues of individual slayings provide the background for the major individual encounters that pit Patroklos against Sarpedon, Kebriones and Hektor. But, although the aristeia is that of Patroklos, the triumph is Hektor's. The death of Patroklos leads to the second movement, the protracted fight over his body.

The body of the fallen warrior that is contested in this final segment returns us to the individual encounter that is at the heart of battle in the *Iliad*. The fight over a body serves as a common transition from one encounter to the next. The motif appears in the first fighting scene, when Elephenor is killed (4.470-2):

So the spirit left him and over his body was fought out
weary work by Trojans and Achaians, who like wolves
sprang upon one another, with man against man in the onfall.

Similarly the Thracians protect the body of their fallen leader Peiros from the attack of Thoas (4.532). Having been sounded in the overture, the motif virtually disappears until Book 13, where Hektor kills Amphimachos in return for Imbrios, but the Achaeans secure both bodies and mutilate that of Imbrios (13.195). Battles rage over the bodies of Alkathoös and Askalaphos (13.496, 526). The motif appears more elaborately in the Patrokleia. The fighting over Sarpedon becomes the subject of speeches by the dying Sarpedon (16.498), Glaukos (544) and Patroklos (559). Fighting over the body is intense (637-44):

No longer
could a man, even a knowing one, have made out the godlike
Sarpedon, since he was piled from head to ends of feet under
a mass of weapons, the blood and the dust, while others about him
kept forever swarming over his dead body, as flies
through a sheepfold thunder about the pails overspilling
milk, in the season of spring when the milk splashes in the buckets.
So they swarmed over the dead man ...

Apollo finally removes the body from the battlefield and gives it to Death and Sleep to carry to Lykia for burial (16.676). No such peaceful fate awaits Hektor's charioteer Kebriones. Hektor and Patroklos contend over him with one dragging him by the head and the other by the feet (16.762). Not burial but dust and oblivion is our last view of him 'as he in the turning dust lay/ mightily in his might, his horsemanship all forgotten' (16.775-6).

These occurrences of the theme are shaped with a view to its fullest version in the fighting over the body of Patroklos. The entire Book 17 is a gigantic elaboration of the initial theme: *ep' autôi d' ergon etuchthê argaleon Trôôn kai Achaiôn*, 'and over his body was fought out weary work by Trojans and Achaians' (4.470-1).

While the fighting over the body of Patroklos is confusing in the wealth of its detail, the outlines are simple. At the beginning there is a focus on individual encounters. Menelaos successfully protects the body against Euphorbos but retreats from Hektor, who strips the body of its armour but yields in turn to Aias before realising his purpose of beheading the body and throwing it to the dogs. There follows a general fight in which now one and now the other side is successful (17.262). This is most vividly expressed in the grotesque simile in which Patroklos 'becomes' a bull's hide stretched by tanners (17.389; below, p. 104), a simile that signals the climactic position of the fight over Patroklos' body and goes much farther than the corresponding passages about Sarpedon and Kebriones to express the transformation of living warrior into mere thing. At length Zeus gives victory to the Trojans (593), and in a passage richly studded with similes the poet describes the retreat of the Achaeans, with Meriones and Menelaos carrying the body while the two Aiantes provide cover (722).

It is a characteristic feature of the final phase of the third day that it moves towards reversals. The smashing of the wall and the setting of fire to the ship of Protesilaos had been climaxes towards which the narrative had moved steadily. But the aristeia of Patroklos ends with his death, while the fight over his body moves towards a triumph of Hektor that is suddenly aborted. The organised retreat of the Achaeans seems to fail before his insistent pursuit. Three times he seizes the foot of Patroklos, but while beaten back on each occasion he persists in his attempt, like a lion who will not let go of a carcass (18.155). The narrative moves to the 'almost' of his taking possession of the body when the apparition of Achilles routs the Trojans. With the rescue of Patroklos' body general fighting in the *Iliad* comes to an end. What remains is the personal vendetta of Achilles. His aristeia celebrates in the most monumental form the individual encounter that is at the core of heroic fighting.

4

The Similes

Simile and metaphor are so common in poetry of all kinds that their occurrence as such in the *Iliad* calls for little comment. More specifically, heroic poetry of all ages and countries has found it easy to illustrate qualities of the warrior through reference to animals and other phenomena of nature. It is not surprising, therefore, to find that warriors in the *Iliad* are as fierce as lions or boars, as aggressive as hawks, as swift as horses or as persistent as dogs, and that their fighting rages with the violence of a forest fire or a sea storm. What is surprising is the frequency with which such comparisons are elaborated into the 'Homeric simile', the elaborately wrought comparison that pursues a usually traditional metaphor for several lines. Out of more than 300 comparisons in the *Iliad*, close to 200 are of the extended kind. The 'simile with a tail', as Charles Perrault called it in the seventeenth century, has for us become so integral a part of the epic that it is hard to imagine that it may well owe its privileged standing to an idiosyncrasy of the poet of the *Iliad*. There are many more similes in the *Iliad* than in the *Odyssey*, and they occur for the most part in the books of fighting. It is natural to infer from this that the extended simile was a standard feature of battle poetry, designed to add variety to a type of narrative in which repetition was unavoidable and diversity at a premium. But there are two other considerations that give pause. First, the roughly 700 lines taken up by similes contain many 'late' phrases and constructions that cannot be assigned to traditional diction. Moreover, internal repetition among this corpus is much lower than for the *Iliad* as a whole. Second, the similes relate to their immediate and wider narrative contexts in remarkable detail. There is hardly a simile of any complexity that cannot be shown to fit its context with subtle propriety. The linguistic evidence of lateness and the literary evidence of close fit suggest that in its Iliadic form the extended simile was a Homeric speciality, a virtuoso device developed by the poet of the *Iliad* from much simpler materials to provide a suitably brilliant and extensive form of decoration for his monumental epic. If lost epics from the time of Homer were to turn up, we should not expect them to show anything like the complexity of Iliadic similes, not to speak of the skill with which they are woven into the narrative.

The narrative function of the similes

Similes discharge some of their most important functions by virtue of their position in the narrative, quite apart from any particular content. They are a kind of narrative punctuation mark and paragraphing device. One might also call them 'narrative particles'. Ancient Greek is studded with little words or particles that articulate the relationship of clauses and modify the meaning of the statement in various ways. What particles are to the sentence, similes are to the Homeric narrative, and their syntactic function must be grasped before one can talk about the content of individual similes.

At the simplest level the simile marks its context as worthy of special attention. Whenever Homer wants to say something important he slows down the pace of the narrative – a procedure that has been much misunderstood. We are all familiar with the term 'epic length', a term which implies that the epic world, unlike the world of drama, is always leisurely and that the urgency of action is subordinated to a stately and imperturbable flow of narrative. The opposite is the case. Homeric narrative has a keen sense of narrative tension and hierarchy, but slowing down is its major tool of emphasis (Austin, 1966). Its seeming digressions and endless descriptions are, like still shots or slow-motion sequences, moments of heightened suspense. When Pandaros prepares to shoot Menelaos, half a dozen lines are given over to an account of how he made his bow (4.106-11). The description underscores the gravity of the broken truce. The elaborate account of Agamemnon's arming (11.16-45) signals the opening of the Great Battle. The description of Achilles' arms, including 130 lines about his shield, pushes the principle to its extreme.

Like these descriptions, the similes arrest the reader's attention and by their mere presence make him recognise a momentous point in the narrative. Similes occur predominantly in battle scenes. Here they articulate change and are found when a warrior joins or withdraws from battle, defeats his opponent or is defeated by him. When Sarpedon joins the attack on the wall, his entrance is marked by the unusually long simile of a hungry lion attacking the stable (12.299-306). The longest lion simile in the *Iliad* marks the re-entry of Achilles into battle (20.164-73). The retreats of Aias and Menelaos are marked by the identical simile of a lion beaten back by herdsmen (11.548 = 17.657). The fall of a major warrior is an important moment. Simoeisios, important only because he is among the very first to fall, receives a tree simile (4.482). Asios, Sarpedon and Euphorbos have their narrative role confirmed when a tree simile accompanies their fall (13.389 = 16.482, 17.53). The temporary fall of Hektor at the hands of Aias merits no less than the image of an oak struck down by lightning (14.414).

The point of decision can be seen from the perspective of victory or of defeat. The latter, illustrated by the previous examples, is the standard procedure when the fallen warrior is of any note. To honour him with a simile or necrologue is the least the poet can do for him. Similes of victory occur at lesser moments and mark the warrior's progress towards a final encounter. Thus Agamemnon and Hektor are lions singling out a cow from a stampeding herd (11.172, 15.630). The victim in both cases is of no consequence.

While the simile generally marks change, it will sometimes focus on a state of equilibrium that is the result of an extraordinary expenditure of energy on both sides. Thus the first clash of armies is compared to a confluence of torrents (4.452). In the fight over the wall the Achaeans and Trojans have at each other noisily but indecisively. The event is compared to a snowstorm that blankets both land and sea. Indeed, the image appears twice, and its elaboration on the second occasion marks the growing intensity of the battle (12.156-8, 278-86).

Two similes of precise measuring mark the balance of battle before Hektor smashes the gate of the wall. In the first, two men dispute the proper location of a boundary stone (12.421); in the second a poor woman measures wool on a pair of balances

(12.433). Some of the most vivid similes in the *Iliad* illustrate intense but indecisive fighting over the body of a fallen warrior. The dead Sarpedon is hidden from view in the heat of the fighting while the noise of battle about him is compared to the work of woodcutters and the warriors swarm around him like flies around a milkpail (16.633, 641). The most remarkable instance of a fiercely contested draw occurs in the fight over the body of Patroklos (17.389-97):

> As when a man gives the hide of a great ox, a bullock,
> drenched first deep in fat, to all his people to stretch out;
> the people take it from him and stand in a circle about it
> and pull, and presently the moisture goes and the fat sinks
> in, with so many pulling, and the bull's hide is stretched out level;
> so the men of both sides in a cramped space tugged at the body
> in both directions; and the hearts of the Trojans were hopeful
> to drag him away to Ilion, those of the Achaians
> to get him back to the hollow ships.

If one simile is not enough to underscore the significance of the moment, the poet can use two or more. The most stunning example of this technique occurs in the *Odyssey*. At the climactic moment of Odysseus' revenge on Polyphemos, at the point when the smouldering tip of the olive staff is plunged into Polyphemos' eye, the poet transforms this instant of agonising pain into a detached technological description: the rotation of the staff is compared to a shipbuilder's drill; the sizzling of the eye to a redhot axe tempered in cold water (*Odyssey* 9.384).

In the *Iliad*, the most effective double simile is used on the occasion of Aias' reluctant retreat on the morning of the Great Battle. First he appears as a lion who after a night of being beaten back by men and dogs abandons his attack on a herd of cattle (11.548). Immediately afterwards, he is a stubborn donkey who goes into a cornfield (11.558-62):

> in despite of boys, and many sticks have been broken upon him,
> but he gets in and goes on eating the deep grain, and the children
> beat him with sticks, but their strength is infantile; yet at last
> by hard work they drive him out when he is glutted with eating;

Here the wonderful contrast of heroic frustration and comic satisfaction serves to underscore both the reluctance of Aias' retreat and the ambiguity of heroic existence: if you can limit your desire to corn rather than meat, you will get what you want.

The most elaborate simile cluster in the *Iliad* occurs in Book 2 when the marshalling of the army on the plain of Skamander is expressed through a sequence of five similes. This unique cluster expresses not only the sheer mass of the army but also the process by which the confused multitude is turned into an orderly force (2.455).

Similes are often found in complementary distribution balancing one another – not unlike the *men ... de* of the typical Greek sentence. Thus at the opening of Book 3 the progress of the armies towards each other is marked by a simile for each side (3.3, 10). As the armies approach, Paris and Menelaos jump ahead of their men, and each of them receives a simile (3.23, 33). The procedure is repeated in the encounter of the armies in Book 4, where a simile describing each side is followed by a simile describing their clash (4.422, 433, 452). In the final duel of Hektor and Achilles, the initial position of each man is marked by a simile. Hektor is a hissing snake waiting for its attacker (22.93), Achilles is seen at the moment of Hektor's flight as a hawk pursuing a trembling dove (22.139). The race that delays their encounter receives three similes, and in the encounter itself each man is once more defined by a simile. Hektor, no longer the trembling dove, has turned into a high-flown eagle (22.308-10), but Achilles has been removed from the world of nature altogether and has become a cosmic force (22.317-20):

> And as a star moves among stars in the night's darkening,
> Hesper, who is the fairest star who stands in the sky, such
> was the shining from the pointed spear Achilleus was shaking
> in his right hand with evil intention toward brilliant Hektor.

To these instances in which the placement of similes articulates the structure of a particular scene, we must now add instances in which a chain of similes underscores narrative continuity through successive scenes. The most striking example is the chain of similes that associate Achilles' re-entry into battle with fire and range from a burning city to the light of the stars. The simile quoted above is the final link in this chain and prefigures night in its choice of constellation. The chain begins with the apparition of Achilles that puts a sudden end to the fighting over the body of Patroklos. There the divinely caused radiance (*selas*) from his head is compared to fire signals sent by a beleaguered city (18.207). When he receives his new armour from Thetis, the Myrmidons dare not look at it, but Achilles' eyes light up with fire (*selas*) as he gazes at it (19.16). The same word is mentioned in the arming scene, where the brilliance of his shield is compared to a mountain fire seen by sailors in distress, and his helmet shines like a star (19.375). In the aristeia of Achilles the fire metaphors are 'reliteralised' when Hephaistos in his elemental form helps Achilles in the fight with the river. After this literal interlude the metaphors resume. The slaughter Achilles causes among the Trojans becomes a burning city doomed by divine wrath (21.522). As Priam watches Achilles' approach to the city he sees him as the Dog Star (22.26). Hektor is turned to flight by the brightness from Achilles' spear 'shining like fire or the rising sun' (22.135). (Note how rising sun and evening star frame the duel itself!)

This chain of images associating the aristeia of Achilles with various forms of fire is framed by two images of a burning city, which provide a prologue and epilogue to the chain. As Menelaos and Meriones carry the body of Patroklos towards the ships the fighting around them is compared to fire that rages through a city (17.737). The simile is clearly proleptic and looks ahead to the conflagration of Troy that begins when Achilles learns about the death of Patroklos. The epilogue shows us the smouldering ruins of Troy in a simile that illustrates the desolate laments of the Trojans when Hektor dies (22.410).

The content of similes

Similes are drawn from a wide range of phenomena but with a very uneven distribution. A handful of simile families account for well over two-thirds of all occurrences. By far the largest group is made up of hunter-hunted similes. Here we may further distinguish between a smaller group in which the hunter is human and a much larger group in which he is an animal. The latter category is dominated by lion images but also includes birds of prey, dogs, wolves and, on one occasion, dolphins (21.22). The most interesting of the hunted animals is the boar because it allows the poet to represent a strong and aggressive animal in a posture of defence or counterattack (11.324, 414, 12.146, 13.471). Odysseus surrounded by Trojans turns on them like a savage boar (11.414); a little later, when he is injured, exhausted, and lost but for the timely help of Aias, the poet sees him as an injured stag (11.474).

Not all animal images involve hunting. We also find bleating sheep (4.433), flies around a milk-pail (2.469, 16.641), swarming bees (2.87), goats (2.474), wasps attacking boys who disturbed them (16.259), prancing horses (6.506 = 15.263), a cow giving birth (17.4), snakes attacking or waiting for a passer-by (3.33, 22.93), a donkey shrugging off the sticks of little boys (11.558).

Vegetation imagery is dominated by the family of tree images. The warrior falls like a tree (4.482, 13.178, 13.389 = 16.482). The first occurrence of this simile is particularly moving. Simeoisios falls at the hands of Aias and 'did not repay his parents' care for him' (4.477). He crashes to the ground like a poplar that a carpenter cut down for use in making a chariot. The implicit contrast with the uselessness of the corpse continues the theme of wasted care. The falling tree can be elaborated in the direction of pathos or terror. When Hektor is felled by Aias he is like an oak uprooted by a thunderbolt (14.414), but the half-grown Eurphorbos is compared to a sapling tended carefully by a man in a lonely place and torn up by a sudden gust (17.53). The simile casts a shadow over Thetis' comparison of her son to a young tree (18.57). Trees do not always fall: Leontes and Polypoites, defenders of the wall, are like sturdy oaks that no storm can uproot (12.131). If the falling tree is the chief image of violent death, the cycle of leaves is a haunting reminder of the ephemerality of human life (6.146).

The weather, especially in its violent forms, provides the subject of a loose and extended simile family. Wind and water combine in images in which warriors are seen in various phases of a wave (2.144, 209, 394, 13.795, 15.381, 618, 624). There are dust storms (13.334), snow storms (12.156, 278), rivers in spate (4.452, 11.492), lightning (13.242), and forest fires (2.455, 14.396). From violent weather it is only a step to catastrophes such as earthquakes, mentioned once in a simile (2.781) and once directly in the preparation for the battle of the gods (20.57). Sometimes the weather spells relief in the form of a clear night (8.555) or a helpful breeze (7.4). When Patroklos beats back the attack on the ships, Zeus in his frequent role as weather god suddenly lifts clouds from a mountaintop (16.297). But for the Trojans the intervention of Patroklos is an almost apocalyptic flood sent by Zeus to punish wicked mortals (16.384). On two occasions, uncertainty of mind is expressed in the striking image of the sea torn by winds from different directions (9.4, 14.16).

It is often said, and with some justice, that the similes are drawn from a wider experience of the world than the narrative itself reveals. It is more questionable to argue that the major collective function of the similes is to add variety and provide some relief from the grim and monochromatic business of battle. The dominant simile families of hunter-hunted and violent weather are themselves drawn from a very narrow segment of the world and one that is very close to the phenomena of war the similes are meant to illustrate. Rather than provide variety and relief, the dominant simile families underscore the austerity of the poem and intensify its obsession with force and violence. Redfield has interpreted the *Iliad* as an inquiry into the paradoxical place of war in human society: dedicated to the preservation of a particular culture, it is an activity opposed to the work of culture as such. He points out (p. 189) that many of the similes are located *agrou ep' eschatiên*, in the marginal zone between human habitation and the wilderness. The collective effect of the dominant simile families is to establish the battlefield as a similar marginal zone.

One way of developing this theme further is to look at the role of eating in the similes and in the narrative. The frequent descriptions of food are a justly famous element of Homeric style, but it is well to remember how little the poet says about eating itself. Take the following example. When the Achaean delegates come to Achilles they are first treated to a dinner. Chines of mutton, goat and pork are carved, put on spits, salted, and roasted when the fire has died down. The meat is put on platters and served together with bread in 'beautiful baskets'. After sacrificing to the gods (9.221-2),

> They put their hands to the good things that lay ready before them.
> But when they had put aside their desire for eating and drinking ...

No less than fifteen lines are devoted to food (9.206-20), but eating occurs in the space between one line and the next. In the narrative of the *Iliad* eating is a purely cultural phenomenon the natural basis of which is taken for granted and ignored. By contrast, the hunting similes often stress the hunger of the predator and sometimes conclude with the image of a feeding animal (3.23-6; 11.175-6; 18.161-2):

> like a lion who comes on a mighty carcass,
> in his hunger chancing upon the body of a horned stag
> or wild goat; who eats it eagerly, although against him
> are hastening the hounds in their speed and the stalwart young men:

> First the lion breaks her neck caught fast in the strong teeth,
> then gulps down the blood and all the guts that are inward;

> And as herdsmen who dwell in the fields are not able to frighten
> a tawny lion in his great hunger away from a carcass,

The *Iliad* thus shows a contrast between immediate and mediated satisfaction of physical needs. Mediation is specifically human: in the ritual eating scenes of the *Iliad* it has reached such a degree that the 'original' purpose of the mediated activity is almost forgotten. Despite the frequency of meals in the *Iliad*, one cannot really say that the warriors like to eat. The opposition between mediated and unmediated food clarifies the role of the animal images of the *Iliad*, which do not simply show that the warrior is as strong as a lion, swift as a hawk or dangerous as a boar. Rather they say that he has returned to a state of nature and has abandoned the mediations of law, custom and ritual that make up human society. It is fully in keeping with this theme that Achilles in his fury expresses a desire to eat Hektor raw (above, p. 69), but that the action of the poem comes to a close with the ceremonious meal of Achilles and Priam (24.621).

An odd simile in Book 11 appears in a new light from this perspective and permits some further modification of the food theme. Odysseus has been injured but is saved by Aias. This situation generates the following simile (11.473-81):

> They found Odysseus beloved of Zeus, and around him
> the Trojans crowded, as bloody scavengers in the mountains
> crowd on a horned stag who is stricken, one whom a hunter
> shot with an arrow from the string, and the stag has escaped him, running
> with his feet, while the blood stayed warm, and his knees were springing beneath him.
> But when the pain of the flying arrow has beaten him, then
> the rending scavengers begin to feast on him in the mountains
> and the shaded glen. But some spirit leads that way a dangerous
> lion, and the scavengers run in terror, and the lion eats it;

Odysseus is the wounded stag. But to persist in this identification raises difficulties. First he is eaten by his enemies, which is not true because he does not die, and then he is eaten by his friend, which is absurd. Clearly this is not the way to read the simile, but neither can we read the detail as gratuitous elaboration. While not homologous with the immediate context, the simile fits into the wider theme of the brutalising power of war, sounded by the poet when in his proemium he envisages the warriors' corpses as food for dogs and carrion birds. If we are in a speculative mood we may go farther and ask why the fate of being eaten twice should happen to Odysseus of all warriors. The question leads to the exceptional relation of Odysseus to food, both in the *Iliad* and in the *Odyssey*. Odysseus is the only Homeric warrior whom we ever see eating and drinking (*Od.* 12.177, 14.109). He speaks of his belly as an independent and shameless agent who cannot be gainsaid (*Od.* 7.216). He is on one occasion compared to a haggis, a stomach filled with blood and meat, turning over the fire (*Od.* 20.25-7). These are of course Odyssean passages that fit into the wider theme of Odysseus as the survivor. The brainiest of the warriors, he has also the most accepting attitude towards the body. But even in the *Iliad* Odysseus is the one warrior who stresses the physical necessity of food. After the reconciliation of Achilles and Agamemnon he insists, against the impetuosity of Achilles, that the army must eat before going into battle. This unique connection between Odysseus and food remains striking, whether or not we see it as related to the simile in which he is a stag eaten first by dogs and then by a lion.

The function of detail: the lion similes

There is an old question about the degree to which detail in similes is relevant to narrative context. It was raised with polemical intent by Charles Perrault, who in his *Parallèle des anciens et des modernes* ridiculed the 'simile with a tail' (Perrault, 3.65-7). The tail for him is the elaboration that does not contribute to the point of the simile. Thus in the simile that illustrates the thigh-wound of Menelaos (4.141) he does not object to the basic conceit of comparing the blood on the white thigh to a piece of ivory stained with purple. But why does the poet tell us that the piece was stained by a Maeonian or Karian woman, that it is a cheek-piece for a horse, that many horsemen desire it, that it lies in the king's treasure chamber, and that it brings beauty and prestige both to the horse and to the horseman? What has any of this to do with the simple notion of 'red on white'? The question depends on two premises of dubious merit. The first is that every simile is dominated by a specific point of departure. The second premise is that the point of departure governs a homological relationship between simile and narrative hammered out in close detail just as Shakespeare's Richard II in his prison cell hammers out the conceit of the prison-as-world. Because Perrault cannot reconcile the subsequent detail of the simile with its alleged point of departure he shrugs it off as useless. But the search for a dominant point of departure and for a hierarchy of corresponding detail often leads nowhere with Homeric, as indeed with later, similes. It is more useful to think of the simile as an entity with its own structure capable of illuminating the immediate or wider content of narrative without being isomorphic at every point. It is also important to distinguish between the point of departure of a simile and its main idea. Often the two are the same, but sometimes they are not. Thus 'red on white' is not the central element in the purple ivory simile, which develops a precious mood that stresses the triviality of the injury and ironically undercuts the hysterical despair of Agamemnon's reaction to his brother's wound.

A good way of sharpening our eyes for the manner in which detail is relevant is to look at the individual simile in relation to its siblings and ask whether it could be interchanged with them or whether its individual features are strongly motivated by the particular narrative context. My discussion of tree and fire images has already given some answer to that question, but the demonstration can be made more systematically by a survey of the two dozen lion similes, by far the largest and most complex family of similes in the *Iliad*.

The lion either wins or loses. The class of winning similes is differentiated by the nature of the victim: fawn, cow, bull or boar. The differentiation fits the hierarchy of victims in the narrative. The hapless warrior on whom Agamemnon and Hektor fasten in their rout of the enemy is a cow (11.172, 15.630). Euphorbos, greatest of the minor warriors, is also a cow when he falls to Menelaos. But, unlike the random victims in the other two examples, he is the 'best cow' (17.62). Sarpedon is a bull (16.487), Patroklos a boar (16.823). The ascending hierarchy is completed in the only simile that pits a lion against another lion and ends in a draw: it applies to Patroklos and Hektor as they fight over the body of Kebriones (16.756).

The simile in which the victims of the lion are fawns deserves special attention. Agamemnon kills Isos and Antiphos, whom Achilles on a previous occasion had captured and ransomed. They are like the helpless young of a hind who helplessly looks on while they are killed in their lair (11.113). The pathos and cruelty of this simile are relevant to the characterisation of Agamemnon in his aristeia and throughout the poem. In the scene following the killing of Idos and Antiphos, Agamemnon denies ransom to the sons of Antimachos. The scene recalls the earlier supplication of Adrestos that Menelaos was willing to grant but Agamemnon denied (6.37). On that occasion Agamemnon's hatred of the Trojans culminated in the desire to bring death to all of them, including the infant in the mother's womb (6.58). Given the poet's way of expressing Agamemnon's cruelty through its effect on children, there is an ironic justice when the pain of the injured Agamemnon is compared to labour pains (11.269).

Other birth images in the *Iliad* bear suggestive links to the Agamemnon images. Menelaos stands over the body of Patroklos like a heifer over her first-born calf (17.4). War gives birth to death, and Patroklos is first-born because with him the war begins in a radically different way. The simile also looks forward to the inadequacy of Menelaos as a protector: like the hind in the Agamemnon simile, the cow will be unable to guard her calf against assault. The retreat of Menelaos from the body is described in the simile of a retreating lion (17.109). Then Aias takes over and protects the body (17.133-6):

> like a lion over his young, when the lion
> is leading his little ones along, and men who are hunting
> come upon them in the forest. He stands in the pride of his great strength
> hooding his eyes under the cover of down-drawn eyelids.

The relationship of this to the previous simile requires no comment. The final birth image once more casts Patroklos as the lion cub. But this time the cub is dead, killed by a hunter during the lion's absence (18.318). Grieving and seized by fierce anger the lion goes in search of the hunter. The simile describes the grief of Achilles as he keeps watch over the body of Patroklos, and it looks forward to his aristeia on the following day. The precise internal shadings of the group are noteworthy: the cub or calf is seen alive as long as the body of Patroklos is fought over and in need of protection. The death of the cub is reserved for Achilles, in keeping with the perspective that governs the representation of Patroklos' death (above, p. 55).

The theme of Patroklos as the child of war is linked to the Agamemnon images through the suppliant scenes, which are restricted in the *Iliad* to Agamemnon and Achilles. Thus all Iliadic similes that deal with birth and the fate of the very young are related to the pivotal events – the wounding of Menelaos and the killing of Patroklos that set the war on a course of savage destruction. Aeschylus showed himself a very good reader of Homer when he figured the hubris of Agamemnon in the omen of the eagle devouring the young of the hare (*Agamemnon* 115).

Some curious features occur in similes that show a lion and a carcass. A fairly elaborate version occurs when Menelaos' joy at seeing Paris is expressed through the image of a lion who finds a carcass and will not let go of it in despite of hunters and hounds (3.23). A second and sketchier version occurs when Hektor hangs on to the body of Patroklos like a hungry lion whom herdsmen cannot frighten away from a carcass (18.161). In Book 16, Patroklos and Hektor fight over the body of Kebriones like lions over a dead deer (16.756). The three similes share the only Iliadic occurrences of the word *peinao*, 'to be hungry'. The similes of Books 16 and 18 are easily related to each other since they occur at the beginning and end of a narrative stretch that leads from the death of Patroklos to the rescue of his corpse. If we add to these similes the lion-boar simile (16.823), we get a short chain that transforms Patroklos from equal opponent through noblest of the vanquished into mere body. The simile in Book 3 at first resists integration into any pattern, and the potential identification of Paris with a carcass seems to humiliate him even more than he deserves. One is tempted to shrug it off as one of those similes that do not fit very precisely, but for a curious verbal echo between Books 3 and 17. The same line is used to describe the near success Menelaos and Hektor have in dragging Paris and Patroklos to their side (3.373 = 18.165). Were it not for the intervention of Aphrodite, Paris would suffer the ignominious fate of being dragged away by Menelaos – not unlike a carcass being dragged away by a lion. If we now recall the prominent and ironic role that Menelaos plays in the fighting over the body of Patroklos (above, p. 68) we begin to see a thematic connection between the carcass similes. Because Menelaos does not fulfil the expectation raised in the first lion-carcass simile, Patroklos must die and almost suffers the fate of being dragged away like a carcass.

Not all lion similes fit into such elaborate contexts. Two similes of a lion chasing away other predators are applied to Hektor and Aias without any apparent relationship (11.474, 15.271). The two Aiantes carry off the slain enemy Imbrios like two lions carrying off a goat (13.198). The simile bears no relation to, but neither is it interchangeable with, another carrying simile: Menelaos and Meriones carry off the body of Patroklos, like mules dragging a ship's mast down a rocky mountain path (17.742). This version of the felled-tree simile emphasises the value of the thing carried rather than the velour of those carrying it.

The lion does not always get his way. He may be beaten back; he may be injured or killed; he may survive on one occasion only to be killed later. Nine similes focus on temporary setback or ultimate defeat. Two similes describe a lion under pressure from dogs and men. They are both used of Menelaos when he leaves the body of Patroklos, the first time threatened by Hektor, the second time ordered by Aias (17.109, 657). The second simile is also used of Aias in conjunction with the donkey simile to describe his reluctant retreat – one of the rare instances in which a simile is repeated verbatim (11.548).

Only once is the lion killed outright. In Book 5, Krethon and Orsilochos have the temerity to face Aeneas, and they are compared to young but fullgrown lions who kill sheep and cattle until their time comes to be killed (5.554). On two occasions the outcome of the lion's attack is left open but the possibility of death is explicitly stated. The similes refer to Hektor (12.41) and Sarpedon (12.299), both of whom die in turn. On a third occasion, Patroklos is compared to a lion whose courage brings death to him (16.752). The proleptic function of these similes is unmistakable.

Twice the lion is injured. The first time Diomedes, grazed by Pandaros, is compared to a lion whose fighting rage is tripled by his wound: he wreaks havoc among the sheep and escapes without further harm from the terrified shepherd (5.136). The other injured lion occurs in the final and longest lion image in the *Iliad*, which describes Achilles as he embarks on his aristeia and confronts Aeneas, his first opponent (20.164-73):

> From the other
> side the son of Peleus rose like a lion against him,
> the baleful beast, when men have been straining to kill him, the county
> all in the hunt, and he at the first pays them no attention
> but goes his way, only when some one of the impetuous young men
> has hit him with the spear he whirls, jaws open, over his teeth foam
> breaks out, and in the depth of his chest the powerful heart groans;
> he lashes his own ribs with his tail and the flanks on both sides
> as he rouses himself to fury for the fight, eyes glaring,
> and hurls himself straight onward on the chance of killing some one
> of the men, or else being killed himself in the first onrush.

The simile refers to the entire aristeia of Achilles rather than to the specific encounter with Aeneas. It clearly connects with the simile of Book 18 about the grieving lion stalking the killers of his cubs. It is a fuller and more serious version of the Diomedes

111

simile, just as Achilles is a fuller and more serious version of Diomedes. The wound of Diomedes at the hands of Pandaros repeats the wound Pandaros/Paris inflicted on Menelaos. The wound of Achilles is the death of Patroklos, another and more fateful repetition. The lion both times responds to the pivotal nature of the wound, but the five-line description of his response, culminating in the image of the tail furiously lashing ribs and flanks, far exceeds the power of the simple phrase 'stirred up the lion's strength' (5.139). Finally, this simile, too, is proleptic: like Hektor, Sarpedon and Patroklos, Achilles is a lion who will die.

Contrast and significance in the Iliadic image

The typical simile families stay close to the world they illustrate, and within a narrow range of subject-matter they show a high degree of subtle differentiation that is very responsive to simile placement. There are other similes that are no less responsive to narrative context but operate through contrast rather than through resemblance. The heifer and her calf (17.4) or the woman in labour (11.269) come to mind as examples. One of the most affecting similes in the *Iliad* compares the head of a falling warrior weighed down by his helmet to a poppy bent down by rain and the weight of its fruit (8.306). Discrepancy is also the point of two similes that stress the difference between men and gods. The bow-shot of Pandaros, elaborately prepared and disastrous in its final consequences, fails utterly of its intended result, for Athene deflects the arrow like a mother brushing away a fly from her baby (4.130). When Apollo destroys the wall he does so with the ease of a boy tearing down a sandcastle (15.362).

Most of the contrast similes are drawn from the human world and are deeply suffused with ironic pathos. This effect derives from their relation to the common simile families that compare the warrior to an animal. The power and frequency of such similes blur the dividing-line of man and animal: it is a highly charged moment in the poem when Apollo questions the humanity of Achilles and says that in his treatment of Hektor he behaves like a savage lion (*leôn d' hôs agria oiden*, 24.41). In contrast to the blurring function of animal images, similes drawn from the human sphere measure the loss of the warrior's humanity by drawing a line between him and other men. We find this effect when Achilles likens the weeping Patroklos to a little girl begging her mother to be picked up (16.7). Similarly, Hektor considers the possibility of negotiating with Achilles and rejects it in an image that epitomises the world of human conversation from which he is now excluded (22.125-8):

> There is no
> way any more from a tree or a rock to talk to him gently
> whispering like a young man and a young girl, in the way
> a young man and a young maiden whisper together.

The most powerful effect of this kind occurs in an image that is not a simile. The race of Hektor and Achilles takes them from the walls of Troy to the springs, one hot, the other cold, where the Trojan women washed their clothes 'before the coming of the sons of the Achaeans' (22.156). The topographical detail, transformed into a vignette of deepest peace, measures the distance of the warrior from ordinary humanity. Such images, whether or not they occur in similes, perhaps come closer than any other feature of style or narrative to suggest an answer to the question: What is Iliadic about the *Iliad*? Three points suggest themselves. First, as Paolo Vivante (p. 106) has said, the poet knows 'where to look and what to ignore – how to focus his vision upon the vantage points of reality'. Homer's descriptive mastery is less a matter of technique than of the choice of the image in the first place. To focus on the springs is the stroke of genius in the last example, and time and again we observe that Iliadic effects derive from the manner in which the poet simply takes note of certain things, such as Hektor's spear in Paris' house, the lyre on which Achilles plays when the delegates arrive, Andromache's headgear, the flowers she embroiders or – a significant contrast – the loom on which Helen weaves the sufferings of the Achaeans and Trojans (above, p. 74).

Second, the image, by virtue of being noticed, is endowed with a significance that does and does not point beyond itself. Jasper Griffin has written about the 'intrinsic symbolism' of certain Homeric gestures and images (Griffin, 121). Vivante (87) states the same point more fully:

> It was the genius of Homer to draw his images true to life, and at the same time endow them unwittingly with a symbolic significance. Symbolic of what? we may ask. Certainly not of any superimposed value, but of a stress or mode of being which appears native to the objects themselves.

The women at the spring evoke a world of peace and are 'allegorical', in the literal sense in which all poetry is allegorical, that is, 'says something else' beyond what it says. But the Iliadic image possesses to an eminent degree the quality many theorists consider the secret of the poetic image: it resists the interpretation it invites. It is not opaque, but it cannot be interpreted away. Whatever thought is inspired by the women at the spring, our gaze never abandons them. The poet creates significance by foregrounding his image – hence the traditional admiration for the plasticity and lucidity of Homeric narrative – and this foregrounding has an arresting power that keeps the reader from abandoning the lively concreteness of the image.

Third, the significant and arresting image is part of a whole of which it is one extreme and which is conveyed in its wholeness as a contrast of polar opposites. This is an example of the pervasive tendency in Greek culture to think of the cosmos, the order of things, as a balance of opposites. The Iliadic totality, however, is unbalanced and moves towards its destruction in one extreme. In the static image of the shield of Achilles war and peace are evenly balanced, but in the narrative war and destruction prevail. Hence the poignancy of such scenes as Hektor's reminiscence of the conversation of boys and girls, the description of the women at the spring, or the flashback to Andromache's wedding: the poet celebrates beauty and order at the point of their destruction. The greatest example of this technique is, of course, the encounter of Priam and Achilles where the characters share the poet's vision of an order about to be destroyed.

The Homeric simile and the epic tradition

The elaborate form of the epic simile, which may owe its origin to an idiosyncrasy of the *Iliad* poet, became a defining feature of the Western epic. The grand epic must be studded with these jewels of poetic virtuosity, and the poet gained fame by reshaping traditional similes, as in the following unbroken chain of homage and rivalry (6.146-8):

> As is the generation of leaves, so is that of humanity.
> The wind scatters the leaves on the ground, but the live timber
> burgeons with leaves again in the season of spring returning.

> quam multa in silvis autumni frigore primo
> lapsa cadunt folia ... (*Aeneid* 6.309-10)

> Come d'autunno si levan le foglie
> l'una appresso de l'altra, fin che 'l ramo
> vede a la terra tutte le sue spoglie (*Inferno* 3.112-14)

> Thick as autumnal leaves that strew the brooks
> In Vallombrosa, where the Etrurian shades
> High over-arched embower ... (*Paradise Lost*, 1.302-4)

The relationship of the Homeric simile to its successors is often discussed in misleading evolutionary terms. A critic of Vergilian or Miltonic similes will dwell on extensive homology with the immediate and wider context, prolepsis and the interrelation of similes, often with the implication that these are distinct qualities of the post-Homeric simile and that the Homeric simile is by comparison 'simple'. But, as I have shown, the integration of the simile into the narrative and thematic structure of the poem is a cardinal feature for the *Iliad*. It may be possible to prove that later poets use even more elaborate similes just as one can show that Liszt wrote more difficult piano music than Beethoven. But the demonstration is pointless. Once a certain level of complexity has been achieved, the opposition of 'simple' and 'complex' ceases to be a useful analytical tool.

Moreover, the perception of an increase in complexity is often due to false inferences drawn from the revision of Homeric similes by later poets. A poet will often take a marginal element in his model and give it greater weight. Vergil was the great master of this procedure. He read Homer with an eye for unfinished business: his very choice of his hero is an example. Take the following example in which a Vergilian simile serves a more elaborate and structurally significant function that results from moving its Homeric elements to a more central position. Hektor's advance comes to a standstill, and he is compared to a boulder falling down a mountainside until it comes to a rest on the plain (13.137). The simile may be inspired by the memory of the rock with which Hektor had recently smashed the gate of the Achaean wall, but it is only one of many similes that articulate the fighting in the middle books of the *Iliad*, and it does not mark an especially critical moment. Vergil transfers the simile to the end of the *Aeneid*, where it measures Turnus' final decline and interprets it as the inevitable consequence of force without wisdom (*Aeneid* 12.684). To underscore the point Vergil dwells on the stability of Aeneas, who is compared to a rising Apennine mountain (*Aeneid* 12.701). The pair of similes concludes the role reversal of Aeneas and Turnus. The former has been transformed from refugee to autochthonous ancestor; the other has lost his place and is doomed to headlong destruction. The example illustrates Vergil's opportunism and virtuosity in 'stealing the club of Hercules'. But it is a critical error to conclude that, because Vergil makes more of the simile of the falling stone than Homer did, his use of similes is in general more complex than Homer's.

A related argument can be made about the case in which a poet's more elaborate use of a particular kind of simile reflects a difference in purpose rather than an advance in technique. Striking instances of proleptic similes can be found both in the *Iliad* and in the *Odyssey*, but none of them are as resonant or strategically placed as Milton's Leviathan and Proserpina images (*Paradise Lost* 1.200, 4.268). Milton's epic, however, is a meditation on origins, and the centrality of proleptic images derives from the simple fact that the reader's knowledge of the outcome, his own fallen condition, is the point of departure for the work.

Finally, the interpretation of difference in evolutionary terms may derive from the critic's unreflective adoption of the later epic poet's ideology. The epic ambition 'pursues / Things unattempted yet in prose or rhyme' (*Paradise Lost* 1.15-16) and demonstrates its superiority through revisions. But, while the desire to outdo the predecessor has been a constant motive in the epic tradition, it is by no means certain that the results are most usefully studied in a context that values (or devaluates) epic devices according to their complexity. If one takes the most powerful and most strategically deployed similes in the *Iliad* and holds them against their competitors in later epics, one will find little cause to extol or denigrate the Homeric simile on the grounds of its relative simplicity.

5

The Gods

Human and divine motivation

Divine intervention and natural causality

Everything of note in the *Iliad* is the work of a god. One may give a coherent account of the poem's action without any reference to the gods at all. Both these statements are true, and the lack of contradiction between them captures an essential element of the Homeric gods. There is an easy but not entirely satisfactory way of resolving the apparent contradiction. It consists of treating the gods as a redundant system of motivation, whose function consists of metaphorically repeating and thereby clarifying human motives and actions. Thus, when Athene tells Achilles not to kill Agamemnon (1.210), it is 'really' Achilles who changes his mind, but Homer emphasises the sudden and radical nature of Achilles' change of mind by resorting to the rhetorical device of divine intervention. The analysis of the action can proceed without reference to this device, even though its frequent occurrence has an important bearing on the texture of the poem.

This interpretation is inadequate but its possibility tells us something important about the Homeric gods. Their intervention works through rather than against human nature, and with a few uncharacteristic exceptions such interventions do not interrupt natural causality. The divine, far from transcending the natural, is the natural in its most perfect state. The field of divine intervention is the outstanding. Success and failure, courage or loss of nerve, presence of mind or folly of judgement – wherever these are present in an eminent degree the poet and his characters see the hand of a god. The view of the world underlying this habit is less strange to us than the elaborate machinery through which it expresses itself. Wherever risk and skill are at a premium, effort and result are rarely fully commensurate. The Homeric gods operate in that gap, closing or widening it in a manner that is both beyond calculation and yet curiously appropriate to the intention and performance of the agent. When we use phrases like 'I don't know how I did it' or 'I don't know what came over me' we reveal the common ground between our experience and the work of the gods in the *Iliad*.

In the most characteristic form of divine intervention it is possible to subtract the work of the god without altering the result or leaving a residue of unexplained events. The simplest cases are accidents that the poet or his characters attribute to a god. When Menelaos' sword shatters on Paris' helmet, he sees the work of Zeus (3.365). So does Aias when Hektor cuts off his spearhead (16.119). Zeus snaps the bowstring of Teukros (15.461). Athene makes Aias slip on a pile of cow dung (23.774). She also breaks the axle of Eumelos' chariot after Apollo has caused Diomedes to lose his whip (23.384). A god guides the warrior's missile so that it hits its target squarely or fails of its intended result. So Athene guides the spear of Diomedes that kills Pandaros

(5.290), but she also deflects Pandaros' arrow (4.129) and blunts the force of Sokos' spear (11.437) so that Menelaos and Odysseus do not suffer mortal wounds. Poseidon protects Antilochos in a non-specific manner (13.554) and prevents the Trojan spears from penetrating his shield. It is worth stating that these cases are exceptional: most spears and arrows hit or miss their targets without divine assistance.

The ebb and flow of the fighting is often seen as the work of a god. Zeus gives strength to the Trojans or bewitches the Achaeans (8.335, 12.254). The sudden access of energy in an individual fighter – his second wind, as we would say – is also the work of a god. Athene gives speed to Odysseus in the finish of the foot race (23.772), strength and nimbleness to Diomedes (5.122) and Menelaos (17.569), on all three occasions in response to a prayer. Zeus gives Hektor the strength to pick up the boulder with which he smashes the gate of the wall (12.450); the Aiantes feel a surge of power after Poseidon has cheered them on (13.68). By contrast, Aias retreats reluctantly when Zeus inspires fear in him (11.544). In all these cases the reference to a god is in one sense redundant. The same is true of the many passages in which a god offers advice or encouragement to men, whether for good or for ill. The outcome is always an action that is perfectly intelligible in human terms alone, but from the perspective of the character the event may or may not involve a breach of natural causality. On a dozen occasions a god addresses a mortal in the disguise of a fellow warrior. In these scenes the character has no inkling of the divine source of the advice, and nothing prevents us from taking the words as spoken by the human character and attributing to them a power as if they were spoken by a god. On a few occasions, the character has a sense of their divine origin and experiences, with varying degrees of intensity, an epiphany of the god. Aeneas recognises Apollo in the shape of Periphas (17.322). The lesser Aias is elated by the words of Poseidon/Kalchas and claims to discover the divinity of Kalchas by the mode of his departure (13.71). The sudden absence of Deiphobos tells Hektor that he really was Athene (22.294). On a few occasions, the god assumes no disguise at all. When Poseidon speaks to the Achaeans nothing is said about his shape, but we may still imagine him as the Kalchas who had previously spoken to the Aiantes (13.94). Apollo assumes no disguise when he tells Hektor to stay away from Achilles (20.375). To the wounded Hektor he explicitly reveals himself (15.254). He rebuffs Diomedes and Patroklos in his own shape and causes them to retreat (5.439, 16.703). He reverts from the disguise of Agenor when he mocks Achilles (22.7). Athene comes in her own shape to Odysseus and gives him the presence of mind to stop the Achaean panic (2.172). Later she stands beside him in the shape of a herald and hushes the assembly (2.279).

The most epiphanic moment in the *Iliad* is Athene's very first appearance when she tells Achilles not to kill Agamemnon. This is one of only two occasions on which the poet singles out physical details of the god's appearance. Athene moves in from behind him, pulls Achilles by the hair, and as he turns he sees her flashing eyes (1.200). In the other scene Aphrodite addresses Helen in the guise of an old woman but Helen recognises the goddess by her beautiful throat (3.396). In both cases the human respondent is amazed (*thambêse*) but free from terror.

There are some situations in which the subtraction of the god leaves an unexplained residue. Take the chariot race where Diomedes loses his whip and Eumelos' axle breaks. Both of these natural events are attributed to Apollo and Athene. But Athene also returns the whip to Diomedes – an outcome for which there is no natural

117

explanation (23.390). The same is true of the spear that Athene returns to Achilles after he has first missed Hektor (22.276). A rhetorically more emphatic case occurs in the death of Patroklos. Here we may, if we wish, reconstruct a naturalistic sequence in which Patroklos is struck with panic and in the resulting confusion is wounded by Euphorbos and killed by Hektor. A parallel to such a scene occurs when Poseidon strikes Alkathoös with panic and Idomeneus kills him (13.434). It is possible to subtract the god from the latter sequence, but Apollo literally strikes Patroklos with his hand so that he loses his armour piece by piece (16.791). This is not only miraculous, but the violation of natural causality is emphasised and contributes to the pathos of Patroklos' death.

There are a few other passages in which the poet goes beyond nature. In one case, much against his usual practice, Zeus pushes Hektor into battle 'with his big hand' (15.695). Poseidon leads the Achaeans with a magical sword (14.384). Apollo levels the Achaean wall and fills the moat as if it were child's play (15.361). But such excursions beyond the boundaries of nature only confirm the sense that the supernatural is foreign to the *Iliad*. The arms of Achilles are indeed made by a god. They gleam terribly so that Achilles alone can endure to look at them. But they are not magical, and if they are impenetrable it is by virtue of Hephaistos' workmanship. The attitude of the *Iliad* towards the supernatural is perhaps best illustrated by the curious incident of Xanthos, the horse of Achilles (19.404). Hera momentarily gives speech to him, and he predicts his master's death. But then the Erinyes, goddesses of vengeance and guardians of established practice, silence him, as if his momentary eloquence were a violation both of natural causality and literary decorum.

There are two forms of divine intervention that go beyond nature but are so heavily conventionalised that they almost count as natural occurrences. They are the removal of an endangered warrior (always a Trojan) and his sudden healing by a god. A helpful god will cover a warrior in a fog and snatch him away at the moment of imminent defeat. Aphrodite rescues Paris (3.380), but her rescue of Aeneas fails and has to be completed by Apollo (5.311, 432). Aeneas is once more the subject of divine rescue when Poseidon spirits him away from Achilles (20.290). Apollo saves Hektor from Achilles on one occasion (20.443); he also prevents the encounter of Agenor and Achilles (21.596). At the command of Zeus, Apollo removes the body of Sarpedon and hands it to Sleep and Death to carry home to Lykia (16.666). The removals of Aeneas and Agenor involve a substitution. Apollo fashions a phantom of Aeneas' body over which Trojans and Achaeans fight (5.449). After the removal of Agenor, Apollo assumes his shape and leads Achilles on a wild goose chase (21.599).

On three occasions Apollo acts as a healer. The healing of Aeneas (5.445) and Glaukos (16.528) is miraculous, but the third example yields to a natural explanation. Hektor, stunned by the stone Aias threw at him, is carried off by his companions to a safe place, where he vomits blood and faints. When Apollo comes to him he has just regained consciousness and is sitting up. Apollo reveals his protection to him and gives him strength so that he bounces back into battle like a well-fed stallion. Since Hektor's injury was non-specific we may see Apollo's intervention simply as a metaphor of quick recovery from the loss of consciousness (15.239). A quasi-healing occurs when Diomedes prays to Athene after his injury by Pandaros. She gives him strength so that he re-enters battle with increased fury (5.121), but she does not heal his wound, for later in the fighting we see him resting from exhaustion and cooling his wound that is irritated by sweat.

It is part of the natural perspective in the *Iliad* that, although the gods participate in human affairs, conflicts between gods and men are rare. The exceptions prove the rule. When Athene opens Diomedes' eyes she tells him not to attack any of the gods except Aphrodite (5.130). He almost forgets this advice when he attacks Aeneas even after Apollo has taken him under his wing. But it only takes the words of the god to make Diomedes know his place (5.440). Similarly, Patroklos retreats from Apollo when he appears on the walls of Troy and orders him back (16.707). When Apollo casts off the disguise of Agenor and mocks his pursuer, Achilles scolds him but he does not attack the god (22.15). In Book 14 the poet dwells on the general fighting and describes the armies as respectively led by Poseidon and Hektor (14.389). Such asymmetry is unique, and the passage may be spurious. Book 5, which is rich in divine episodes, ends with a scene that pits Diomedes and Athene against Ares and ends in ignominious defeat for the war god. This scene is unique for blurring the dividing-line between men and gods. First Ares kills and despoils an Aetolian (5.842), and then Diomedes wounds Ares in the stomach. But a character in the *Iliad* would see nothing remarkable in the encounter. He would see Ares in his mortal disguise as the Thracian Akamas (5.462) and, given the association of Diomedes with Aetolia through his grandfather Oineus, he would interpret the sequence as a repetition of the end of Book 4, where the Thracian Peiros kills Diorês and is killed in return by the Aetolian Thoas.

Achilles' fight with the river involves a unique and spectacular extension of natural causality. At a natural level we can clearly trace a sequence in which Achilles pursues his enemies into the river, is caught by the swift current, but climbs ashore with the help of an uprooted tree straddling the river banks (21.240). But when the river pursues Achilles beyond the plain the boundaries of nature are left well behind, and the counter-attack of Hephaistos reverses the expected outcome of the clash of fire and water. Poseidon and Athene come to Achilles' rescue in his plight, the former a water god who has seniority over a mere river, the latter a goddess who is superior to the elements. The entire scene sees the hero's triumph over the elements as prior and subordinate to his human conflicts. One may also see in the entire scene a narrative modulation from human conflict to the battle of the gods. Whatever the reason for the temporary indulgence in the supernatural on such a scale, the narrative returns firmly to a natural perspective with the final encounter of Achilles and Hektor, where the presence of the gods as spectators underscores rather than suspends the limits of the natural world.

Divine motivation and human responsibility

Who deserves the credit or blame for the outcome of an action in which a god intervened? The answer to this question is far from simple and rests on premises that were misunderstood even in antiquity. These misunderstandings, to which Plato and Euripides bear witness, are a good point of departure because they are the result of a perspective in some respects closer to ours than to Homer's. In Euripides' *Trojan Women* (860) there is a trial scene in which Helen asserts her innocence by pleading that she was compelled by Aphrodite against her will and is therefore not responsible.

Clearly this defence derives from the Iliadic scene in which Helen refuses to obey Aphrodite's command to return to her husband but complies reluctantly when Aphrodite threatens her. Euripides' Hekabe refuses to accept this defence, and playing on a word she argues that it was not Aphrodite but Helen's *aphrosunê*, her recklessness and lack of control, that caused the disaster (*Hecuba* 989). In the myth of Er at the end of the Republic the souls must choose a fate before returning to earth, and this choice will determine their moral life. As they choose, a voice reminds them: *aitia helomenou, theos anaitios* ('the choice is yours, do not blame the god!').

The polemical thrust of the two passages is unmistakable. Both disapprove of a view according to which a man may disclaim responsibility by shifting the blame on to the gods. The view they attack seems to be fully articulated in the apology of Agamemnon, where he says (19.85-90):

> This is the word the Achaians have spoken often against me
> and found fault with me in it, yet I am not responsible
> but Zeus is, and Destiny, and Erinys the mist-walking
> who in assembly caught my heart in the savage delusion
> on that day I myself stripped from him the prize of Achilleus.
> Yet what could I do? It is the god who accomplishes all things.

He then continues this statement with a long digression showing that even Zeus was subject to Delusion. The standard answer to the problem raised by this and similar passages runs as follows: the problem exists only if you hold a view of responsibility that focuses on intention and consciousness. If you hold such a view, then the apology of Agamemnon appears as a blatant piece of buck-passing, and something like the Euripidean and Platonic polemic is inevitable. But Homer's view of responsibility does not focus on intention, and in fact he is much more interested in liability than in responsibility. It is a characteristic feature of Homeric psychology, demonstrated by Snell and Dodds, that it will motivate an action externally through the intervention of a god while at the same time holding the subject liable for the consequences of an action of which he is not the cause. Hence Agamemnon's invocation of Zeus is not an evasion of responsibility. While there is much truth to this answer, Lesky (1961) has shown that it is not sufficiently sensitive to the nuances of Homeric situations. Agamemnon does not evade liability, but it is remarkable that he should find it necessary to say with such emphasis: 'It was not my fault.' The fact of the denial proves that it is possible to say: 'It was your fault'; indeed, that is what according to Agamemnon the Achaeans did say. Agamemnon's apology is not only Homeric psychology in action; it is also a face-saving procedure quite intelligible in terms of commonsense psychology. Observe first that the poet makes a fuss about the injuries of the Achaean leaders (elsewhere he is apt to forget or ignore previous injuries). Diomedes, Odysseus and Agamemnon hobble into the assembly, visible sign of the humiliation Agamemnon has suffered (19.47). Not leaning confidently on his sceptre, but sitting down, Agamemnon begins to speak (19.76). His speech goes on for ever; its very length suggests that there is something to explain (away). Liability Agamemnon cannot escape – the hobbling warriors are visible proof of his folly – but he can make up a good story to make his responsibility appear in a flattering light: what should poor Agamemnon do if even Zeus could not escape Delusion ...? Nobody is in a mood to challenge Agamemnon's self-restoration, least of all Achilles, who concludes the assembly with pious words that are conspicuously silent about his first prayer, which Zeus granted as a cruel favour (19.270-4):

> Father Zeus, great are the delusions with which you visit men.
> Without you, the son of Atreus could never have stirred so
> the heart inside my breast, nor taken the girl away from me
> against my will, and be in helplessness. No, but Zeus somehow
> wished that death should befall great numbers of the Achaians.

In Book 3 the rhetoric of responsibility appears in a very different light. Helen has gone to the wall, where the old men still respond to her beauty but agree none the less that she should be handed over to the Achaeans. Against this background of disapproval Priam calls out to Helen and is anxious to say something kind to her (3.162-5):

> Come over where I am, dear child, and sit down beside me,
> to look at your husband of time past, your friends and your people.
> I am not blaming you: to me the gods are blameworthy
> who drove upon me this sorrowful war against the Achaians.

Helen recognises the tactfulness of Priam, but for her the proper thing is to insist on her share of responsibility (3.172-6):

> Always to me, beloved father, you are feared and respected;
> and I wish bitter death had been what I wanted, when I came hither
> following your son, forsaking my chamber, my kinsmen,
> my grown child, and the loveliness of girls my own age.
> It did not happen that way: and now I am worn with weeping.

Not a word here of the gods, but a stark acknowledgement of the facts: I followed your son and left my family and friends behind. She concludes her speech with a strong phrase of self-reproach that appears to have the force of the slang usage 'bitch' (*kunôpis*).

The dialogue of Helen and Priam and the speech of Agamemnon suggest that the words of Homeric characters are highly responsive to differences in context. The formal assembly permits, perhaps even requires, elaborate face-saving: the Achaeans have as strong an interest as Agamemnon that the self-image of their king remain intact. In the private encounter Priam displays a kindness that is in character but not required by his office, and to his solicitous manner of removing the problem of responsibility Helen responds by emphatically pointing the finger at herself.

The Helen-Priam scene must also be read together with the Helen-Aphrodite scene that follows shortly. Aphrodite has rescued Paris and deposited him in the safety of his bedroom. Now she approaches Helen in the guise of an old woman and tells her to go to her husband. Helen recognises the goddess and indignantly refuses. Here is the guilt-ridden woman of the conversation with Priam, venting her anger on the goddess: if you are so fond of him, why don't you go with him – he may make you his wife or his slave – but I will not (3.406). But, when the goddess turns on her in anger, Helen yields to the powerful combination of fear and passion Aphrodite represents. The scene is unique in the *Iliad*. No other character rebels against a god; no other god manifests his power by overruling and cowing his subject. But it is Homer who shows the power of Aphrodite, not Helen who claims the goddess as an excuse for her behaviour. In the subsequent scene we find Helen contemptuous of Paris and solicitous for his safety – a contradiction intelligible enough. In later scenes Helen is full of regret, self-recriminations and laments, but never does she offer an excuse.

If we now return to Euripides, we notice that his polemic rests on a systematic distortion of the *Iliad*. His Helen echoes Agamemnon, and the scene between Helen and Hekabe reverses the scene between Helen and Priam. The coarsening of the texture is appropriate to Euripides' polemic purpose, but Iliadic situations are much more ambiguous than their parodies and do not support a view of human responsibility that is the univocal opposite of the Platonic *aitia helomenou, theos anaitios*.

The flexible relationship between divine motivation and human responsibility extends to credit as well as to blame. Ancient writers did not find Homer problematic in this regard, but modern readers have often been uneasy in giving credit to a warrior for a deed in which a god tips the scale. The most notorious example occurs in the duel of Achilles and Hektor, where the trickery of Athene seems to give Achilles an unfair advantage that takes away from the glory of his triumph. The simple cases show clearly that the warrior may take full credit for the result achieved through divine intervention, but not all cases are simple. An unambiguous example occurs when Diomedes, on being wounded by Pandaros, prays to Athene that she may help him in his revenge. Some hundred lines later we see him throwing his spear at Pandaros, and Athene guides the missile towards its target as a reward and confirmation of his marksmanship (5.290). Things are cloudier in the foot race, where Odysseus prays to Athene and she rewards him with speed. His opponent is the lesser Aias, who after the fall of Troy incurred the wrath of Athene for destroying her sanctuary in the citadel. This tradition may be echoed when Aias, who does not pray to Athene, slips on a piece of cow dung, the work of the goddess as the poet tells us (23.774). So does Aias when, covered with cow dung, he exclaims (23.783-4):

> Ah, now! That goddess made me slip on my feet, who has always
> stood over Odysseus like a mother, and taken good care of him.

Do the poet and his character speak with the same voice? Or may we attribute to Aias a touch of jealousy and a suggestion that but for the (unfair) intervention of the god the race would have ended differently?

Whatever doubts we may have about the intention of Aias' words, the death of Patroklos offers unambiguous evidence of divine intervention that detracts from the glory of the human victory. There is nothing in the conventions of Homeric poetry that would prevent Apollo from playing the same role in the defeat of Patroklos that Athene plays in the defeat of Pandaros. But, as Homer shapes that death, the glory of Hektor's achievement is sharply diminished, as Patroklos himself points out in his dying words (16.849-50):

> No, deadly destiny, with the son of Leto, has killed me,
> and of men it was Euphorbos; you are only my third slayer.

What, then, about Athene's role in the defeat of Hektor? She returns his spear to Achilles after his first throw, an action that perhaps has no thematic implications and is a somewhat awkward device for extending the critical encounter beyond the first exchange of blows that usually terminates a duel. In any event, the decisive spear-cast is the work of Achilles alone; Athene neither guides the missile nor adds to its thrust. He takes careful aim – a quite unusual thing to do for a Homeric warrior – and hits Hektor where he knows his armour to be most vulnerable. This emphasis on the independent strength and skill of Achilles contrasts too sharply with the dominant role of Apollo in the death of Patroklos to be accidental. Athene's role is more ancillary than in the aristeia of Diomedes and more closely related to the delusion and final insight of Hektor (above, p. 64). Her presence neither enhances nor detracts from the achievement of Achilles but helps to direct sympathy towards the victim – a characteristically Iliadic motif. Achilles at the moment of triumph is distanced by his formidable superiority. Hektor, no longer the hectoring man of illusion, engages our pity no less profoundly than Patroklos, though in a very different manner.

The Homeric gods and their society

The individual gods: Apollo and Athene

Apollo and Athene intervene in the action of the *Iliad* more often than any other god except Zeus. To some extent the two are the patron gods of Trojans and Achaeans respectively. So it appears in the first fighting when Apollo, 'looking down from Pergamos', rallies the Trojans while Athene is busy among the Achaeans (4.507). The association of Apollo with the citadel of Troy as well as with other surrounding places recurs in several passages, and some historians of religion have seen in it a reflection of the Asian origin of the god. But it would be quite wrong to say that Apollo is a Trojan and Athene an Achaean god. The Trojan bias of Apollo appears less powerfully in his protection of Hektor and the Trojans than in his opposition to Patroklos and Achilles. That opposition transcends the circumstances of the particular narrative and is rooted in the fundamental opposition of man and god. Apollo is the god in whom the characters of the *Iliad* experience the limits of the human. He keeps his distance and in so doing keeps man in his place. Take his first appearance in the poem. Insulted by Agamemnon, the priest Chryses prays to Apollo, invoking him in solemn and ritual terms. Apollo responds by sending the plague on the Achaeans. In the portrayal of the god the poet dwells on his bow as the attribute that reveals the essential nature of the god. In human hands the bow is a suspect weapon, suitable only to minor warriors, but Apollo's bow is the perfect emblem of divine distance, destroying man from a position of remote power (1.43-9):

> So he spoke in prayer, and Phoibos Apollo heard him,
> and strode down along the pinnacles of Olympos, angered
> in his heart, carrying across his shoulders the bow and the hooded
> quiver; and the shafts clashed on the shoulders of the god walking
> angrily. He came as night comes down and knelt then
> apart and opposite the ships and let go an arrow.
> Terrible was the clash that rose from the bow of silver.

This first appearance of Apollo sets his style in the poem. Whenever he speaks to men he draws a line. When Diomedes attacks the injured Aeneas, Apollo intervenes (5.440-2):

> Take care, give back, son of Tydeus, and strive no longer
> to make yourself like the gods in mind, since never the same is
> the breed of gods, who are immortal, and men who walk groundling.

He utters similar words when Patroklos threatens the wall of Troy (16.707). He taunts Achilles with the question: Why do you chase me? I am not mortal (22.8).

Apollo responds to transgressions of sacred order. His role in the poem begins and ends with such a response. The intervention on behalf of Chryses is balanced by his protection of Hektor's body. He urges the gods to attend to Hektor's ransom, not because Hektor is his protégé, but because Achilles' actions are unseemly (24.40). His protection of Hektor's body is related to his function as a god of healing and ritual purity. He also acts in this role when he restores Aeneas, Glaukos and Hektor to health and removes the body of Sarpedon from battle. In the society of the gods the defining attribute of Apollo is not the bow but the lyre, an instrument that likewise depends on controlled tension. His lyre confirms the spirit of harmony among the gods once their unquenchable laughter has dispelled the quarrel of Zeus and Hera (1.603). Apollo is a great benefactor of human life because he sets the limits that define the space of civilised existence: without him all order would collapse. And yet this benefactor acts out of no special concern for mankind. Disdain is his prevailing mood, and man enters his field of vision only when he crosses the line drawn by the god. When the gods fight each other, Hermes and Apollo for very different reasons refuse to be drawn into the quarrel. Hermes, who faces Leto, tells her that it is a dangerous business for a god to attack a bedmate of Zeus. He concedes defeat in advance and urges her to boast of her victory among the gods. This shamelessness worthy of a Falstaff contrasts with the reasons Apollo advances to Poseidon (21.462-7):

> Shaker of the earth, you would have me be as one without prudence
> if I am to fight even you for the sake of insignificant
> mortals, who are as leaves are, and now flourish and grow warm
> with life, and feed on what the ground gives, but then again
> fade away and are dead. Therefore let us with all speed
> give up this quarrel and let the mortals fight their own battles.'

Like Apollo, Athene reveals traces of a more specialised role. She is the goddess of skills – in particular, domestic skills. When the women of Troy offer her a precious robe we catch a glimpse of the weaving goddess about whose competition with Arachne Ovid wrote one of his most famous tales. Achilles rejects the daughters of Agamemnon even if they combined the beauty of Aphrodite with the handiwork of Athene (9.389). The Trojan shipwright Harmonides was her special favourite (5.61). This functionally limited association of Athene with the Trojans pales before her vigorous partisanship of the Achaeans. She is much more emphatically a supporter of the Achaeans than Apollo is a protector of the Trojans, but her partisanship ultimately serves to express another experience of the divine, which Walter Otto has captured by contrasting the 'ever-remote' Apollo with the 'ever-present' Athene. The closeness of the divine embodied in Athene manifests itself in the narrative as support of her favourites and occasionally deception of her enemies.

Once again the god's peculiar being and style manifest themselves in her first appearance. Achilles is on the verge of killing Agamemnon when Athene intervenes. She is not ceremonially invoked nor does she act from afar. She arrives in the nick of time, stands behind Achilles, and with an intimate gesture pulls him by the hair (1.199-203):

> Achilleus in amazement turned about, and straightway
> knew Pallas Athene and the terrible eyes shining.
> He uttered winged words and addressed her: 'Why have you come now,
> o child of Zeus of the aegis, once more? Is it that you may see
> the outrageousness of the son of Atreus Agamemnon?'

The amazement of Achilles is free from all terror, and he addresses her in familiar terms. He obeys her, of course, if obedience is the right term: in the presence of Athene one sees the force of reason and acts on it. Her closeness also inspires presence of mind. So Odysseus in Book 2 is the only warrior not stampeded by panic. As he stands by his ship but refuses to draw it into the sea, Athene arrives once more in the nick of time, and armed with her encouragement he persuades and cudgels the Achaeans back to the assembly (2.166). Odysseus as the special favourite of Athene is not unknown in the *Iliad*, but this theme flowers in the *Odyssey*, where the 'ever-presence' of Athene almost assumes the form of chumminess, as in the long and teasing colloquy on Odysseus' first arrival in Ithaka (13.287).

In the *Iliad* Athene is closest to Diomedes. She is with him at the beginning and end of his aristeia, and she addresses him without disguise. Her proximity to Diomedes in the final attack on Ares is quite literal: with an unceremonious shove she pushes Stheneleus off the chariot and mounts it herself, standing beside her favourite at the moment of his triumph. Familiar she may be, but she is also majestic: the axle of the chariot groans under her weight (5.838).

The close presence of Athene has its dangerous side. She deludes her enemies with destructive intimacy. She is the bright idea that moves Pandaros to break the truce (4.89). She takes the Trojans' wit away (18.311). With heart-rending cruelty she approaches Hektor in the guise of Deiphobos and gives to him, who had broken under the terrifying stress of loneliness, the illusion of fellowship and solidarity (22.226).

Apollo and Athene embody different modes in which man experiences the divine, but they are complementary rather than opposing deities. Within the sphere that Apollo defines as appropriate to human action Athene offers divine assistance. This complementarily emerges very clearly in the aristeia of Diomedes, where Athene gives her protégé the strength to defeat all mortals but warns him to beware of attacking the gods, a warning that he remembers and respects when it is repeated by Apollo. Although the narrative casts Athene and Apollo in the roles of the chief partisans of the opposing sides, the poet never opposes them to one another because there is at the thematic level no conflict between their natures.

The individual gods: Ares and Aphrodite

Athene is openly hostile to Ares and, in conjunction with Hera, is hostile to Aphrodite as well. The complementarity of Ares and Aphrodite and their joint opposition to Athene are a major thematic axis of the poem, no less important to its understanding than the complementarily of Athene and Apollo. Ares and Athene are joined several times as war gods. When the armies first encounter one another, the Achaeans silent in well-ordered advance, the Trojans and their allies in noisy confusion, Ares appears as leading the latter and Athene the former. But the implicit contrast is blunted by the following lines, which describe the presence of weakly personified attributes of war, terror, fear and hate, presumably on both sides (4.440). On three occasions Athene and Ares are joined without any differentiation in phrases meaning 'not even Ares or Athene would belittle/undertake such fighting' (13.127, 17.398, 20.358). Zeus characterises war as the work of Ares and Athene (5.430). But wherever their conjunction is elaborated it turns into the opposition of control and mindless fury.

This point appears clearly when Hera stirs rebellion against Zeus and tells Ares about the death of his son Askalaphos (15.110). Full of outrage, Ares is ready to defy Zeus' command, calls for his horses Fear and Terror and puts on his armour. But Athene, fearing for the safety of the gods, stops him, takes off his helmet, takes the spear out of his hand, and gives him a tongue-lashing. To complete her treatment of him as an ill-tempered brat she makes him sit down. Evidently Ares is not a god whose feelings need to be respected.

The fullest elaboration of the opposition occurs in the aristeia of Diomedes, where Ares and Aphrodite are joined as gods of passion whom Athene subjects to ridicule and humiliation. At the beginning of his aristeia, Athene gives Diomedes permission to attack Aphrodite alone of all the gods. She does so because of the scandalous role Aphrodite had played in the duel of Paris and Menelaos and because in the divine assembly following the abortive duel Zeus had aroused her anger by praising Aphrodite for looking so well after her protégé. Without saying so, Athene seeks revenge through Diomedes, and her opportunity comes when Aphrodite ventures once more on the field of battle, this time to rescue Aeneas, her son by Anchises (5.311). The rescue attempt is given in unusual detail. What covers Aeneas is not the customary dense cloud, but Aphrodite's white elbows and the folds of her shining dress. These, she thinks, will be a 'bulwark against missiles' and keep bronze from her son's chest. But Diomedes is made from other mettle than Menelaos. His spear pierces the gown 'that the graces wove for her' and stabs her wrist so that *ichôr*, the divine blood, flows to the ground. Screaming, she drops Aeneas, and but for Apollo he would be lost, for she is preoccupied with her terrible wrist-wound and implores Ares to drive her back to Olympus. There she finds a sympathetic welcome from her mother Dione, who makes a proper fuss over her, tells stories about other gods who suffered at the hands of mortals, accuses Athene of having egged on Diomedes, and mutters darkly that he will come to no good end. But Hera and Athene have fun at her expense. Now it is their turn to do the teasing, and Athene mocks (5.421-5):

> Father Zeus, would you be angry with me if I said
> something? It must be the lady of Kypros, moving some woman
> of Achaia to follow after those Trojans she loves so hopelessly,

laying hold on the fair dresses of the Achaian women,
tore the tenderness of her hand on a golden pin's point.

Zeus takes the teasing in good spirit but has kind words for Aphrodite (5.428-30):

No, my child, not for you are the works of warfare. Rather
concern yourself only with the lovely secrets of marriage,
while all this shall be left to Athene and sudden Ares.

His words look forward to the repetition of the incident with a different cast. Athene has come to the side of Diomedes, worn out by his previous injury. She scolds him for being less warlike than his father, and he replies: 'I see Ares in the field. Did you not tell me to stay away from the gods except for Aphrodite' (5.819)? But now Ares joins Aphrodite as a target of attack. With the help of Athene, Diomedes attacks the god; his spear, lent additional thrust by the goddess, pierces the abdomen of Ares. He, too, screams, but much louder than Aphrodite (5.859), and flees back to Olympus like a funnel cloud. Where the divine daughter sought refuge with the mother, the divine son seeks out the father. Clearly the sequence repeats the wounding of Aphrodite with a deliberately coarsened crescendo. But the climax is different as the father turns on the son with contemptuous anger (5.889-91):

Do not sit beside me and whine, you double-faced liar.
To me you are most hateful of all gods who hold Olympos.
Forever quarrelling is dear to your heart, wars and battles.

Sex and violence are the stuff of the Trojan war, which begins with the rape of Helen and ends with the burning city. The poet is far from idealising his subject. The cowed submission of Helen and the smouldering ruins of Troy reveal the power of Ares and Aphrodite at their elemental worst. But the poet who acknowledges the power of these gods pays little tribute to them; instead he views them with laughter and disdain. The easy triumph over them by Athene, repeated in the Battle of the Gods (21.391) and echoed in the Odyssean story of Ares and Aphrodite, manifests the Olympian ethos of the *Iliad*, in which the dignity and control of Athene and Apollo count for more than the chaotic passions of love and war.

The individual gods: Zeus

The quartet of Apollo, Athene, Ares and Aphrodite cover much of the range of the divine in the *Iliad*, but we must remember that these gods (as well as all the others) can do little that lies outside the will of Zeus. Indeed, in their most important interventions the other gods are simply the instrument of Zeus. He is the king of the gods in a far more radical sense than Agamemnon is the king of the Achaeans. Power is his defining feature. He likes to boast of it in crudely physical terms. In a famous passage, he challenges the other gods to a tug-of-war with a golden chain and predicts that he would easily pull the chain with all the gods and goddesses, including Earth and Ocean, and hang it from the top of Olympus (8.19). He threatens violence to Hera

(1.565, 15.16) and to Poseidon 15.162, and the fear of his indiscriminate anger leads Athene to stop Ares from avenging his son Askalaphos (15.121).

As with Apollo and Athene, the first appearance of Zeus manifests his being and style. When Thetis visits him she finds him sitting apart on the highest summit of Olympus. Because her mission is secret the poet needs to show Thetis and Zeus by themselves. But the solitude of Zeus transcends narrative exigency and is a defining aspect of his nature. He is usually by himself, imagined either on a mountaintop (8.47, 14.157, 15.151) or nowhere in particular. When he grants the request of Thetis, he nods his head and shakes Olympus (1.528) the passage inspired Phidias to his famous statue of Zeus and is a metaphoric anticipation of Aristotle's unmoved mover.

Unlike the other gods, Zeus never appears on the battlefield, and he never speaks to a human being, whether in disguise or in his own voice. He communicates with men through intermediaries such as Apollo and Athene or the messenger gods Hermes and Iris (4.70, 11.185, 15.146, 24.331). On the other hand, Zeus likes to comment on human affairs. He regrets the death of Sarpedon and weeps bloody tears, a meteorological prodigy without parallel (16.459). He pities Hektor (17.198) and the horses of Achilles (17.441). He prophesies the death of Patroklos and return of Achilles to battle (8.470); on another occasion, he looks beyond the death of Hektor to the fall of Troy (15.69). No other god shares this choric function with him.

Zeus sometimes acts in his original role as lord of the skies. He sends thunder and lightning (8.75, 133, 15.377); he can darken the battlefield with fog and clouds (16.567, 17.268), but he can also send sudden light (17.649). These meteorological interventions, however, are much less common than a more abstract form of intervention that makes Zeus the cause of things par excellence. Here it is useful to take note of the very different knowledge that readers and characters have of divine actions in the *Iliad*. The reader is throughout in the privileged position of Diomedes, to whom Athene gives temporary clairvoyance so that he can see and distinguish the gods. Thus the reader will develop a vivid image of the Olympian gods in their striking individuality. The normal situation of the characters is quite different: they combine a keen sense of divine effects with ignorance of their particular causes. The characters will attribute such effects to 'a god' or 'the gods'. The reader knows that Athene is protecting Diomedes; Pandaros only knows that some god stands by him (5.185). Similarly, Aias knows that one of the Olympians took the form of Kalchas and gave courage to the Achaeans, but he does not recognise Poseidon (13.68). Only in special cases does a character attribute an effect to a specific god. Thus Hektor recognises the absent Deiphobos as Athene, and for the lesser Aias it is clear that Odysseus owes his victory in the foot race to Athene.

The great exception to this rule is Zeus, and perhaps the best measure of his radical superiority is the way in which Homeric characters habitually trace events to Zeus in a manner in which the Christian sees the hand of the Lord. If a god is specified by a character as the cause of an event, it is almost invariably Zeus, and his various names occur more frequently in the *Iliad* than the names of all other gods put together.

The other gods

Other gods than the five discussed so far appear in the *Iliad*, some of them quite frequently. But none of them plays a narrative or thematic role that is distinct and crucial to the structure of the poem. Of these gods, lesser not in rank but in poetic function, Hera and Poseidon are clearly the most important.

There are two important aspects of Hera in the *Iliad*, reflecting her status in the divine hierarchy and her role in the story. As the consort of Zeus she ranks above all the other gods and in some ways stands between him and the others. The poet does not oppose the pair of Zeus and Hera to the rest of the gods. When he insists on the singularity of Zeus he will put Hera with the gods. But she derives from her special situation a licence to contradict him and quarrel with him openly.

The Iliadic Hera is motivated by a bitter hatred for everything Trojan, a hatred so radical that its satisfaction leads her to abandon her favourite cities of Argos, Mycenae and Sparta to the later wrath of Zeus as long as he will guarantee the destruction of Troy. No wonder, for the judgement of Paris and the rape of Helen offend her in a triple capacity: as woman, as guarantor of marriage, and as patroness of the city of Menelaos. Despite the intensity of her hatred, her narrative function is quite limited because the translation of her anger into action is the work of Athene. Hera and Athene are great plotters on Olympus, but Hera recedes into the background as soon as the action begins. Thus Hera is much less central to the *Iliad* than Juno is to the *Aeneid*, where her relentless anger resists the fulfilment of Aeneas' mission at every stage. The only action that is planned and carried through by Hera is the deception of Zeus in Book 14.

Poseidon presides over the counter-offensive of the Achaeans in Books 13 and 14 but, considering his status as one of the three lords of the universe, he plays a marginal role in the *Iliad*. He supports the Achaeans because the Trojans under King Laomedon did not reward him when he built a wall for them (21.441). This motive is a rather thin justification for his presence, especially in comparison with the *Odyssey*, where he and his crude son Polyphemos represent the furious revenge of the elements once man intrudes on them. In fact, Poseidon is somewhat out of place in the *Iliad* in a twofold manner. He is literally out of his element; he is also behind the times. He remembers the division of the universe into three parts of which Zeus, Poseidon and Hades were to be coequal rulers. He grumbles at, but lacks the power to challenge, the supremacy of Zeus. His exit from the scene develops that theme in considerable detail (15.184). The poet gives Poseidon playing-time according to his status, but he is ultimately a superfluous presence. One can imagine an *Iliad* without Poseidon.

The other gods appear in either marginal or sharply restricted contexts. Thus Leto and Artemis help in healing Aeneas and appear briefly in the battle of the gods (5.447, 21.470). Iris is always the messenger of the gods and nothing else. Hermes in his safe conduct of Priam combines his traditional roles of god of wayfarers and thieves and conveyor of the dead (above, p. 73). Hephaistos is the god of fire, appearing both in its elemental form and as the artificer who controls and uses it.

A survey of the gods in the *Iliad* should not pass over personifications, which sometimes owe their divinity to editorial fiat. Hebe is youth personified; her personhood and divine status in the poem are unquestioned (4.2, 5.722, 905). But some personifications have a more ambiguous existence. Take the following lines (4.440-5):

> and Terror drove them, and Fear, and Hate whose wrath is relentless,
> she the sister and companion of murderous Ares,

she who is only a little thing at the first, but thereafter
grows until she strides on the earth with her head striking heaven.
She then hurled down bitterness equally between both sides
as she walked through the onslaught making men's pain heavier.

Here 'Eris', 'Hate', is clearly personified, as she is at the beginning of Book 11, where she stands on the ship of Odysseus and rouses the Achaeans to battle. Are Terror and Fear similar daemons, deserving of capital initials, or should they be just lower-case nouns? The same question arises about the companions of Ares in Book 5 (5.592-3):

and Ares led them with the goddess Enyo,
she carrying with her the turmoil of shameless hatred

The translator here denies to *kudoimos* the status that the editor gives to it. *Enuo* and *kudoimos* are both very obscure words; the latter occurs in contexts where personification is clearly inappropriate and in others where it may be intended (11.52).

In many of these cases it is impossible to tell (nor does it matter very much) whether a noun is personified and whether such personification rests on religious practice or is a matter of poetic convention. It is certainly wrong to take such forms of speech as in themselves providing evidence about the belief in or cult of divine entities. Nowhere is it more important to resist this temptation than with the group of words, often vaguely and sometimes strongly personified, that imply some sort of deterministic outlook. Most prominent in this group is the word *moira*, which means *share* or *lot*. The word *aisa*, derived from a semantically similar root, is also common. Homer uses *moira* in sentences where it is the subject of an action, either by itself or in conjunction with another noun or god, as in:

But *moira* and the son of Leto killed me (16.849)
Destructive *moira* forced Hektor to stay in the same place (22.5)
Purple death and strong *moira* seized him (5.83)
But Zeus and *moira* and mist-walking vengeance (19.87)

Who or what is *moira* (or *aisa* and similar words)? What is its relationship to human decisions and to the gods? What is Zeus up to when he deliberates whether he should prolong the life of Sarpedon, whose *moira* it is to be vanquished by Patroklos (16.434)? What about Apollo, who repulses Patroklos on the grounds that it is neither his *aisa* nor that of Achilles to conquer Troy (16.707)? In what sense are the premature return of the Achaeans (2.155), the death of Aeneas (20.336) or the conquest of Troy by Achilles (20.30, 21.517) 'against fate'? Does Zeus make a decision or a discovery when he weighs the lots of Achilles and Hektor and the latter's *aisimon êmar*, 'day of aisa', falls (22.212)?

The demand for systematic and coherent answers to questions of this kind wrongly imputes to Homer a concern with philosophical and theological problems of determinism. Homer was not Boethius. His characters are all fatalists of a pragmatic kind, and their lives, defined by generations of story-tellers, were full of events that 'had to happen'. But from the fact that the *Iliad* has a rich language of fate it does not follow that either Homer or his characters used that language with more precision or greater metaphysical claims than we do when we say 'It was bound to happen' or 'That's the

130

way it is'. To mystify such simple words as *aisa* and *moira* and to catch through them a glimpse of a demonic and comprehensive agency of fate is to misunderstand the clarity, nobility and unsentimental realism with which Homeric warriors recognise and accept their mortal lot. Not for them the endless arguments of Milton's devils about 'providence, foreknowledge, will, and fate, / Fixed fate, free will, foreknowledge absolute' (*Paradise Lost* 2.559-60).

The society of the Olympians

The gods of the *Iliad* have their residence on Mount Olympus. They form a society that is more than the sum of its parts and breathes a style and ethos of its own. Athene and Apollo are the Olympians par excellence. Ares and Aphrodite are not Olympian at all in spirit. They are admitted to Olympus to reflect within its boundaries the opposition against which the Olympian spirit defines itself with laughter and disdain. Homer is aware of gods that are not admissible to Olympus because they challenge it too radically. One of these gods is Dionysus, to whom the *Iliad* refers briefly on two occasions (6.132, 14.325). The Dionysus of Euripides' *Bacchae* or the Aphrodite of the *Hippolytus*, a much more Dionysiac force than her namesake in the *Iliad*, cannot be contained within the limits of Olympus, and the worshipper's ecstatic union with the god, which is at the heart of the Dionysiac cult, is equally foreign to the severe distance of Apollo and to Athene's illuminating proximity.

The gods of the underworld are also banished from Olympus. Death is final in the *Iliad*. Precisely because the poem is so insistent on this point it can have no truck with chthonic forces or with the cult of the dead that attributes to the deceased ancestor a continuing power to bless or curse. In the *Oresteia* Apollo and Athene are the winners in the conflict with chthonic forces, but their victory is precarious and yields to a harmonious and mysterious settlement. The Aeschylean Athene does not dare treat the Erinyes as Homer's Athene treats Ares and Aphrodite. A comparison of the modes of her triumph in the *Iliad* and the *Oresteia* tells us much about the character and limits of the Homeric Olympus.

Zeus is the only god to carry the epithet 'Olympian'. It occurs half a dozen times in the *Iliad*, and on a dozen occasions 'the Olympian' is a sobriquet for Zeus. Both usages have their origin in the role of Zeus as the sky god, but it would be wrong to infer from them that Zeus is the most Olympian of gods. Although his power guarantees the continuance of Olympian society, he is in some important respects not an Olympian at all. When Zeus scolds Ares for his quarrelsome and barbarian nature he speaks like a true Olympian, but the *Iliad* attributes to Zeus fits of indiscriminate anger that go beyond anything Ares is capable of. Hephaistos remembers one such occasion when Zeus flung him from Olympus (1.591). Hypnos suffered a similar fate (14.257). Zeus reminds Hera how he hung her from the sky and weighted her feet with anvils (15.18). The past violence of Zeus and the threat of its repetition serve to limit the Olympian society no less than the exclusion of Dionysus and the chthonic deities. Olympian society owes its existence to a censorship Victorian in its rigour, if not in its prudishness. The censorship rests on the poet's commitment to the Olympian values embodied in Apollo and Athene, but he knows too much about the world not to give us a sense of the continuing existence and force of what he excludes.

The attitude of the *Iliad* towards Olympus is a curious mixture of admiration, envy and condescension. It is determined by the manner in which the poet defines the opposition between human and divine society. The human world is shaped by conflict. To such a world one could oppose Paradise or Elysium, a world of unchanging bliss and devoid of conflict. Alternatively, if conflict is seen as the result of passion, one could oppose to the human world a rational order, such as that of Swift's Houyhnhnms. Olympus is unlike Paradise and unlike the world of the Houyhnhnms, for the gods are not always rational, and they are far from peaceful. But, conflict-ridden as their society is, it differs from the human world in that their struggles always yield to reconciliation and never have irreversible consequences. The quarrel of Agamemnon and Achilles rages unchecked until it claims Patroklos as its victim. The assembly in which their quarrel erupts is balanced by a divine assembly in which Zeus and Hera have a frightful row, but the mediation of Hephaistos resolves the tension in peals of divine laughter.

The outrageousness of the gods reaches its high (or low) point in the theomachy, the battle of the gods that takes place after Hephaistos has stopped the attack of the river god on Achilles (21.385). The reader who expects a solemn catastrophe or *Götterdämmerung*, will be sorely disappointed, for the theomachy is more in the nature of a tavern brawl. Ares seeks revenge on Athene, but she lays him flat with a stone. This is the only encounter that bears any resemblance to heroic fighting. As for the others, Athene gives Aphrodite a push as she conducts Ares from the battlefield so that both lie on the ground – probably an allusion to their amours. Hera takes Artemis' arrows and slaps her face with them. Hermes freely admits his cowardice and refuses to fight. So does Apollo, for whom the occasion is altogether too undignified. And Zeus, who shed tears for Sarpedon and generally follows human events with serious concern? He laughs (21.385-90):

> But upon the other gods descended the wearisome burden
> of hatred, and the wind of their fury blew from division,
> and they collided with a grand crash, the broad earth echoing
> and the huge sky sounded as with trumpets. Zeus heard it
> from where he sat on Olympos, and was amused in his deep heart
> for pleasure, as he watched the gods' collision in conflict.

The sublime frivolity of the gods relates them to mortals in a twofold manner. From one perspective their youth, beauty, power and immortality make them immeasurably superior to man – a theme stressed in the famous image of the fallen leaves (6.146, 21.464). But from another perspective poverty, ephemerality and exposure to risk are a source of human dignity and significance. Because the gods are protected against risk, their experience is finally void, for value is created by risk and the possibility of loss. From this perspective, the 'easy lives' of the gods are looked on with conde-scension. The perspectives of despair and condescension are intimately related. To daydream about a life free from the constraints of sickness, age and death is very human. Sarpedon does so in his famous exposition of the heroic code. If we were gods, he says there, we would not fight but would live in perpetual pleasure. But we are not and must earn pleasure and recognition by risking our lives (12.322). When Achilles daydreams about a peaceful life on his estate in Phthia, what is this but a secularised version of the life of the gods? He learns that the choice is impossible, and once the inevitable choice is confirmed ironic denigration colours the picture of the easy life.

The *Odyssey* illuminates the *Iliad* in this respect. If we except the song of Ares and Aphrodite, distanced by virtue of its being a song within the song, the Odyssean gods are less glamorous and more moral than the gods of the *Iliad*. The world of desire and daydreams takes intermediate shapes that lack the prestige of Olympus and can be rejected. Thus Scheria is a quasi-divine world, more decorous and less sublime than but just as frivolous as the Iliadic Olympus. When a conflict erupts, as in Euryalos' boorish challenge to Odysseus, it is easily resolved and serves only to stress the freedom of this world from toil and strife (8.158, 396). Nausikaa, though native to this world, is bored by it, and Odysseus is not tempted for a minute. For he had rejected a similar opportunity in a more glamorous form. Kalypso had promised him immortal youth, but Odysseus chose Penelope and rocky Ithaka (5.215). The world of mortality and labour to which the Bible condemns mankind as a result of the Fall appears in the Homeric vision as the object of deliberate choice. In different ways Odysseus and Achilles both reject divinity and choose mortality. Here, as in Freud's celebrated essay on *The Merchant of Venice*, the possibility of human dignity arises from the ability to transform the inevitable into the freely chosen. The Homeric Olympus is a mirror in whose glittering surface mankind discovers that dignity.

Justice and the gods

The history of Homeric criticism begins with attacks on Homer's representation of the gods. The sixth-century poet-philosopher Xenophanes wrote: 'Homer and Hesiod have attributed to the gods everything that is a shame and reproach among men, stealing and committing adultery and deceiving each other' (fr. 169; Kirk, 1957, 166). Plato in the *Republic* elaborated this attack. Because it was inconceivable to him that justice and the divine would not completely coincide, and because this is evidently not the case in Homer, he drew the radical consequence of banishing Homer from his Utopian commonwealth, which had room only for a poetry strictly committed to celebrating the gods as guardians of justice. The Platonic attack had a considerable effect on the development of the Western epic as the most prestigious and political form of poetry. The epic poet had to think of himself as answering the Platonic charge on behalf of all poetry. Milton as usual shows the most explicit awareness of the epic poet's task when he asks the spirit for illumination:

> That to the height of this great argument
> I may assert eternal providence,
> And justify the ways of God to men.

The reader who, steeped in the epic tradition, looks in the *Iliad* for theodicy will be disappointed. The gods are not just in any ordinary sense of the word. He may attribute the lack of theodicy to the fact of polytheism. A system of many gods is much better at representing the manifold conflicts of the world than at establishing an overriding principle of justice. But this answer founders on the pre-eminence of Zeus, which gives rise to the expectation that the conflict of particular gods is part of some overarching design. The proemium of the *Iliad* endorses this expectation when it concludes its summary of events with the phrase *Dios d' eteleieto boulê*, 'and the design of Zeus was fulfilled'.

Some scholars have argued that the poet of the *Iliad* does not justify the ways of god to men because he does not yet have a concept of justice. They point out that the root for the word 'just' and its derivatives in the classical period is rare in the *Iliad* and is used more restrictively. Also the characters in the *Iliad* invoke Zeus as protector of particular rights (hospitality, oaths) rather than as guarantor of a comprehensive principle. Social justice is a theme in the *Odyssey*, and even more so in Hesiod, but when in an Iliadic simile Zeus punishes the wicked with a flood, not unlike the Old Testament god, the sentiment and language of the passage stick out like a sore thumb (16.384). The 'not yet' theory sees in the behaviour of the gods the reflection of an aristocratic code based on a self-regarding competition for goods. Men are to gods what the poor and weak are to the rich and powerful. Men, or the lower classes of them, as the case may be, must suffer the fallout from the dealings of their betters. Nowhere does this situation appear more starkly than in the divine deliberations about the fate of Troy, which falls victim to the horsetrading of Zeus and Hera (4.1). In the poem's final vision Zeus appears as the random dispenser of good and evil.

From an evolutionary perspective the recalcitrance of the *Iliad* to theodicy appears as a moral deficiency. But such a perspective is highly questionable. The significant differences in outlook between the *Iliad* and the *Odyssey* reflect different purposes and generic constraints rather than moral and intellectual evolution. These differences are most marked when it comes to justice. The *Odyssey* is a model tale of poetic justice. Odysseus tells how he punished Polyphemos for his violation of hospitality, but through Odysseus Homer tells his story of Odysseus' unwarranted intrusion into the brutal but innocent world of the Kyklops, and he derives from it the interpretation of the subsequent adventures of Odysseus as punishments. Transgression and punishment figure prominently in the Aiolos and Thrinakia adventures that seal the fate of the companions. In the story of the homecoming, loyalty is tested and disloyalty provoked into insolence; in the final reckoning, the virtuous are rewarded and the guilty are punished.

The poet of the *Iliad* is perfectly familiar with the explanatory scheme that underlies the *Odyssey*. He does not deny that the fall of Troy is the divinely sanctioned punishment for the rape of Helen; this premise accounts for the bitter irony of the scene in which Hekabe in her search for the most valuable gown to offer to Athene picks one that Paris had brought home from his fateful voyage (6.286). But such explanatory patterns are peripheral to the *Iliad*. The poet is more interested in the logic of events than in their justice, and what interests him most of all is the discrepancy between the intentions that trigger an act and the consequences that follow from it. The 'plan of Zeus' that is fulfilled in the *Iliad* is the order of events that becomes intelligible to the human mind only in retrospect. It is an order of events, rather than a chaos, and it provides, among other things, for justice of a rough kind. The poet of the *Iliad* does not justify the ways of god to men, but he shows the gods in their bewildering contradictions as guarantors of the logic of events. That is a theodicy of sorts, and by claiming less it may be truer to the facts of our experience.

6

Homeric Repetitions

Repetitions are about counting. How many of them are there? How often are they repeated? Homeric philology has a long acquaintance with counting and gave to the world the term *hapax legomenon*, or 'nonce word'. Wilamowitz, the greatest classical scholar of the early twentieth century, coined the evidentiary rule 'einmal ist keinmal, zweimal ist immer' ('once is never, twice is always'). In the following pages I do a lot of counting and take advantage of digital technology to give a quantitative and statistical overview of phrasal repetition in the *Iliad*, with some glances at the *Odyssey* to highlight differences that throw a light on the *Iliad*. I look at aggregate data before turning to individual repetitions because it is useful to know whether a given event happens twice, a dozen, or 500 times. By the same token, it is helpful to know how many distinct events happen twice or 500 times. Frequency is a very interesting property of many phenomena, computers have made it simpler and quicker to assemble accurate data across large data sets, and such data provide very useful ways of framing questions and assessing probabilities. I have rounded many figures to make it easier to compare magnitudes.

My data come from the Chicago Homer, a database that systematically counts and classifies repeated phenomena in Early Greek epic. Not all repeated phrases in Homer are poetic idioms or 'formulae' of the kind I discussed in Chapter 1 (pp. 21ff.). In the Chicago Homer, a repetition is defined as any string of two or more words that occurs more than once in the corpus of Early Greek poetry, which includes 16,000 lines of the *Iliad*, 12,000 lines of the *Odyssey*, and about 2,300 lines each of Hesiod and the *Homeric Hymns*. The program that extracted these repetitions did not operate on the inflected forms of the words in the text but on the 'lemma' or dictionary headword form to which the inflected forms were mapped. In the resultant database you can search for literally repeated phrases or for lemmatised versions in which grammatical variance is ignored.

Any string of more than two elements contains substrings: the string 'abc' contains the substrings 'ab' and 'bc', and so forth. The longer the string, the larger the number of substrings. For the purpose of counting repetitions substrings are ignored in the Chicago Homer unless they occur independently. The following example illustrates the problems of this accurate but redundant way of recording repeated strings. A phrase saying that the priest Chryses 'came to the swift ships of the Achaeans' is repeated once. Four of its nine possible substrings recur independently between 10 and 59 times:

2x	*êlthe*	*thoas*	*epi*	*nêas*	*Achaiôn*
10x		*thoas*	*epi*	*nêas*	*Achaiôn*
15x		*thoas*	*epi*	*nêas*	
36x			*epi*	*nêas*	*Achaiôn*
59x			*epi*	*nêas*	

It may be counterintuitive to process this five-word string as 122 tokens of five different repetition types, but there is no obvious way of declaring some of these repetitions as more 'real' or 'relevant' than others. Counting repeated strings and independent substrings in this fashion yields ~36,000 repeated lemma strings or types that account for ~192,000 occurrences or tokens in Early Greek epic. You get an idea of the inflation built into this way of counting substrings if you add up the number of words in all repetition events. Their sum is ~515,000, well more than twice the number of words in the corpus. But since this inflation works equally across all parts of the corpus, you can confidently compare figures derived from this consistent way of counting repetitions.

There are considerable advantages to building a lexicon of repeated phrases from a dumb algorithm that simply counts the number of cases where the same words reappear in the same order. No assumptions are made in advance about what counts as a formula or otherwise significant repetition, and the investigator learns much about meaningful repetitive phenomena by isolating them from a background of 'noise'.

Table 5. Homeric repetitions by length and frequency

Length in lines	Frequency									Total by length
	2	4	8	16	32	64	128	256	>256	
0.25	1908	1883	1490	880	486	204	75	36	14	6976
0.5	8979	6099	2653	999	295	79	17	5		19126
0.75	1957	1015	316	110	25	8	3			3434
1	813	376	116	36	6	3				1350
1.5	378	137	11	6						532
2	333	77	6	1						417
3	105	13								118
4	33	3								36
> 4	51	3	1							55
Total by frequency	14557	9606	4593	2032	812	294	95	41	14	32044

Repetitions can be classified by length, frequency, and type. In Table 5 they are classified by metrical length and frequency. Well over half of the short repetitions consist of function words only or of a content followed or preceded by a function word. It is tempting to exclude them as 'junk repetitions', but one man's junk is another man's food, and in any event the distributional patterns are the same whether you include or exclude them. The table has a characteristic shape. The number of distinct repeated strings is inversely proportional to their length and to their frequency. There are many short repetitions that occur a few times, and a few short repetitions that occur many times. There are far fewer long repetitions, and none of them is repeated very often. Repetitions that are less than half a line in length and occur four times or less account for almost 60% of all repetitions and 50% if you exclude function word repetitions.

An interesting property of repetitions emerges clearly from a simple chart that shows the distribution by length and frequency (Figure 1). Doublets are the most common repetitions, and the number of frequently repeated strings drops quickly. By contrast, there is a sharp increase from repetitions that fill less than a quarter of a verse to repetitions between a quarter and half of a verse. From that spike, the numbers by length drop even more precipitously than the numbers by frequency.

Figure 1. Repetitions by length and frequency

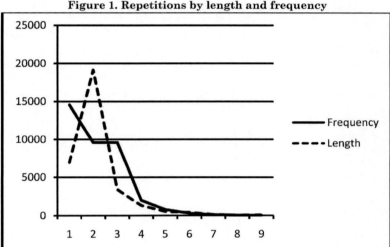

The lessons from this chart nicely square with Egbert Bakker's work, especially in *Poetry in Speech*. The hexameter is a very long metrical form and typically divides into two or more prosodo-syntactic units or 'cola'. Bakker approached these cola from the perspective of linguists who have studied the way people tell stories. Linguists break down such everyday narratives into minimal units as if they were frames of a film. Such units are two- or three-second events, just the right 'bite size' for the human brain to take in and process in a single step.

Bakker's basic point is that the Homeric 'colon' is a narrative event of this size and type. He demonstrates this point very strikingly by printing stretches of Homeric narrative not in the usual line-by-line manner, but in a colon-by-colon or frame-by-frame manner. The distribution of repetitions by length shows in a similar fashion that Homeric narrative works with building blocks that fit the constraints of human memory. It is also easy to see how building blocks of that size fit Sinclair's ideas about an idiom principle that is rooted in a 'natural tendency to economy of effort'(Sinclair 1991, 110).

The distribution of repetitions across the poems

Repetitions differ in length and frequency. They are also distributed quite unevenly across the Homeric poems. There is a crude but effective way of measuring the degree of repetition: you chop the poems into word pairs or bigrams and count the number of repeated bigrams that are found in each line. Thus the opening of the *Iliad,*

137

mênin aeide thea Pêlêïadeô Achilêos
oulomenên

turns into the bigrams *mênin aeide, aeide thea, thea Pêlêïadeô* etc. *Pêlêïadeô Achilêos* is repeated seven times in the *Iliad*. You can ignore or account for the frequency of repetition, but the results do not differ very much. In the following I just count the number of bigrams that are repeated, which means that the first line of the *Iliad* gets a repetition score of 1.

Crude as they are, the resultant scores tell interesting stories. A Homeric line is either spoken by a character or by the narrator. Aristotle admired the protodramatic quality of the *Iliad* and *Odyssey* and praised the poet for 'bringing on a character and letting him speak'. About 2,200 or 8% of all Homeric lines are 'speech tags' in which the author marks the beginning or end of a speech. The average repetition score for narrative lines (3.61) and spoken lines (3.68) differ by only 2%. But the repetition score for speech tags (5.49) is higher by 50%. Speech tags do a lot more work in the *Iliad* and *Odyssey* than do 'quoth' or 'said he' in later narrative, and they justly strike us as a highly characteristic feature of Homeric narrative. But in their extraordinary degree of repetition they are actually quite untypical, and it is misleading to extrapolate from them to the poems as a whole.

Different patterns of repetition in the *Iliad* and *Odyssey*

Whether they read Homer in English or Greek, modern readers are likely to encounter the *Odyssey* before the *Iliad,* and they are likely to form their impression of the Homeric through the *Odyssey,* and more particularly through Odysseus' long narrative of his adventures. But the *Odyssey* differs significantly from the *Iliad* in its use of repetitions, and some repetitive features of Odysseus' narrative have no counterpart anywhere else in Early Greek epic.

To begin with, the *Odyssey* as a whole is somewhat more repetitious. We can divide each poem into respectively 625 and 482 'sliding' text windows of 100 lines that move through the poems at 25 line intervals. The number of repeated bigrams for these segments range from 254 (*Il.* 2.490ff.) to 524 (*Od.*17.78ff.) While the averages for the *Iliad* (370) and the *Odyssey* (396) differ only by 6%, the difference assumes more significance if you look at the quartile distribution of the segments (Table 6). The *Iliad* has twice as many low-repetition segments and half as many high-repetition segments. This distribution marks differences that are clearly noticeable by listeners or readers, and the clusters of particular dense repetitions have been noticed by scholars since the nineteenth century. In the *Iliad* they come mostly from Books 8, 1, and 7. The two most repetitive 100 line stretches of the *Iliad* begin at 24.112 and 1.426.

Table 6. Quartiles of repeated bigrams in 100-line
segments of *Iliad* and *Odyssey*

Repeated bigrams	254-348	349-377	378-408	409-524
Iliad segments	196 (31%)	169 (27%)	155 (25%)	106 (17%)
Odyssey segments	80 (17%)	105 (22%)	122 (25%)	173 (36%)

6. Homeric Repetitions

The rosy-fingered dawn effect

The sun rises thirteen times in the *Iliad* in ten different lines, three of which are repeated once. In the *Odyssey* it rises 32 times. Twenty of them are marked in the famous line:

êmos d' êrigeneia phanê rhododaktulos Êôs

which occurs twice in the *Iliad*. The difference is striking, but it is not an isolated effect. For instance, Homeric verses often end with a cadential phrase 521-522 610-620 that consists of '*eni* + dative noun', as in *eni oikôi*. In the *Iliad* a phrase of this type occurs roughly every 300 lines, whereas in the *Odyssey* it occurs every 100 lines. This audible difference is reinforced by the fact that in the *Odyssey* a few phrases are repeated frequently, as emerges clearly from the tabulation of the eight most common instances of this phrase type:

Phrase	Translation	*Iliad*	*Odyssey*
eni oikôi	in the house	2	34
eni thumôi	in the mind	10	23
eni dêmôi	among the people	2	7
eni chôrôi	in the space	1	8
eni pontôi	on the sea	0	8
eni nêusin	in the ships	3	3
eni boulêi	in the assembly	3	1
eni nêi	in the ship	0	4

Phenomena of this kind are quite pervasive in the *Odyssey* and account for a marked difference between the two epics in the type/token ratio of their repeated phrases. Wherever you find related repetitions, there is a noticeable tendency in the *Odyssey* to cluster a majority of the tokens around a few subtypes. By contrast, in the *Iliad* tokens are more evenly distributed across the subtypes, making for a distinctly more varied verbal texture.

Rondo and ritual in the Odyssey

In Odysseus' flashback narrative a certain type of repetition becomes part of a deliberate rhetorical strategy. You may think of Odysseus' adventures as a rondo in which the recurring theme of departure and arrival divides the episodes. Three times Odysseus marks the transition from one adventure to the next with a two-liner about sailing on while grieving for lost companions (9.62-3 = 9.565-6 = 10.133-4.) Five times the companions follow orders to get into the boat, sit down, and beat the grey sea with their oars (9.103-4 = 9.179-80 = 9.471-2 = 9.563-4 = 12.146-7). There is a five-line stretch about eating and drinking all day, nightfall, sleeping on the beach, and dawn that appears with very minor variations on five occasions (9.161, 9.556, 10.183, 10.476, 12.29).

These repetitions acquire the resonance of refrains as the toils and routines of travel find an 'answerable style' in the narrative of the 'much-suffering' Odysseus. The rhetoric takes a deliberately ghoulish turn in the Polyphemos story. The giant is a creature of pastoral habits, and we learn much about his ways of looking after his sheep. But he breaks the iron law of Homeric hospitality and eats rather than feeds his guests. He seizes two companions, dashes their heads together so that their brains splatter about, cuts them up, and eats them raw, like a mountain lion (9.288-93). This is one of the most gruesome moments in the epic. He does the same thing on the following morning and evening, but now the event has been incorporated into his daily ritual and is described in a repeated two-liner that merges elements from the first and more extended description (9.310-11 = 9.343-4):

> But after he had briskly done all his chores and finished,
> again he snatched up two men, and prepared them for dinner.

In Odysseus' flashback narrative, repetition is not a by-product of oral composition. It is part of a distinctive rhetorical strategy to communicate a distinctive view of the world, and it achieves effects that are neither sought nor found in the *Iliad*. This is a very important point to remember when thinking about general aspects of Homeric repetition.

Classifying repetitions by type: who speaks?

While length and frequency are useful criteria for getting a first overview of phrasal repetition, a richer classification system is needed to account in a satisfactory way for the diversity of phrasal repetition. I have focused on the speaker's awareness in encoding or decoding an utterance as a repetition. The speaker may be thought of in alternate and overlapping ways as a character, the language, the genre, or the composer. Speaker's awareness exists on a continuum whose endpoints are marked by the complete presence or absence of individual awareness. At least four types of repetition emerge from such a model:

1. Explicit repetitions are spoken and intended by some character in the poem.
2. Functional repetitions are spoken by the language itself.
3. Idiomatic repetitions, the 'formulae', are spoken by the genre.
4. Interdependent repetitions are spoken by the poet or more generally a mind that remembers details from the context of one passage while composing another.

Explicit repetitions

Complete awareness is found in explicit repetitions where A tells B to deliver a message X to C. B then goes to C and repeats exactly those words. In a subtype of this pattern A tells B to do X. The execution of the order is then described in terms that are almost identical to the order itself.

The paradigm of this type is found on the four occasions when Zeus dispatches his special messenger Iris, and most particularly in her errand to Poseidon (*Il.* 15.158-9):

> *bask' ithi Iri tacheia, Poseidaôni anakti*
> *panta tad' angeilai, mêde pseudangelos einai.*

140

6. Homeric Repetitions

Go on your way now, swift Iris, to the lord Poseidon,
and give him all this message nor be a false messenger.

There are only about three dozen examples of this pattern in the Homeric poems, but as a limiting case, this type is important because it shows that the speakers and listeners of epic are familiar with the idea of repeating the same words in the same order. The convention may be seen as a way of showing the concept of fixed utterance in action, and it presupposes a theory of information that values speed (*tacheia*), completeness (*panta*), and lack of distortion (*pseudangelos*).

For a reader, the redundancy in the exact repetition of the message may seem clumsy. In a novel, for instance, a letter might be a structural equivalent of a message, but its complete text would appear only once, and further references to it would occur through quotation or citation. Typographical devices might authenticate the documentary status of the letter. In Homeric epic, verbatim repetition serves this authenticating function and establishes the identity of the messages. But while from the perspective of a reading culture, such repetitions may seem redundant, they are not puzzling. Readers may not know what to make of the fact that Agamemnon and Hektor repeat a three-line passage predicting the fall of Troy (4.163-5 = 6.447-9) or that the story of Penelope's ruse is told three times in the same way (*Od.* 2.94-111 = 19.139-56 = 24.129-46). They may wonder whether there is a purpose behind the fact that the deaths of Hektor and Patroklos are narrated in a three-line passage that does not recur (16.855-7 = 22.361-3). But they have no trouble understanding what happens when Zeus gives an order to Iris and she carries it out to the letter. Thus the simplicity and clarity of this quaint practice of repeating long orders serves as a useful point of departure for assessing the uncertainty of purpose that surrounds other forms of extended verbatim repetition in Early Greek epic.

In the *Iliad* the most extreme case of such explicit repetition is Agamemnon's offer of damages to Achilles. It takes Agamemnon 36 lines to enumerate his gifts (9.122-57), and Odysseus repeats them with minimal grammatical changes. (9.264-99).

Functional repetitions

At the other end of the awareness spectrum there are functional repetitions, the Greek versions of 'but if', 'of the', 'the man' and other combinations of functions words or content + function words through which utterances are bound together. The language itself is the speaker of such strings: you do not intend them but cannot say anything without their largely tacit use.

On the other hand, language never speaks outside a particular discursive context with its own needs for words or phrases. Some functional repetitions therefore will not only occur more often in some environments, but will become active markers. Thus the filler phrase *d'ara,* which occurs 13 times as often in narrative as in speech, is a powerful marker and in its aggregate proclaims that 'narrative is going on here'.

It is hard to think of a less interesting phrase than the combination of the two most common words in Early Greek epic, the particle *de* and the pronoun *ho*. It is not surprising that the resultant phrase, meaning something like 'and|but he|him|she| her|they|them', is the most common Homeric repetition. With its 2782 occurrences, you are likely to come across it once every ten lines. But if you look at its distribution you see that half of the time the word occurs at the beginning of a line and that the 493 instances of verse-initial *ton d'* and its prosodic sibling *ton de* ('but him') are more than twice as common as the next phrase. If you hear '*ton de*' a few times at the beginning of a line you know are in the presence of epic.

Thus the distribution of functional repetitions is far from semantically inert. They weave a fabric that says 'epic'. Moreover, this fabric differs from work to work. There are phrases that are distinctly more common in Iliadic narrative, such as *ou ti, hos te, de te,* and *hos rha.* Phrases more common in Odyssean narrative include *autar epei, d'aute, all' hote, d'ara.*

In this context one might also mention the shaping power of simple but common prepositional phrases, such as *eni megaroisin* (in the house, 203x), *epi nêas* (towards the ships, 156x), *eni stêthessi* (in the breast, 106x), *para nêusi* (by the ships, 102x), *eni phresi* (102), or *kata thumon* (57), both of which refer to mental operations.

Idiomatic repetitions

We arrive at last at 'rosy-fingered Dawn', 'swift-footed Achilles', 'winged words' and the many other phrases that people associate with Homeric repetition. They are the main topic of the critical subdiscipline of Homeric scholarship that investigates the 'formulaic' structure of Early Greek epic. I call them poetic idioms. One can of course think of idioms as the formulae of everyday language. Whatever the terminology, it is important to approach these strange features of Homeric diction as much as possible from what we know about the use of ordinary language by ordinary people.

Idiomatic repetitions have semantic, syntactic, and prosodic properties. The semantic and syntactic dimensions of *rhododaktulos Êôs* are well captured by the traditional translation 'rosy-fingered Dawn'. The peculiarly referring function of the accusative in such phrases as *boên agathos Menelaos* or *podas ôkus Achilleus,* literally 'good|swift (with regard to) shout|feet', is reasonably well captured by English phrases like 'swift-footed' or 'of the great war cry'. Prosodic properties, which are a prominent feature of technical discussions, are very difficult to follow in any detail without a good knowledge of Greek on the part of the reader, and for the most part I ignore them in this discussion.

Frequency, distribution and metrical status of idiomatic repetitions

Because idiomatic repetitions are repeated it makes sense to take their frequency as a point of departure. If a phrase is repeated only once or twice in Early Greek epic, we do not know whether it is idiomatic or not. If it occurs a dozen times or more, we can be sure that it is. There are ~180 phrases that occur at least a dozen times in the *Iliad,* some of them with minor variations. Their frequency ranges from 242 to 12, and they account for ~4000 repetition events: a phrase of this type occurs on average once every four lines.

That is a lot of repetition. Consider Homer and Shakespeare as prime examples of works that were composed for aural consumption but ended up as highly canonical reading matter. Homer and Shakespeare have approximately the same lexical density, if you define that concept as the number of distinct content words processed by a listener per minute. You cannot directly compare word counts because a lot of grammatical work that is done by suffixes in Greek is done by function words in English. By a rough calculus, seven Greek words correspond to ten English words. A comparison of random 700-word Homeric and 1,000-word Shakespearean samples reveals little difference in the number of distinct lemmata per segment. The Phaeacians who listened in rapt silence to Odysseus' narrative and the spectators in the Globe Theatre faced comparable tasks in following the story.

While the lexical density of Shakespeare does not differ much from that of Homer, the incidence of fixed phrases is much lower. The Shakespeare corpus is roughly five times the size of the *Iliad*. In the *Iliad* there are ~50 common adjective/noun combinations with some 1200 occurrences. In the Shakespeare corpus we find 75 such combinations with ~1800 occurrences. Simple arithmetic shows that the density of such combination is more than three times as high in the Iliad.[1] But that calculation understates the differences. First, the Shakespearean phrases are much less salient and consist for the most part of very common adjectives ('good', 'sweet', 'noble') combined with very common nouns ('man', 'lord', 'heart'). Among the idiomatic repetitions of the *Iliad*, there are only twenty unremarkable combinations of common nouns with common adjectives, such as 'quick ship', 'dear son', 'great glory' or 'beautiful weapons'. Secondly, the Homeric text includes many idioms that combine different word classes. Frequent combinations of this kind are very rare in Shakespeare. Thus one may say with some confidence that with regard to idiomatic repetition the *Iliad* differs from Shakespeare (and similar texts) by a whole order of magnitude. This difference in degree is a difference in kind.

The salience of idiomatic repetitions is underscored by their strong metrical definition. A phrase of a given shape could theoretically fit into several positions in a verse. In practice, however, a very strong form of Sinclair's idiom principle is at work: the great majority of repeated phrase occur exclusively or predominantly in one position. Consider the phrasal pattern 510-521-522-610-620, of which *dios Achilleus* and *huies Achaiôn* are the most common Iliadic examples. Such phrases, which occupy the last third of the hexameter, have a strong cadential force. Of 50 phrases of this type with a dozen or more occurrences, 29 always occur in verse-terminal position. The other 21 types have 58 occurrences elsewhere, but overall only 5% of occurrences move from the favoured position of 510. In summary, metrical properties powerfully shape the idiomatic status of a repeated phrase. A Homeric idiom is mostly the same phrase occurring with mostly the same syntax and in mostly the same metrical position.

Semantic properties of idiomatic repetitions

References to speech acts, heroes and gods make up the largest group of common phrases. There is some overlap in the categories since references to gods and heroes occur characteristically in speech tags. From one perspective there is nothing remarkable about phrases of the 'he said' type. They are bound to be common, and they may be expected to display relatively little internal variation, just as they do in later fiction.

---

[1] I use Shakespeare because I have precise and very granular data. There is good reason to believe that with regard to the distribution of lexical and phrasal phenomena Shakespeare does not differ very much from other English authors.

On the other hand, a frequency-oriented perspective draws our attention immediately to the fact that talking is by far the most common activity in the *Iliad*.

Speech closers
There are three kinds of talking phrases: speech openers, speech closers, and repartee tags. Speech closers display little variety. That makes sense because the narrator wants to get on with the story. By far the most common phrase in the *Iliad* is *hôs ephat'* and its close cousins (242-242).[1] Next comes a bundle of phrases that define a speech and response pattern:

> *hôs ephath' hoi d'* (90-110)
> *hôs ephath' hoi d' ara* (35-35)
> *hôs ephath' hoi d' ara pantes* (18-25)

These phrases point to the forensic quality of Homeric speech: an individual addresses a group that responds. The typical nature of this situation is further emphasised by the fact that the phrase *hoi d' ara pantes* ('all of them') never occurs outside the context of a speech and response phrase. All these phrases are relatively more common in the *Odyssey,* but two distinctly Iliadic extensions combine *hôs ephat'* with *oud' apithêse* ('nor disobeyed', 21-2) or *euchomenos* ('boasting/praying', 13-15).

In two phrases the end of the speech is tucked away in a participle and subordinated to the ensuing action. *Hôs ara phônêsas* and its variants are more common in the *Odyssey* (37-34) while *hôs eipôn* dominates in the *Iliad* (91-49). Unmotivated differences of this sort are individually without interest, but in the aggregate they contribute to the distinct lexical and phrasal fabric of each epic.

Winged words
Speech openers are more elaborate and varied affairs than speech closers. They include the famous phrase *epea pteroenta,* which is by a considerable margin the most common noun-epithet phrase in Homer (61-64) and nearly always occurs in the verse-terminal phrase *phônêsas epea pteroenta prosêuda.* Flight is an ancient human ambition, often recorded in myth. To see words as birdlike and endow them with the power to cross distance with the speed and ease that elude the earthbound speaker is to articulate in the imagination a goal that has inspired profound technological innovation. But writing, the telegraph, the telephone, and lately the Internet are ultimately extension of a power of language recognised and beautifully articulated in the famous phrase that anticipates the subsequent technological extensions of that power.

To interpret *epea pteroenta* in this way is certainly to go beyond the rhetorical power it has in any particular context. But it would be wrong to think of it simply as a long way of saying 'said'. Why did this rather than some other phrase turn out to be the most frequent noun-epithet combination, and why did this particular way of thinking about language lead to the most famous of ornamental phrases in Homer? Interpreting Homer often takes the form of going back to first things, not because

---

[1] The figures in parenthesis refer to counts in the *Iliad* and *Odyssey*. Where a third figure appears it reports the count in Hesiod and the Homeric Hymns. The *Iliad* is longer than the *Odyssey* by a third. Thus if the counts are equal or approximately equal, the phrase is relatively more common in the *Odyssey*.

Homer is first, but because he is first to us. For the modern reader in the midst of a communications revolution of astonishing rapidity there is prophetic wisdom in the description of words as 'winged'.

Other speech openers and repartee tags
Since the phrase *epea pteroenta* introduces only 10% of Homeric speeches, it is reasonable to ask whether the phrase provides some special framing for what follows. There are 680 speech openers in the *Iliad*. No more than half are accounted for by frequent phrases, and not many phrase types occur a dozen times. *Muthon eeipen* (33-20) is a phrase with a somewhat Iliadic flavour. *Makron aüsas* ('shouting loudly', 19-1) is obviously a phrase for a war poem.

Two phrases with an interestingly gendered dimension are *epos t' ephat' ek t' onomaze* ('spoke the word and named it', 17-26) and *anchou histamenê* ('standing close', 18-6). The former occurs in contexts of conversational intimacy, is often accompanied by a phrase about touching, and is preferred in cross-gender speech. The latter is distinctly more common in the *Iliad*, where it describes the way in which Athene (6x) and Iris (5x) approach their interlocutors. It is not used more than once of any male speaker, and whether by accident or design, the phrase appears gendered, and it is the most literal expression of Athene's 'closeness', whether as a helper or deceiver.

Almost a third of Iliadic and not quite half of Odyssean speeches follow immediately on a preceding speech and are introduced by a repartee tag. Of the four most common repartee tags three are more common in the *Odyssey* and one in the *Iliad*:

> *ton d' apameibomenos prosephê* (36- 70)
> *ton d' aute proseeipe* (43-57)
> *ton d' êmeibet' epeita* (48-24)
> *antion êuda* (17-55)

Anger is the only emotion commonly identified in a repartee tag – and it is strikingly marked as a facial expression of looking from below: *hupodra idôn* (17-9). Not surprisingly it is somewhat more common in the *Iliad*. There are smiling repartee phrases in Homer, but they do not make it into the top list.

Phrases commonly used by Homeric characters
Ô philoi, an appeal to friends, is the most common way to begin a speech (21-23). The second most common phrase expresses surprise: *ô popoi* (29-22) or *ô popoi ê* (20-13). Since the two epics have almost the same number of spoken lines, the figures show that expressions of surprise are more common in the *Iliad*. Respect for old age appears in the phrase 'old sir' (*ô geron*, 8-11). The phrase *hêgêtores êde medontes* (*leaders and counsellors*, 14-10) is sometimes found in narrative, but it occurs typically as a formal speech opening. Falling below the threshold of a dozen occurrences in the *Iliad* are various phrases that mean 'let me tell you', 'tell me', 'no need', or 'well said'. *Homo homericus* clearly shares some of our speech habits.

Phrases about warriors
Next to speech phrases, name phrases for warriors make up the largest group of common repetitions. Such phrases are overwhelmingly in the nominative case. For

personal names, the case ratios of nominative and accusative (40%-17%) reverse the ratios for nouns (22%-38%). But this trend is even more pronounced with name phrases. Only four of them occur with any frequency in other cases than the nominative. The decoration of a name with a phrase is a powerful device for stressing the agency of a character.

It is an important guide to the value system of Early Greek epic that warriors are frequently identified as the sons of their fathers. The most common phrase for the Achaeans identifies them as *huies Achaiôn* (53-11), and we find the following phrases referring to a variety of individual warriors: *philon huion* ('dear', 32-34-6) *aglaos huios* ('shining', 19-8) *alkimos huios* ('valiant', 15-0) *phaidimos huios* ('splendid', 4-12).

Aglaos huios is used in the *Iliad* to add some lustre to minor warriors such as Pandaros (7x) or Eurypylos (4x) and Nestor's son Antilochos (2x). *Alkimos huios* is used once for three different warriors in the *Iliad*, but it is chiefly a way of referring to Patroklos as *Menoitiou alkimos huios* (12x).

While *aglaos*, *alkimos* and *phaidimos* focus on the son as splendid warrior, the phrase *philon huion* (32-34) functions somewhat differently. It is often said that in many contexts the adjective *philos* is a substitute for the possessive pronoun so that the phrase *hon philon huion* is simply a metrically expanded way of saying [*his/her*] *son*. But this cannot be true. In six of the ten occurrences a mother (Aphrodite, Thetis, Hera, Penelope) rescues, finds, or addresses 'her dear son'. In the other four occurrences, Hektor kisses the baby Astyanax (6.474), Zeus arranges for the burial or mourns the labours of his sons Sarpedon (16.447) and Herakles (19.132), and Odysseus addresses Telemachos for the last time in the poem (*Od.* 24.505). So it appears that *hon philon huion* is a highly affect-laden phrase.

The Achaeans appear in several other phrases as 'well-greaved' (*eüknêmides Achaioi*, 31-5) or 'bronze-armoured' (*Achaiôn chalkochitônôn*, 22-2), and they are envisaged collectively as 'all' (*pantas Achaious*, 15-10) or the 'people' (*laon Achaiôn* (25-0). Perhaps the most striking epithet is *karê komoôntes* ('flowing-haired', 26-3). This phrase, which is also used of the manes of horses (8.42 = 13.24), points to the aesthetics of war and includes proleptically the famous anecdote about the Spartans combing their hair before the battle at Thermopylae.

There is no collective phrase for the Trojans that is used more than six times, although there are two phrases that contain their name: 'Trojans and Achaeans' (*Trôôn kai Achaiôn*, 22-1) and 'fight with the Trojans' (*Trôsi machesthai*, 18-2). The most resonant Troy phrase is the name for the city itself: 'sacred Ilion' or *Ilion hirên* (22-2).

There are two very common phrases to specify a leader. *Anax andrôn* ('lord of men', 50-2) refers to Agamemnon in 47 of its 52 occurrences. The phrase *poimeni laôn* ('shepherd of the people', 44-12-2) is applied to Agamemnon (11-3) and Nestor (4-3), but in well over half of its occurrences it applies to a wide variety of men, and it is the most generic phrase for a leader. The metaphor is obvious but deep and reveals that Early Greek epic and the Bible alike are rooted in a world where 'The Lord is my shepherd' and about which Robertson Smith wrote with unmatched eloquence in his *Religion of the Semites.*

Name phrases for warriors
Diï philos ('dear to Zeus', 17-0) is a general honorific attached to Achilles (5), Hektor

(4), Odysseus (3), and five other warriors. The Iliadic characters who are associated with special phrases are Achilles, Agamemnon, Hektor, Odysseus, Menelaos, Diomedes, Hektor, Aias, and Nestor, as represented in Table 7.

Table 7. Common epithets for warrior

Achilleus	*dios Achilleus* (57-0) *podarkês dios Achilleus* (21-0) *podas ôkus Achilleus* (30-0)
Agamemnon	*anax andrôn Agamemnôn* (44-2) *kreiôn Agamemnôn* (40-1) *Atreïdêi Agamemnoni* (21-4)
Hektôr	*Hektora dion* *koruthaiolos Hektor* (37-0) *phaidimos Hektôr* (29-0)
Odysseus	*dios Odusseus* (23-80) *polumêtis Odusseus* (14-66) *polutlas dios Odusseus* (5-37) *Odussêos theioio* (3-24)
Menelaos	*boên agathos Menelaos* (16-9) *arêïphilos Menelaos* (20-1) *xanthos Menelaos* (16-15)
Diomedes	*boên agathos Diomêdês* (21-0) *krateros Diomêdês* (20-0)
Nestôr	*Gerênios hippota Nestôr* (21-10)
Aias	*Telamônios Aias* (22-0)

It is of course the case that these epithets address specific aspects of a warrior's quality or story. Achilles is 'swift-footed' because the narrative climax involves a race around the walls of the Troy. But it is even more instructive to look at the epithets without reference to their specific carriers and see in their aggregate a reflection of the priorities of a heroic value system. Warriors are close to the gods (*dios*) and splendid (*phaidimos*). They love or are loved by the god of war (*arêïphilos*). The leader (*anax andrôn*) rules by strength (*kreiôn*), and warriors are strong (*krateros*). Various uses of the patronymic point to the importance of the father-son theme. Warriors are swift (*podas ôkus*, *podarkês*) and can shout (*boên agathos*). They protect their heads (*koruthaiolos*), bodies (*chalkochitôn*), and legs (*eüknêmides*). Their favourite animal is the horse (*hippota*).

Phrases about gods
Gods are the referents of the next largest group of phrases. Zeus is in a class by himself. Athene, Apollo, Hera, and Poseidon each have several common phrases attached to them. Aphrodite, Hermes, and Iris, each have one. Frequency turns out to be an excellent guide to hierarchy in this case. Phrases about gods are usually in the nominative, just like phrases about heroes.

In talking about gods it pays to take a look at Hesiod and the *Homeric Hymns*. 'God talk' is much more common in these explicitly 'theological' works, but from the greater absolute and relative frequency of common phrases in these poems an interesting light falls on the human focus of Homeric narrative.

The most common phrase for the gods as a whole is *athanatoisi theoisi*, 'the death-less gods' (18-19-22). Almost as common are various collocations of *theos* with *makar* ('blessed') before or after (29-28-30). Finally, there is *theôn aieigenetaôn* ('the ever-lasting gods', 8-4-6). By contrast, the most common phrase for humans is *thnêtôn anthrôpôn* ('mortal men', 6-4-22).

The place of the gods is the broad sky (*ouranon eurun*, 12-21-12), and half the occurrences of this phrase refer to some gods 'who own the sky' (*hoi ouranon eurun echousi* (2-16-2). The Odyssean flavour and distribution of this phrase are noteworthy. The inhabitants of the sky are an inscrutable 'them' rather than named gods about whom one knows something. The *Iliad* prefers to locate the gods in a specific and named place: the gods 'have their residence on Olympos' (*Olumpia dômat' echontes*, 10-3-13). The other common phrase about Olympos, *makron Olumpon* (11-4-6) is likewise more common in the *Iliad*. The 'starry sky', however (*ouranon asteroenta*, 7-4-12) is much more common in Hesiod's *Theogony* (8).

Zeus

Zeus is most commonly addressed or spoken of as the father of the gods, and the phrase *patêr andrôn te theôn te* (father of men and gods) is often a substitute for his name (12-3-6). There is a group of collocations in which the name Zeus is followed or preceded by the word *patêr*. Thus we find the invocation *Zeu pater* (21-11-1) and the dative *Diï patri* (17-7-4).

Distinctive to Zeus are three epithets with an archaic nominative ending in '-*a*':

nephelêgereta (cloud-gatherer, 22-8-4)
mêtieta (designing, 16-3-14)
euruopa (wide-seeing, 13-7-11)

The first of these is distinctly Iliadic; the second and third are relatively more common outside of Homer. The nonce word *steropêgereta* ('gathers the thunder-flash') is also used of Zeus (16.298). There appears to a consistent association of this archaic nominative with the semantic concept 'old'. Thus the heroic epithets *hippota* and *hippêlata* are used of heroes who belong to an earlier world.

Other phrases for Zeus include *Diï Kroniôni* ('Zeus the son of Kronos', 12-2-3) and two phrases that are more common in the Odyssey as well as in Hesiod and the Hymns: *Dios megaloio* (great Zeus, 6-10-6) and *Diï terpikeraunôi* (thunder-delighting Zeus, 5-7-5).

Of particular interest is the collocation of Zeus with *aigiochos* (*aegis-holding*), which is found in the following combinations:

Dios aigiochoio (14-10-11)
aigiochoio Dios (11-2-4)
Dios ... aigiochoio (11-5-6)

6. Homeric Repetitions

On more than half of its occurrences (5-9-5) the sequence *Dios aigiochoio* is preceded by a form of the word *kourê* ('young woman') and refers to daughters of Zeus, whether Athene (10), the Muses (5), nymphs (3), or Helen (1). In ten of its seventeen the phrase *aigiochoio Dios* is followed by *tekos* (*child of aegis-holding Zeus*, 8-2). This phrase always refers to Athene and may be followed by her special and obscure epithet *Atrutônê* (4-2).

The collocation Zeus + word + *aigiochos* occurs most commonly in the verse-terminal construction *Dios* + word + *aigiochoio* (10-4-5). *Noos* ('mind') is the word in ten of those occurrences; the other nine are divided between seven different words. Thus the phrase 'mind of aegis-holding Zeus' has a clear resonance, and there is a cluster of phrases that link Zeus with Athene and thought through the epithet *aigiochos*.

Athene

In both epics, Athene follows Zeus as the most frequently named god, but in the *Odyssey* she follows much more closely on her father's heels (222-160) than in the *Iliad* (489-161). On the other hand, *glaukôpis Athênê* (91) is the most common phrase for a god, and after *epea pteroenta* (136) and *dios Odusseus* (103) it is the most common noun-epithet combination in Early Greek epic. In more than half of its occurrences, *glaukôpis Athênê* (28-51-12) occurs in the expanded phrase *thea glaukôpis Athênê* (19-32-5). *Glaukôpis* can also appear without the name of Athene (2-8-4), but it always refers to her.

The expanded phrase *thea glaukôpis Athênê* appears more often in speech openers (32-24), whereas the shorter phrase more often marks Athene as an agent (12-43). This difference is even more marked in the verse-terminal *Pallas Athênê* (24-18-2). Except on one occasion, this phrase never introduce Athene as a speaker, and when it occurs in a speech closer (4-9) it marks what she does in response. Thus *Pallas Athênê* is the quintessential phrase for Athene as agent, and this is also true of its verse-initial variant *Pallas Athênaiê* (4-8-4).

Apollo

Apollo is most often referred to as *Phoibos Apollôn*. This phrase occurs most frequently as a verse-terminal nominative (32-2-14), but it can also appear in the verse-initial genitive *Phoibou Apollônos* (4-1-6). In structure and sound, this phrase is obviously similar to *Pallas Athênê*, but Apollo is sometimes just called *Phoibos* (9-0-11), whereas *Pallas* never appears by itself.

Apollo shares with Herakles, Hermes, and Sarpedon the epithet *Dios huios*, which is discussed below. His most distinctive epithet speaks very clearly to his *modus operandi*. He is the god who 'works' (*hekaergos*) or 'shoots' from afar (*hek[at]êbolos*). What look like three distinct epithets is better seen as forms of a single epithet-noun lemma (39-7-44) that make up a particularly robust declensional system to meet various metrical constraints:

> Nominative: *hekaergos Apollôn* (9-1-8)
> Genitive: *hek[at]êbolou Apollônos* (10-2-12)
> Dative: *hekêbolôi Apollôni* (6-0-5)
> Accusative: *hek[at]êbolon Apollôna* (10-2-12)
> Vocative: *hekatêbol' Apollon* (4-2-7)

Ares
Although the god of war ranks fourth in the number of references to him in Early Greek epic, none of his various epithets occurs more than eleven times: *thouros* ('wild', 11), *brotoloigos* ('man-destroying', 7), *obrimos* ('heavy', 6), *aatos polemoio* ('insatiable of war', 4), *poludakrus* ('causing many tears', 3). The chief reason is that he only speaks twice and thus is not often found in the situation that causes the decoration of the name. But the absence of a dominant epithet also says something about his status in the hierarchy of the gods.

Hera
Hera is either *leukôlenos* ('white-armed', 24-0-6) or *potnia* ('august', 24-1-5). The former phrase is usually expanded into *thea leukôlenos Hêrê* (19-0-1); the latter into the famous phrase about 'cow-eyed' Hera that most readers associate with her: *boôpis potnia Hêrê* (14-0-3). Neither of these epithets is specific to Hera. *Potnia mêtêr*, for instance, is more common than *potnia Hêrê* (36-30), but the two phrases are semantically and phonetically related. *Leukôlenos* is used of eight other women, including unnamed servants (4-11-2). Verse-medial *boôpis* is restricted to Hera, but in verse-terminal position the epithet is used of five other mortal and divine women (3-0-2).

Poseidon
Poseidaôn enosichthôn (14-10-1) is the most common epithet phrase for the god of the earth and sea. It is obviously related to the more common noun *ennosigaios* (20-6-7). It may be doubted whether Homer's listeners had a clear idea of what the first part of this word means, but it must refer something you do to the earth, which is the meaning of the second components *chtôn* and *gaia*. Poseidon's less common epithets are semantically more transparent: *gaiêochos* (12-6-3) means 'holder of the earth', and *kuanochaitês* (6-3-4) means 'dark-maned' – probably a reflection of Poseidon' s strong association with horses. The three words *ennosigaios*, *gaiêochos*, and *kuanochaitês* are used as names or epithets and combined in various ways. None of these combinations is as common as *Poseidaôn enosichthôn*, but together they set up a strong network of phrases.

Iris, Hermes and Aphrodite
Iris, the messenger of the gods in the Iliad, is the epithet sister of Achilles. She is either *podas ôkea Iris* (9-0-1) or *podênemos ôkea Iris* ('wind-footed', 9-0-1). The latter phrase is metrically equivalent to *podarkês dios Achilleus*.

Hermes is known separately as *argeïphontês* ('Argos-slayer', 6-6-16) or *diaktoros* ('conductor of the dead', 0-3-4), but in Homer the two words are more commonly combined to form the distinctive phrase *diaktoros argeïphontês* (8-7-3).

The most common phrases for Aphrodite are *chrusêi Aphroditêi* ('golden Aphrodite', 6-5-7), the more striking *philommeidês Aphroditê* ('fond of smiles', 4-1-5), and the generic *Dios thugatêr* or 'daughter of Zeus'.

Phrases applied to other gods
Dios huios (16-5-18) and *Dios thugatêr* (14-6-5), referring to a son or daughter of Zeus, are honorific epithets used of gods and semi-divine heroes. The former is used of Apollo (19x), Herakles (12x), Hermes (3x), and the mortal Sarpedon (4x). In the

Iliad it is a major epithet for Apollo (11-2-7), especially in the verse-terminal expanded form *anax Dios huios Apollôn* ('Lord Apollo the son of Zeus', 7-1-5). Herakles, an obvious and frequent referent outside of Homer, is only passingly identified in the *Iliad* as a son of Zeus (1-2-9), but it is a singular mark of distinction for Sarpedon that he receives the other four Iliadic references, and it is fitting that Zeus entrusts his burial to his 'brother' Apollo. *Dios thugatêr* (14-6-6) refers once to Atê, Helen, Persephone and the Muse, but is primarily a phrase for Aphrodite (8-1-4) and for Athene (4-3-1).

Body and soul
The most common Homeric words for parts of the ensemble of body and soul are, in descending order:

thumos (853)
cheir (hand, 729)
phrên (478)
pous (foot, 329)
stêthos (chest, 209)
menos (energy, 206)
ômos (shoulder, 180)
kephalê (head, 161)
ophthalmos (eye, 141)
haima (blood, 123)
gonu (knee, 129)
êtor (heart,111)
dakruon (tear, 106)
kara (head, 101)

Four of the six most common words are psychological rather than anatomical. *Thumos* and *phrên* are emotional or rational organs that have no clear anatomical correspondence. *Stêthos* (chest) is typically used as the seat of emotions, and *menos* is probably closest to what we would call *adrenaline*. Hands and feet are the most prominent body parts. Blood and tears are the most common body fluids. Important priorities of Homeric narrative are quite clearly expressed in this simple frequency based list.

Common phrases reinforce those priorities. *Thumos eni stêthessi* (37-24) is the most frequent psychological phrase and refers to an energising force inside. The *thumos* commands (*thumos anôgei*, 12-8) and is proud (*thumos agênôr*, 9-15) or 'great-hearted' (*megalêtora thumon*, 11-6). The most common set of phrases for killing means 'to take away the *thumos*' ([*apo|ek*] + *thumon* + *helesthai*, 13-4). Without the *thumos* a man is a lifeless lump, as witnessed by the most common dying phrase, which imitates the sound of the body slumping to the ground (*doupêsen de pesôn*, 19-2).

In the phrase *kradiên kai thumon* ('heart and *thumos*', 9-5) two emotional organs reinforce each other. But to ponder a matter in terms of its cognitive and emotional aspects is to ponder it *kata phrena kai kata thumon* (10-11).

'Knowing well' (*eü eidôs* 26-18) is a cognitive phrase. So are the variants of the phrase *en|epi* + *phresi* + *tithêmi*, which means 'putting something in your mind' (7-11). *Philon êtor* (18-22), verse terminal in all but eight occurrences, is an emphatic way of saying 'heart' at the end of the line. It may not be accidental that *philos* bonds more closely with *êtor* than with any other word.

You do things with your hands, and *cheir* is the only physical body part that appears in a variety of phrases such as

chersin echontes (holding in one's hands, 23-16)
meta chersin echôn (holding in one's hands, 6-7)
chersin helôn (taking with one's hands, 23-16)
en chersi tithei (put in one's hands, 12-10)
cheiri pacheiêi (with a thick hand, 13-5)
cheiras anaschôn (holding up one's hands (12-5)
hoi d' ep' oneiath' hetoima prokeimena cheiras iallon (they stretched out their hands
    towards the food prepared in front of them, 3-11)
cheiras aaptous (untouchable hands, 10-3)

An emphatic way of *seeing with your own eyes* appears in the collocation of the verb *idein* with *ophthalmos* preceding (10-7) or following (8-14).

Suffering and tears
Things that happen are for the most part bad. Common phrases include half a dozen phrases of suffering, but no phrases of pleasure. Thus we find *kaka polla* ('many evils', 10-13), *aipun olethron* ('sheer disaster', 14-11), *kêra melainan* (black fate, 10-8), *potmon epispein* (complete one's fate, 7-16), *polla pathôn* (7-17) or *polla mogêsas* (4-16-1) ('suffering/toiling much') or *algea paschôn* ('suffering pain', 5-11-1). Most of these phrases are distinctly more common in the *Odyssey*.

In both poems nothing is shed as frequently as tears. We find *dakru + cheô* (20-16). Tears are shed by women on seventeen, and by men on twenty-three occasions. Given the fact that the ratio of male:female name occurrences is almost 4:1, women cry more often in Homer than men. But it is also the case that tears come easily to Homeric men, and 'hot tears' (*dakrua therma*, 4-2) are in fact a male prerogative.

Ships and horses
'Ship' (*naus*, 589-414) follows 'man' (*anêr*, 590-449) as the most common noun in Early Greek epic. *Anêr* is not a word that appears in many phrases – it is a generic word that complements the repertoire of name phrases – but *naus* is rich in phrases. Ships are most commonly fast (*nêa thoên*, 19-36), hollow (*glaphuros,* 30-1, *koilos,* 17-9), or black (*nêï melainêi*, 16-37). The blackness of a ship refers to its threat rather than its colour, as is apparent from the other nouns with which *melas* closely bonds, such as *kêr* (deadly fate), *haima* (blood), *nux* (night), and *thanatos* (death).

In the *Iliad* ships are closely associated with the Achaeans (*nêas Achaiôn*, 58-1). Ships are also 'well-benched' **nêas eüsselmous*, 13-8) and 'even' (*nêas eïsas*, 9-10).

The common phrases for the 'wine-coloured sea' (*oinopa ponton*, 6-12) and the beach (*rhêgmini thalassês* 4-10; *thina thalassês*, 2-15) are distinctly more frequent in the *Odyssey*, as befits a poem in which there is much coming and going by sea. Horses are more common in the *Iliad* and play an important role in battle. Epithets for them emphasise speed (*ôkeas hippous*, 28-3-3) or the distinctive mane, which may be distantly related to the warrior's flowing hair (*mônuchas hippous*, 33-1).

Weapons and fighting
Weapons are sharp, merciless, and made from bronze. They are also aesthetic objects. Offence prevails over defence, and the spear is much more important than the sword. Thus we find:

oxeï chalkôi	sharp bronze	26-11
oxeï douri	sharp spear	17-3
chalkeon enchos	bronze spear	18-5
dolichoskion enchos	long-shadowed spear	21-4
douri phaeinôi	shining spear	22-0
kluta teuchea	famous arms	16-2
teuchea kala	beautiful arms	17-3
nêleï chalkôi	merciless bronze	11-8
xiphos oxu	sharp sword	5-12
aspida pantos' eïsên	the shield even around	17-0

Note the distinct Odyssean preference for *xiphos oxu*.
Closely related to phrases about weapons are general phrases about war, the most common of which are:

kraterêi husminêi	strong battle	32-1
thouridos alkês	fierce valour	21-0
stichas andrôn	rows of men	16-0

A handful of phrases literally denoting approach or encounter are typically used in situations of hostile approach or standing one's ground:

antios êlthe	came opposite	19-1
enguthen elthôn	came close	12-7
asson imen	come closer,	10-8
schedon elthemen	come close,	12-6
authi menôn	remaining in place	14-6

Given the ubiquity of fighting in the *Iliad* it is instructive to see that there are not many common phrases that describe injury or death. *Doupêsen de pesôn* imitates the thudding noise of the dead warrior hitting the ground (19-2), and on six occasions the phrase is followed by a phrase describing the clatter of his armour (*arabêse de teuche' ep' autôi*). There is a phrase about a spear injury (*akontise douri phaeinôi*, 14-0) and a phrase about darkness covering the eyes of the fallen warrior (*ton de skotos osse kalupse*, 12-0). But in the approximately 150 individual encounters there is considerable emphasis on rhetorical variety, and we do not find the distinctly Odyssean 'rosy-fingered Dawn' effect.

Rare repetitions, clustering and interdependence

The more often a phrase is repeated the less sense it makes to ask about its specific function in any particular context. Its narrative or thematic contribution will be global rather than local, subject to some version of Sinclair's idiom principle (see above, p.

22). But the question remains what to make of the many phrases that are repeated once or twice. How do they fit into an aesthetic that depends primarily on pervasive resonance?

You can answer this question on the analogy of the definition of a stranger as a friend you have not yet met. We have some 30,000 lines of epic from what must have been millions. Rare repetitions therefore may largely be a function of what we have lost. If we had three million lines, many strangers would turn out to be old friends. And so they would, except that the number of rare repetitions would increase rather than decrease. From a lexical perspective, as Harald Baayen has demonstrated, language is characterised by a 'large number of rare events'. In a linguistic corpus of any size, the number of unique lexical items is always larger than the number of items that are repeated once or more often. As a corpus increases, the absolute number of unique items increases, and their relative number does not decline sharply.

What is true of lexical items is true of their combination as well. However many 'rare' repetitions would be revealed as idiomatic repetitions in a hypothetical larger corpus, their number would be overbalanced by new rare repetitions some of which would be turn out to be idiomatic on a further expansion of the corpus, and so forth *ad infinitum.* If we had two dozen Early Greek epics we would know much more than we now do about the distribution of idiomatic repetitions within or across works, authors, or the tradition as a whole. But we would still face the question of whether to interpret rare repetitions as instances of unknown idioms, random occurrences, or intentional acts that establish a specific connection between one occurrence and another.

The following table illustrates this point. In the world of repetitions, the equivalent of the *hapax legomenon* or singleton is the phrase that occurs twice or is repeated once. The distribution of Homeric and Shakespearean lemmata is fairly similar: singletons account for roughly a third of the lexicon, and the percentages drop by a factor of two or more as you go towards doublets and triplets. The distribution of Shakespearean lemmata is quite similar to that of other written documents: in a corpus of any size, the percentage of *hapax legomena* will range between a third and more than half, and the percentage of *tris legomena* will be less than 10% of all lemmata.

If we now compare Homeric repetitions with Homeric lemmata, we are not surprised to see that there are more single repetitions of lemma strings than there are distinct lemmata. More interesting is the observation that the decline from singletons to multiple repetitions is even sharper with phrases than with lemmata.

Table 8. Distribution of rare lemmata and repetitions

occurs or is repeated	13,000 Homeric repetitions	8,000 Homeric lemmata	18,000 Shakespearean lemmata
once	7300 (56%)	2600 (33%)	7000 (39%)
twice	2800 (22%)	1200 (15%)	2200 (12%)
thrice	1200 (9%)	700 (9%)	1300 (7%)

Are there criteria on the basis of which you can identify repetitions that are unlikely to be unknown idioms or random occurrences? It is instructive to look at the different distributions of repetitions within and across particular works. In the following table we look at repetitions that the *Iliad* shares only with itself or with the *Odyssey*. If an Iliadic phrase is repeated only once, the odds are 2:1 that its other occurrence will also be in the *Iliad*. If it is repeated more than once, the balance shifts sharply. If a phrase is repeated twice, there is an even chance that one of its occurrences will be in the *Odyssey*. If it is repeated thrice, the odds are 3:2 that one of its occurrences will be in the *Odyssey*.

Table 9. Repetitions within *Iliad* and across *Odyssey*

Iliad shares with	*repeated*	*typeCount*
Iliad only	once	3246
Odyssey	once	1895
Iliad only	twice	1003
Odyssey	twice	1062
Iliad only	thrice	365
Odyssey	thrice	566

It would be easier to interpret these findings if we had just one other epic of approximately the size of the *Iliad* or *Odyssey*. Comparisons with the other remains of Early Greek epic are in various ways problematical. There are seven texts that by the crude criterion of length can be thought of as Homeric 'books': the *Theogony* and *Works and Days* by Hesiod (~1,000 lines each), the pseudo-Hesiodic *Shield of Achilles*, and the *Homeric Hymns* to Demeter, Apollo, Hermes, and Aphrodite. Hesiod was a rough contemporary of 'Homer', but his poems are not narratives in the Homeric sense. The dates of the *Shield of Heracles* and the *Homeric Hymns* are uncertain, but *grosso modo* they behave like Homeric narratives. If with these reservations you treat these seven texts as Homeric 'books' and run statistical tests on the resultant 55 'books' of Early Greek epic the results are always the same: except for the Aphrodite hymn, the seven non-Homeric books lie outside or at the margins of the range defined by the highest and lowest Homeric scores. The Aphrodite hymn, which is a story about the conception and birth of Aeneas, could statistically pass for a Homeric book, and the figures give some support to Reinhardt's charming speculation that the hymn is a piece of courtly flattery composed by the poet of the *Iliad* for a ruler in the Troad who liked to trace his family tree back to Aeneas – the genealogical game that Vergil made famous and many European dynasties imitated.

Whatever the origin of the Aphrodite hymn, quantitative tests across the corpus of Early Greek epic always show that the books of the *Iliad* and *Odyssey* are much closer to each other than they are to non-Homeric texts. But we do not have good enough data to make very firm statements about far from or close to each other the *Iliad* and *Odyssey* would be in a hypothetical document space of Greek narrative poetry between 750 and 650 BCE. In the absence of better evidence, it is therefore hard to gauge the significance of the clear fact that as soon as a phrase is repeated more than once its chances of being repeated across a single work improve dramatically. The appearance of a phrase in more than one work certainly provides some evidence for its idiomatic status. But if we follow the trail of evidence suggesting that the *Iliad* and *Odyssey* are linked in particularly close ways, we may conclude that repetitions across those two poems are not very different from repetitions within them.

Length and various forms of clustering provide the strongest evidence against the idiomatic status of a repeated phrase. By idiomatic status I mean that a given phrase is not owned by a particular author or tied to the context of a specific utterance. Nobody owns the phrase 'Happy Birthday', although the tune has a composer and may still be under copyright. An idiomatic phrase is used freely in the sense that its felicitous application requires nothing beyond the minimal context specified by the meaning of the words: as long as somebody has a birthday, 'Happy Birthday' is a proper thing to say.

Clustering occurs whenever such free use is restricted in some fashion. For instance, a phrase may in its three occurrences refer to the same person. Or a rare phrase may occur only in the vicinity of another rare phrase. Such 'name associations' or 'neighbourhood effects' raise doubts about the idiomatic status of a phrase and provide evidence for the alternate hypothesis that two passages are interdependent in specific ways.

Long repetitions and the 'cut-and-paste' model of composition

The longer a repetition, the less likely it is to be idiomatic. We saw earlier that the majority of repetitions are of a length that human memory can process as a single chunk. There are a number of common one-liners where short idioms have combined to form a fixed longer phrase. While more common in speech tags, this pattern is also found in such narrative or spoken lines as

> *hôs hoi men toiauta pros allêlous agoreuon* (8-16)
> Thus they talked with each other
>
> *êmos d' êrigeneia phanê rhododaktulos Êôs* (2-20)
> When early and rosy-fingered Dawn appeared
>
> *autar epei posios kai edêtuos ex eron hento* (7-14)
> But when they had driven out the desire for food and drink
>
> *all' age moi tode eipe kai atrekeôs katalexon* (4-13)
> Tell me truly
>
> *allo de toi ereô su d' eni phresi balleo sêisin* (7-7)
> But I will tell you something else
>
> *hoi d' hote dê schedon êsan ep' allêloisin iontes* (11-0)
> When they had approached each other closely

Notice that lines of this type are distinctly less common in the *Iliad* (38-70). It is easy to square this type of line with a 'natural tendency to economy of effort' (Sinclair 1991, 110). One may even extend this tendency to include two-liners such as the predominantly Odyssean

6. Homeric Repetitions

hoi d' ep' oneiath' hetoima prokeimena cheiras iallon.
autar epei posios kai edêtuos ex eron hento (3-8)

They put their hands to the good things that lay ready before them.
But when they had put away their desire for eating and drinking,

But it is difficult to square longer exact repetitions with a tendency to economy of effort in an environment of improvisational composition. The point about Mary Poppins' 'supercalifragilisticexpialidocious' is that words do not scale that way. Neither do idioms. Longer repetitions, however, become economical in a 'cut-and-paste' compositional environment that involves writing, whether by the poet, scribes who take dictation, or copyists and editors who add this and that for this or that reason.

There are 197 passages of two lines or more that are repeated at least once in the *Iliad*. As the following table shows, only 17 are repeated more than once:

Table 10. Frequency of long repetitions in the *Iliad*

	2x	*3x*	*4x*
2 lines	63	8	
2-4 lines	80	6	2
4-6 lines	23	1	
6 six lines	4		
> 6 lines	10		

If you work your way down from the longest cases, ignoring explicit and therefore unproblematical repetitions, you encounter first two passages that have since the nineteenth century generated countless hypotheses about the composition and genesis the *Iliad*: Agamemnon's 'cut and run' speeches in *Iliad* 2 and 9 and and the joint expeditions of Hera and Athene in *Iliad* 5 and 8.

In the second book of the *Iliad* Agamemnon tests his troops in a speech of 30 lines, urging them to abandon the expedition (2.110-41). Unfortunately they follow his advice, and it takes the intervention of Odysseus and Athene to prevent an ignominious departure. In Book 9 Agamemnon makes the same suggestion but this time in earnest. His speech consists of the first nine and the last three lines of his speech in Book 2 (9.17-28).

In *Iliad* 5 there is an elaborate account of how Hera and Athene prepare for their mission to help Diomedes (5.733-52). The first five and last eight lines of that account constitute the preparations for their second intervention (8.384-96). Zeus orders them to return and teases them mercilessly, which provokes a six-line account of Hera's indignant impotence that is also found in *Iliad* 4 (4.20-5 = 8.457-462).

Both of these cases are textbook example of 'cut and paste' composition: either the shorter versions have been expanded by adding a middle or – more plausibly – the longer versions have been cut. But whatever their origins, the pattern of resemblances between the passages – extended verbatim sequences in the same order – is very difficult to reconcile with a practice of independent composition according to a traditional narrative schema.

Typical scenes of arming and feasting

Some form of 'cut and paste' composition is also present in the extended arming and eating scenes that since Walter Arend's book on the subject have been discussed under the heading of 'typical scenes.' It is one thing to recognise the presence of narrative schemata that govern the description of recurring events, such as 'arrival, sacrifice and eating, journeys by sea or land, arming and dressing, sleep, hesitation before decision, … assembly, oath, and bath' (Parry 1987, 404). But it is another to assume that such scenes are most typical when they use the same lines in the same sequence to describe recurring events. At least in Iliadic narrative, the multiple repetition of the same lines in the same order is an uncommon event. While fighting scenes depend heavily on narrative schemata and are shot through with recurring phrases, they rarely consist of the same lines in the same order. The arming and ritual meal scenes, in which we find spectacular instances of such exact repetition, are in fact untypical in that regard.

There are six closely interrelated scenes in which a warrior arms for battle:

Paris arms for the duel with Menelaos (3.330-9)
Agamemnon arms for battle (11.16-46)
After having his bow smashed, Teukros arms for regular battle (15.479-82)
Patroklos puts on the armour of Achilles (16.130-44)
Achilles puts on the armour Hephaistos has made for him (19.367-91)
Odysseus arms after running out of arrows (*Od.* 22.122-5)

In each of these scenes the warrior arms from the feet up and puts on, in that order, his greaves, body armour, sword and shield, and helmet. Finally he picks up a spear. Table 11 shows the interrelation of the six scenes. Line numbers preceded by a tilde refer to passages with slight differences in wording. Lines in parenthesis are functionally equivalent but different in wording. From this table it appears that the arming scenes of Agamemnon and Achilles decorate the plain model that appears in the cases of Paris and Patroklos and that an abbreviated version of the pattern appears with Teukros and Odysseus. In the case of Agamemnon, the source of his armour, the nature of his sword, and his shield are described in considerable detail.

The source of Achilles' armour is left blank, presumably because it has been described in the previous narrative in great detail. There are several lines on the effect of the shield. The description of his helmet breaks the pattern that is followed in all other cases. The arming of Achilles adds some lines about trying out the armour. This makes sense because it is new. There is a relationship to the arming scene of Patroklos. Both elaborate on the spear of Achilles – in the case of Patroklos describing the spear that he does not take because only Achilles can wield it. The Teukros and Odysseus scenes both abridge the standard pattern in the same way. Both scenes describe a warrior having to change from archer to spear fighter on the run.

The relative ease with which these scenes can be fitted into the straitjacket of a table may itself be evidence for cut-and-paste composition. There is no question that these passages are embedded in some traditional motif of 'the warrior arming'. But it is not only possible but quite probable that the very tightly structured system with its purposeful additions and omissions is a distinctly Iliadic feature. Richard Janko in his commentary on *Iliad* 16 has an illuminating discussion of why Zenodotus athetised

6. Homeric Repetitions

Table 11. Arming scenes

	Il. 3 Paris	*Il.* 11 Agamemnon	*Il.* 16 Patroklos	*Il.* 19 Achilles	*Il.* 15 Teukros	*Od.* 22 Odysseus
greaves	330	17	131	369		
	331	18	132	370		
armour	332	19	133	371	479 =	=122
source of armour	333	(20-8)	134			
sword	334	~29	135	372		
more about sword		(30-31)				
shield	335	-32	136	373		
more about shield		(33-40)		(374-9)		
helmet	336	~41	137	(379-83)	480	123
helmet tassel	337	42	138		481	124
trying out the armour				(383-6)		
spear(s)	~338	~43	~139	387	~482	~125
more about spears			140			
			141-4	388-91		

the passage in the Patroklos scene and Aristarchus in the Achilles scene (Kirk 1985, 3:335). Much of the history of Homeric scholarship is epitomised in this disagreement. One may despair of the possibility of discovering which of two passages is earlier, and one may judge that both belong where they are. But that does not change the fact that one is the source of the other.

Clustering provides corroborative evidence for the view that the single Odyssean version of the pattern is likely to be a reuse of the Iliadic passage: both the Teukros and Odysseus scenes include phrases that sound innocuous but are not in fact found elsewhere:

alla mnêsômetha charmês (15.477 = Od. 22.146)
Let us remember battle

bê d' ienai mala d' ôka (15 483 = Od. 22.246)
He went quickly

A complex system of interrelated repetitions is found in a number of scenes that describe sacrificial meals. The following are the main scenes:

The ritual meal of reconciliation after Chryseis has been restored to her father (1.458-69)
The feasting of the Achaean chieftains after the nearly disastrous assembly (2.421-32)
The feasting of the Achaean chieftains after the duel of Hektor and Aias (7.317-20)

159

The sacrifice of a cow to Athene by Nestor (*Od.* 3.430-63)
The futile sacrifice to propitiate Helios after his cattle have been slaughtered (*Od.* 12.359-65)
The sacrificial meal prepared by Eumaios for the beggar (*Od.* 14.418-38)
A meal Telemachos and Odysseus share at the house of Eumaios (*Od.* 16.478-80)
The feasting at the house of Autolykos after the child Odysseus has been injured by a boar (*Od.* 19.420-7)

Table 12. Ritual and meal scenes

	Il. 1	*Il.* 2	*Od.* 3	*Od.* 12	*Il.* 7	*Od.* 19	*Od.* 14	*Od.* 16
the animal		402			314			
		403			315	420		
summary preparation					316	421		
barley casting	458	421						
skinning	459	422		(359)				
cut thigh pieces	460	423	(456-7)	360				
put raw meat on folds	461	424	458	361				
burn thigh	462	(425)	459	(362)				
pieces and libation	463	(426)	460	(363)				
tasting vitals	464	427	461	364				
putting meat on spits	465	428	462	365	~317	~422	430	
roasting the meat	466	429			318	423	431	
preparations finished	467	430			319			478
they feasted	468	431			320	425		479
honouring a special guest					~321		~437	
after eating enough	469	432			323			480

In Table 12 I have grouped passages so as to make their relationships more easily visible. Several points very clearly emerge from this table. First, the accounts in *Iliad* 1 and 2 are much the fullest and are virtually identical. Second, the less complete accounts stand in quite precise relationships to each other. Thus the sacrifice at Nestor's palace and on the island of Thrinakia are quite different in some ways. The former is the most elaborate ritual description in Homer, and the latter is an explicitly mutilated account in which you learn that they poured libations with water since they had no wine. But both pick a sequence of lines from the middle of the full description. By contrast, the feasts in *Iliad* 7 and *Odyssey* 19 select lines from the end of the full description and splice them to the beginning with a special and shared connecting line.

The case that with regard to these six scenes we are in a world of cutting and pasting is strengthened by the fact that there are other meal preparation scenes in which this strict pattern is not followed. Even in the tabulated materials, the sacrifice at Nestor's palace and the meal at the cottage of Eumaios for the most part go their own way (and share some interesting features with each other). The meal prepared by Patroklos for the Achaean delegates (9.205-22) has no parallel, but ends with the very Odyssean meal closing couplet in which the act of eating occurs literally between the lines (9.91-2, 221-2, 24.627-8; *Od.* 8x):

> *hoi d' ep' oneiath' hetoima prokeimena cheiras iallon.*
> *autar epei posios kai edêtuos ex eron hento,*

> They put their hands to the good things that lay ready before them.
> But when they had put aside their desire for eating and drinking,

The meal finally shared by Priam and Achilles is in narrative terms a cursory affair. It begins with two spitting and roasting lines from *Iliad* 7, and ends with the meal closing couplet (24.623-4 = 7.317-8; 627-8 = 9.221-2). But in the middle we find these lines, whose components are not found elsewhere in the *Iliad* (24.625-6 = 9.216-7)

> *(Patroklos men| Automedôn d' ara) siton helôn epeneime trapezêi*
> *kalois en kaneoisin, atar krea neimen Achilleus.*

> (Patroklos|Automedon) took the bread and set it out on a table
> in fair baskets, while Achilleus served the meats.

If we think of Patroklos as a ghostly and intertextual presence, the meal in *Iliad* 24 turns out to be an abbreviated but poignantly reminiscent version of the earlier meal in Achilles' tent.

A four-line block describing washing and libation appears in three different scenes:

The decision to send a delegation to Achilles (9.175-8)
Telemachos' visit to Nestor (*Od.* 3.338-42)
Odysseus as beggar asks permission to try the bow (Od. 21.270-3)

Parts of that block of lines appear in three other scenes:

The feasting after the successful return of Chryseis (1.470-1)
Athene's visit to Telemachos (*Od.* 1.146-8)
Odysseus at the court of the Phaiakians (*Od.* 7.183-4)

Table 13 shows the pattern:

Table 13. Libation scenes

	Il. 9	*Od.* 3	*Od.* 21	*Il.* 1	*Od.* 1	*Od.* 7
heralds bring water	~175	335	270		146	
young men bring wine	176	339	271	~470	148	
bowls are filled	177	340	272	471		183
pouring and drinking	178	342	~273		184	

The meal and feasting scenes are the most extended web of repeated lines shared between the *Iliad* and *Odyssey*. As such they provide important evidence for how to think about the relationship of the two epics. If you think that the verbatim repetition of lines in sequence is simply part of a tradition of oral verse-making, there is no problem. Nor is there a problem if you think that the passages are in fact interdependent but that they are the work of the same poet. Problems arise if on the one hand you think that these passages are interdependent but on the other hand you believe that different but single authors composed each poem. You then need to account not only for the general relationship between two unknown poets but, and perhaps more interestingly, you need to answer the question why verbal resemblances between the poems cluster in certain parts of the *Iliad*, and particularly in the framing books, a question to which we will return.

A quick glance at a particular type of feasting scene in the *Odyssey* usefully draws attention to some patterns of repetition not found in the *Iliad*. The most often repeated long Homeric repetition is a seven-line passage describing how a maid brings water for washing hands, the table is set and food is put before the guest. All seven lines are repeated once (*Od.* 1.136-42, 4.52-8), and the first five lines appear in four other Odyssean books (7.172-6, 10-368-72, 15.135-9, 17.91-5). With one exception, the component lines of this passage do not occur in other contexts, and one can say with great certainty that this block of lines was composed on one occasion and then copied in other environments. Repetition of this kind does not occur in the *Iliad*.

Repetition clusters

We have seen in the previous sections that long repetitions are not easily accounted for in terms of an idiom principle. They yield much more readily to a 'cut-and-paste' model of composition, which directly or indirectly makes writing an agent in the process of composition. While this evidence is persuasive, it is also limited and open to a very simple 'so what?' objection. By the count of the Chicago Homer, ~1,400 lines of the *Iliad* consist of repetitions of two or more lines. Once you adjust for the overcounting – much less for long repetitions – and subtract the odd but unproblematic 'explicit' repetitions you are left with 500-700 lines that may stand in some need of explanation. Some of these lines are more consequential than others. If you remove the lines about Achilles' spear from the arming of Patroklos or Achilles, you make a significant local change, but the larger narrative is not disturbed. The two occurrences of Agamemnon's 'cut and run' speech each begin a very consequential sequence of events, and there is no local surgery to fix this problem, if it is a problem. But the majority of long repetitions are more like the lines about Achilles' spear than the 'cut and run' speech. So you could concede that the evidence of long lines is quite compelling, but that it does not prove very much beyond the likely origin of the ~5% of lines in the *Iliad* from which it is derived.

A more substantial challenge to the idiomatic status of at least some repetitions is posed by evidence of clustering. There are ~4600 phrases or passages that are repeated once in the *Iliad*. If you measure the distances between the first and second occurrence and use a statistical normality test to review their distribution you discover a marked 'neighbourhood effect.' In almost a quarter of all cases the second occurrence of phrase is found within 600 lines of the first occurrence, and in 700 cases (15%) it is found within 200 lines. You can argue that a situation that prompts the use of an idiom will also create the conditions for its reuse. Or you can argue, more plausibly in my view, that particular situation prompt new coinages from conventional materials, and that such coinages are likely to be reused immediately. Explicit repetitions almost by definition are repeated within a short distance. But there are not enough of them to account for the marked presence of a neighbourhood effect.

A more complex and telling form of clustering happens when two doublets are found within a short distance of each other in both their occurrences. Some cases of such 'doublet pairs' will happen on a random basis. But if there are too many of them you discount coincidence and look for the reasons that cause the clustering of doublet pairs in certain sections of the *Iliad*. Measuring such clusters is a little more complicated, but its results provide quite striking quantitative confirmation of observations made by Homeric scholars since the nineteenth century.

You begin with a list of all Iliadic doublets, measure the distance of each phrase from every other phrase, and through a series of filtering steps end up with some 5,000 cases where two phrases are repeated within 200 lines of each other in two different parts of the *Iliad*. You now classify these doublet pairs in terms of the books of the *Iliad* between which they establish a link, e.g. 3-7 or 5-8. There are 276 such 'book links'. Now it is a straightforward matter to count the number of doublet pairs in each of these book links, but there are two complicating factors. First, since the books of the *Iliad* are of unequal length, the text areas created by each combination differ considerably in size, from 885 lines for 3-19 to 1806 lines for 5-23. Thus you will want to normalise counts to some measure, such as count per 1,000 lines. Secondly, you can either count just the number of links or you can factor in the length of the repetitions and express your results as the number of lines per 1,000 lines that contain repetition links.

The two methods give results that differ in intelligible ways. Both methods show that repetition links are very unevenly distributed. The standard deviations are large relative to the mean, and the top values are much larger than the median. Factoring in the length of repetition accentuates difference: the ratio of top value to median is 6, as compared with 3.5 for repetition counts.

Table 14. Doublet pairs by count and combined length

	Mean	StDev	Min	Q1	Med	Q3	Max
RepCount per 1,000 lines	13	7.8	0	7.2	12.0	17.8	41.7
RepLength per 1,000 lines in hexameter feet	8.9	7.0	0	4.3	7.0	11.5	41.8

If we run a normality test on repetition counts, we see five clear outliers: 5-16 (41.7), 11-16 (37.3), 16-17 (36.9), 13-15 (36.6), and 20-21 (34.1). If we run the same test on repetition length, the number of values identified as statistical outliers increases to 18, and the five top values are 3-7 (41.8), 5-8 (38.9), 11-16 (35.9), 4-8 (32.2), and 11-17 (31.1).

These figures make considerable sense. They identify the resemblances between the Paris/Menelaos and Hektor/Aias duels of *Iliad* 3 and 7 as a highly unusual case (Kirk 1978). Not far behind are the notorious echoes between *Iliad* 5 and 8, which have exercised scholars since the nineteenth century.

Table 15 shows the dozen top book links by length and compares them with the rank by count. The first thing to note is that doublet pairs are predominantly a feature of the fighting books. All the book links in the top dozen come from the fighting books of the *Iliad,* and in the 70 book links of the top quartile, there are only eight that do not involve fighting books.

Secondly, you notice the special status of Books 8, 11, and 16, which appear three or four times. Third, you notice the discrepancy in count vs. length ranking for the book combination 4-8. If you look at 4-8 together with 5-8 and 3-7 you notice that in these cases – and only in these cases – the length/count ratio is significantly higher than 1. *Iliad* 8 is in fact a statistical outlier in its frequency of long repetitions: 17.5% of its lines – almost three times the average of 6.5% – consist of repeated passage longer than two lines.

The main lesson, however, to draw from these crude quantitative tests is that the web of Iliadic repetition links creates quite specific relationships between particular books. These relationships are sometimes ignored in criticism that focuses on traditional or oral methods of composition. They were very much on the minds of earlier generations of scholars, and the close agreement between their observations and digitally assisted statistical tests is quite striking.

Table 15. *Iliad* books with the highest frequency of shared repetitions

Iliad books	*Rank by length*	*Length per 1000 lines in hexameter feet*	*Rank by count*	*Count per 1000 lines*
3-7	1	41.76	6	31.81
5-8	2	38.92	15	28.49
11-16	3	35.88	2	37.32
4-8	4	32.16	86	16.23
11-17	5	31.10	14	28.59
8-11	6	30.96	8	31.14
20-21	7	28.24	5	34.11
16-17	8	26.26	3	36.86
13-15	9	25.58	4	36.64
11-20	10	25.20	22	25.17
13-16	11	24.57	23	24.65
5-16	12	24.28	1	41.67

Name association in fighting lines

In the previous section we looked at the aggregate effect of doublet pairs and the evidence they provide for interdependence among different fighting sections in the *Iliad.* This is a very abstract or distant form of reading, but it provides a useful frame for evaluating observations at the ground level of the text. The fighting books of the *Iliad* are full of mini-scenarios in which individual warriors inflict or avoid injury. There is no reason why such mini-scenarios should be associated with particular warriors. In practice, however, we find a lot of 'name association': if a mini-scenario is repeated there is a strong likelihood that it will either involve the same or a closely related warrior. There is only a limited number of warriors who appear with any frequency – a dozen Achaeans and half a dozen Trojans. Thus you would expect some name association on a random basis. But name association is a very pervasive phenomenon, and it suggests that many repetitions of mini-scenarios owe their existence to the fact that a particular sequence of lines or events is composed in one context and then transferred to a closely related context. We are not dealing with a situation in which $r_1, r_2 \dots r_n$ are independent creations of a motif R. Instead the genesis of r_1 and r_2 involves a specific relationship between two contexts. It is, however, very difficult to determine just what went on in the mind of a composer who remembered one passage while composing another. There is a wide range of options from unconscious reminiscence to purposeful allusion.

It is also important to remember that proof of interdependence and proof of priority are very different things. Evidence that is sufficient to establish interdependence is usually insufficient to establish priority. Interdependence can often be established with a high degree of confidence through close comparisons of passages in their contexts. But this internal evidence is of little use for priority arguments, and in fact proof of priority typically requires external evidence that establishes which passage came first. But the pervasive presence of interdependent repetitions puts significant constraints on plausible hypotheses for the composition of the Homeric poems and is strong proof that the composition of many passages presupposes a mind that remembers the existence of other passages in their current form or something very close to it.

Aeneas
In five of six longish doublets, a phrase is associated with Aeneas in both of its occurrences.

1. *bê [d'|rh']imen an te machên kai ana klonon encheiaôn* (5.167 = 20.319) This line describes a warrior walking through the battle and throng of spears. It is used of Aeneas when he goes in search of Pandaros, and later it is used of Poseidon when he sets out to rescue Aeneas from Achilles.
2. *mastiga kai hênia sigaloenta/ dexai egô d' hippôn apobêsomai ophra machômai* (5.226-7 = 17.479-80). A warrior asks another warrior to take the reins and guide the horses while he descends to fight on foot. In the first occurrence Aeneas speaks to Pandaros. In the battle over the dead Patroklos Automedon asks Alimedon. They are then attacked by Hektor and Aeneas.
3. After killing Pandaros, Diomedes picks up a huge stone, which 'two men as they now are could not lift' and hurls it at Aeneas. In his encounter with Achilles, Aeneas picks up and hurls the same stone (5.302-4 = 20.285-7).
4. *aichmê d' Aineiao kradainomenê kata gaiês/ ôichet', epei rh' halion stibarês apo cheiros orousen.* A spear thrown by Aeneas at Idomeneus or his henchman Meriones misses its target, and is stuck in the ground where it continues to shake (13.504-5 =

16.614-15). The genitive forms of other warrior names would fit into the metrical slot 210-220-310-321 taken up by *Aineiao*.

5. *entha ken aute Trôes arêïphilôn hup' Achaiôn Ilion eisanebêsan analkeiêisi damentes*. The weak Trojans would have retreated back to the city from the warlike Achaeans if Helenos or Apollo had not given advice to the team of Aeneas and Hektor (6.73-4 =17.319-20).

6. *all' age mêketi tauta legômetha nêputioi hôsm* 'let us not talk foolishly'. This is spoken by Idomeneus on one occasion and by Aeneas on another (13.292 = 20.244). There is no name association here, unless you want to associate the passage with Aeneas' attacks on Idomeneus and Meriones (no. 4), which is a stretch.

Aias, Antilochos and Menelaos
Aias is 'the greatest of the Achaean warriors after Achilles' (17.280). Once Agamemnon, Diomedes, and Odysseus are injured, he is the only major warrior left and dominates fighting on the Achaean side. Given his ubiquity, one might expect repeated phrases to link him to everybody and therefore to nobody in particular. But in practice a network of doublets and triplets ties him to himself or to Antilochos and Menelaos.

1. His first victim is Simoeisios, a minor warrior seen briefly through an almost pastoral perspective, who 'did not return his parents' nurturing care' (*oude tokeusi/ threptra philois apedôke, minunthadios de hoi aiôn/ epleth' hup' Aiantos megathumou douri damenti*). The same haunting phrase occurs in the fighting over the body of Patroklos when Aias kills Hippothoös (4.477-9 = 17.301-30).

2. The beginning of the Hippothoös scene includes a two-liner that had first appeared in the death of Kleitos, a warrior killed by Teukros in direct response to encouragement by his half-brother Aias (15.449-50 = 17.291-2).

3. Within twenty lines of the Simoeisios scene, there is a three-liner describing the death of a warrior at the hands of Antilochos, and a victim of Aias is described by the same three-liner at the opening of Book 6 (4.459-61 = 6.9-11).

4. *Aias d' aspida nuxen epalmenos:* [*hê de|oude*] *diapro/ êluthen encheiê, stuphelixe de min memaôta* (7.260-1 = 12.404-5) This two-liner describes how Aias' attack does or does not pierce the shield of Hektor or Sarpedon but stuns him anyhow. There is no other major warrior whose name could be combined with the phrase *d' aspida nuxen epalmenos*, and from that perspective one might think of this as a conventional Aias phrase. But this constraint does not apply to the other components of this two-liner, which easily could, but in fact do not, occur elsewhere.

5. A similar argument for an Aias specific line can be made about a line that describes him approaching and carrying his shield as if if it were a tower: *Aias d' enguthen êlthe pherôn sakos êüte purgon* (7.219 =11.485 = 17.128). The middle of that phrase does not occur elsewhere in the *Iliad* but is found in an Odyssean line that describes a herald bringing a lyre for the singer Demodokos: *kêrux d' enguthen êlthe pherôn phorminga ligeian* (*Od.* 8.261). It is very tempting to see in the substitution of the lyre for the shield a purposeful allusion to a particularly heroic and Iliadic line.

6. A line from the gift exchange between Aias and Hektor describes the trophy Diomedes receives after the competition with Aias for the armour of Sarpedon (7.304 = 23.825)

7. The retreating lion, one of only three repeated similes, is used of Aias' retreat in *Iliad* 11 and of Menelaos following the command of Aias (11.550-5 = 17.659-64).

8. Within thirty lines of the Aias-lion passage is a line about a warrior who retreats but turns when he reaches his companions. This is used of either Aias, Antilochos or Menelaos (11.595 = 15.591 = 17.114).

9. A line about a warrior cheering on his companions is first used of Paris, but then of Aias and Antilochos (13.767 = 17.117 = 17.683)

Against these nine passages we must set five passages in which there appears to be no name association between the different characters. These passages include Aias, Hektor, or Thoas beaten back by a group of opponents (4.535 = 5.626 = 13.148), a short lion simile applied to Diomedes and Aias (5.782 = 7.256), a stone picked up by Aias and Athene (7.264 = 21.403), and a line about 'purple death and strong Moira' (5.82 = 16.333 = 20.476). The evidence as a whole shows quite persuasively that if Aias is associated with a doublet or triplet on one occasion, a majority of cases will display an association with him or a related character on the other occasions.

The case is almost as strong for Antilochos. In addition to the four passages that associate him with Aias and Menelaos, a line about a warrior gasping for breath while falling off his chariot is in both occurrences a victim of Antilochos (5.585 = 13.399). But three lines about Antilochos in *Iliad* 13 are used elsewhere of other characters that are not related to Antilochos (5.324 = 13.401, 13.371 = 13.397 4.522 = 13.548).

The association between Menelaos and Aias is most obvious in the rich web of repetitions that link the Paris/Menelaos and Hektor/Aias duels. A three-liner describing Menelaos' counterattack on Paris reappears when Menelaos counterattacks Euphorbos (3.348-350 = 17.44-46).

Menelaos and Agamemnon
There are several striking instances of name association between the brothers Agamemnon and Menelaos.

1. Menelaos and Agamemnon receive the same five-line plea from a warrior asking to be ransomed (6.46-50 = 11.131-135).

2. A two-liner about a spear cast by the son of Atreus missing its target applies once to Menelaos and once to Agamemnon (11.232-3 = 13.604-5).

3. Menelaos' most significant – and not entirely unproblemtical – achievement is the killing of Euphorbos, the very young warrior who first injured. One passage from this scene is also found in Agamemnon's killing of the notably young Iphidamas (11.235 = 17.48). Menelaos is compared to a lion killing a cow on that occasion, as is Agamemnon in his pursuit of the Trojans in *Iliad* 11. Two lines from the Agamemnon simile appear in the Menelaos simile – a striking parallel given the rarity of long repetitions between similes (11.175-6 = 17.63-4).

4. A slightly displaced association of Menelaos with Agamemnon appears in the battle over Patroklos' body when Automedon first calls Aias and Menelaos to his help and then attacks a Trojan in a four-line passage of which the first two lines echo Menelaos' attack on Paris (3.355-6 = 17.516-17) and the second two lines appeared previously in a description of a Trojan killed by Agamemnon (5.538-9 = 17.518-19).

Diomedes

Diomedes appears in some twenty long doublets or triplets. A complex web of name associations links him to himself, Achilles, Patroklos, and Hektor as their common enemy. This web, covering at least two thirds of those passages, is more easily understood by remembering the major scenes it involves:

Pandaros and Aeneas team up against Diomedes but he kills the former and wounds the latter (5.166ff.)
Hektor and Diomedes nearly encounter each other (5.590 ff.)
Diomedes and Glaukos recognise each other and do not fight (6.119 ff.)
Diomedes fights Hektor and taunts him (11.343 ff.)
Achilles and Aeneas talk and fight (20.176 ff.)

1. The career of Pandaros is a foreshortened version of the Trojan War. He re-enacts the offence of Paris when he breaks the truce and injures Menelaos with an arrow. His death at the hands of Diomedes and Athene is a proleptic version of the death of Hektor. Diomedes' final words to him are identical to words Achilles addresses to Hektor (5.288-9 = 22.266-7):

> *prin g' ê heteron ge pesonta*
> *haimatos asai Arêa talaurinon polemistên.*

but one or the other must fall before then
to glut with his blood Ares the god who fights under the shield's guard.

The latter part of that passage is also used by the poet to describe Achilles when he sets out on this blood-thirsty quest for Hektor (20.78).
2. Pandaros falls out of his chariot while his armour clatters about. This happens to another victim of Diomedes (5.294 = 8.2.260).
3. Pandaros' horses shy away and his strength and life are dissolved. This is also the fate of Hektor's first charioteer killed by Diomedes (5.295-6 = 8.122-3).
4. A counterfactual speculation about impending disaster involves Diomedes in both of its occurrences (8.130 = 11.310).
5. A variant in the first person plural of a common cheerleading line is spoken by Diomedes on one occasion and by Hera when she and Athene set out on a support mission that focuses on Diomedes (4.418 = 5.718).
6. After Diomedes kills Pandaros he turns back an attack by Aeneas. A three-liner describes how he hurls a huge stone at Aeneas, and a two-liner describes how Aeneas is stunned by the blow. When Apollo comes to the rescue of Aeneas, Diomedes attacks him three times before yielding to the god's warning. Somewhat later in the same book Hektor attacks and causes Diomedes to shudder. Elements from these two scenes reappear in the scene that leads to Diomedes' injury. Hektor once more attacks him (5.590-1 = 11.343-4). Diomedes 'shudders', as he had done on the previous occasion (5.596 = 11.345), but proceeds to stun him with his spear just as he had previously stunned Aeneas with a stone (5.309-10 = 11.355-6).
7. After Diomedes has stunned Hektor with a spear throw he taunts him in a six-line

passage, which is repeated verbatim by Achilles shouting after Hektor, when Apollo physically removes him from battle (11.362-7 = 20.449-54).

8. *Iliad* 6 contains the famous scene in which Glaukos and Diomedes recognise each as other as guest friends and exchange presents rather than fight. Several lines from their encounter turn up in the scene in which Aeneas and Achilles exchange both words and blows. A line about the warriors approaching one another with hostile intent is not only used on those two occasions, but also describes the encounter of Diomedes and Aias at the Funeral Games for Patroklos (6.120 = 20.159 = 23.814).

9. A two-liner of extremely conventional materials appears in that combination of phrases only in the Glaukos-Diomedes scene and in the encounters of Achilles with Aeneas, Asteropaios and Hektor (6.121-2 = 20.176-7 = 21.148 = 22.248).

10. Diomedes and Achilles boast that the children of unhappy parents encounter their might (6.127 = 21.151).

11. The Trojan interlocutor in both scenes offers an elaborate genealogy and concludes it with the same line (6.150-1 = 20.213-14, 6.210 = 20.241).

12. When the encounter of Achilles and Aeneas turns to fighting, we recognise other Diomedes echoes. Aeneas throws at Achilles the stone Diomedes had thrown at him (5.302-4 = 20.285-7).

13. Agastrophos, a victim of Diomedes, is described in the same words as Polydoros, a victim of Achilles (11.343 = 20.412).

14. The association of Diomedes with Achilles that is apparent in these long repetitions also extends to Patroklos. Aeneas learns from Pandaros that Diomedes is a particularly threatening warrior, and in the same words Sarpedon wants to find out about the identity of a warrior who turns out to be Patroklos (5.175-6 = 16.424-5).

15. Patroklos attacks Sarpedon in a three-liner that precisely echoes Diomedes' attack on Phegeus (5.16-18 = 16.478-80).

16. Finally, Patroklos' attack on Troy and rebuff by Apollo are described in the same language as the attack by Diomedes on Aeneas (5.438-9 = 16.705-6; 5.443.444 = 16.710-11).

Compared with the wealth of passages that display strong name association, there is only a handful of long repetitions in which Diomedes is not paired in a significant fashion with another character:

1. There are two horse and chariot lines used of Diomedes and Hektor. They have no narrative interest but could be part of the Hektor-Diomedes pattern (4.366 = 11.198; 8.320 = 23.509).

2. Agamemnon, Diomedes, and Odysseus kill a warrior in a slightly varied three-liner (5.40-4 = 8.258-60 = 11.445-7).

3. A short simile comparing warriors to lions or boars is used of Diomedes and Aias (5.782-3 = 7.256-7).

4. The injured Agamemnon and Diomedes withdraw from battle in the identical two-liner. A neighbourhood effect is at work (11.273-4 = 11.399-40).

Hektor
Hektor is the most frequently named human character in the *Iliad*. He tends to be around whenever there is fighting of any kind, and there are about three dozen long

repetitions in which he is subject or object. There is an unusually large number of very long repetitions strongly or exclusively associated with him.

1. Take the following line that is repeated seven times and describes a warrior who responds to a speech by jumping off a chariot in full armour.

autika d' (4)
ê rha kai (2)   *ex ocheôn sun teuchesin alto chamaze*
Hektôr d' (1)

Represented in this fashion, this looks like a generic one-liner. But on a closer look it turns out that the line applies to Hektor on four of its seven occurrences. On three occasions it is part of a four-liner that extends into a fifth line and describes how Hektor rallies his troops (5.494-7, 6.103-6, 11.214-17). On a fourth occasion, it also describes Hektor's response to Poulydamas (12.81). But it is also used of Menelaos (3.29) about to challenge Paris, of Sarpedon (16.426), and of Diomedes (4.419).

2. Similarly, the one-liner *aneres este philoi, mnêsasthe de thouridos alkês is* virtually owned by Hektor. He uses it five times, and its remaining two occurrences are associated with Aias and Patroklos, as they rally the Achaeans and Myrmidons specifically against Hektor. The line typically concludes a three-liner that includes a speech tag and address phrase.

3. In the fighting of *Iliad* 8 Hektor loses a charioteer to Diomedes and another charioteer to Teukros in a repeated three-liner (8.122-4 = 8.314-17).

4. The fate of an overeager follower of Hektor, killed by Aias and Teukros is remembered in the same two-liner (15.449-50 = 17.291-2). Hektor's chariot moves nimbly among the Trojans and Achaeans (11.198 = 17.458).

5. The same line describes the horses of Achilles moving towards and away from Hektor (16.383 = 16.866).

6. A line about the even state of battle marks a shift of focus towards Hektor in both of its occurrences (12.436 =15.413).

7. A wonderful passage about the confusion of war sounds and missiles pouring against the enemy both times has Hektor and the Trojans as its agents (8.158-9 = 15.589-90).

8. Twice Hektor is the warrior angered by a spear that misses its target (14.406-7 = 22.291-2).

9. There is a handful of passages that are used of Hektor and a brother or other close relative. Thus the line describing Paris' challenge to Menelaos reappears in the duel of Hektor and Aias (3.20 = 7.40).

10. The elaborate stallion simile, one of three repeated similes, is used of Paris and Hektor (6.506-10 = 15.263-8).

11. The two brothers use the same line to assert their resolution not to flee (11.590 = 18.307).

12. Priam and Hektor issue identical instructions about appointing guards (7.371 = 18.299).

13. The injured Deiphobos and Hektor are carried out of battle in the same four-liner (13.535-8 = 14.429-32) .

6. Homeric Repetitions

The deep associations that link the deaths of Hektor and Patroklos have been discussed above (p. 64). Is it coincidental that a line about unbounded noise near the ships marks two turning points in the action, Hektor's smashing of the wall and Patroklos' entry into battle (12.471 = 16.296)? Catalogue killings by Hektor and Patroklos are introduced with the same line (15.328 = 16.306). A three-liner describes the smashed head of victims of the two warriors (16.412-14 = 16.578-80). Finally, it is noteworthy that the two human killers of Patroklos, Euphorbos and Hektor, are killed by a spear that cuts through the soft part of the neck (17.49 = 22.327).

Against this web of passages with strong name associations, some of them extended, there are some shorter passages about which not much can be said, although a neighbourhood effect is at work in a few of them:

Aias, Hektor, and Thoas are rebuffed in trying to despoil the body of a warrior they have killed (4.535 = 15.626 = 13.148)

Agamemnon and Hektor pursue the fleeing enemy (8.342 = 11.178) and fight along the wall (11.48 = 12.76)

Diomedes and Hektor stand near their chariots (4.366 = 11.198).

Aias and Hektor say that they will go into battle and return (11.368 = 13.752).

Odysseus and Hektor share a scolding line (14.95 = 17.173)

A line about a spear shaft driven in the ground is associated with Idomeneus, Meriones, and Hektor (13.443 = 16.612 = 17.528)

Hektor and the dying Sarpedon express concern about the Achaeans despoiling the body of the fallen warrior (15.427 = 16.499)

Athene and Hektor express their hope about dead enemies being food for dogs and birds (8.379-380 = 13.831-832).

Perhaps the most famous of multi-line repetitions associated with Hektor is the sublime passage in which he predicts the fall of Troy to Andromache (6.447-9 = 4.163-5):

eu gar egô tode oida kata phrena kai kata thumon:
essetai êmar hot' an pot' olôlêi Ilios hirê
kai Priamos kai laos eümmeliô Priamoio,

For I know this thing well in my heart, and my mind knows it.
There will come a day when sacred Ilion shall perish,
and Priam, and the people of Priam of the strong ash spear,

This is of course not a fighting passage, but it is repeated on another occasion by Agamemnon when he musters the Achaean troops. The two passages are almost certainly interdependent, and their repetition raises difficulties for most modern readers, who are likely to find its anticipation by Agamemnon a grating distraction from the effect it has in the mouth of Hektor. This is one of the most interesting illustrations of how the study of Homeric repetitions shapes and is shaped by an aesthetics of reading.

An argument from silence

It is, I think, apparent from this survey that repeated long phrases are much more likely to be associated with particular names or individuals than their wording requires. Anybody could be killed by a spear piercing the soft part of the neck, but in practice it is the two human killers of Patroklos. Because there is a limited number of notable warriors in the *Iliad*, one would expect in a random distribution a certain number of name associations that give the appearance of thematic significance. But while it may be difficult to construct a formal probability model from the evidence, the survey shows that cases in which name association seems significant are much larger in number than cases where such association seems arbitrary.

A look at the aggregate of some patterns suggests that name association reduces variety of expressions that are theoretically possible. Consider the thirteen occasions in the *Iliad* where we find a phrase that goes

Seeing (him|them) + there (shuddered, rejoiced, scolded, noticed, pitied,) + name phrase 321-620.

An example is *ton de idôn rhigêse boên agathos Diomêdês* (5.596). The verb forms in this pattern are *eleêse* (3), *ôkteire* (3), *rhigêse* (3), *gêthêse* (2), *noêse* (1), *neikessen* (2). The agents are Achilles (3), Agamemnon (3), Zeus (2), Hera (1), Patroklos (1), Menestheus (1). Metrically and semantically any of the names could go with any of the verbs, but in fact the names and verbs are bound tightly to each other. The verb forms *eleêse* and *ôkteire* mean roughly 'took pity on', but the former is used of Zeus and Hera while the latter is used of Achilles or Patroklos. Only Agamemnon rejoices, and on two of three occasions Diomedes does the shuddering. There is probably some name association between Diomedes and the very minor character Menestheus: they are next in line to each other in Agamemnon's muster of the troops and they are both scolded by him (4.336, 4.368).

Another example of such restriction occurs in a type of phrase of the form

verse-initial nominative patronymic with caesura at position 210 + something.

An example is a line describing a spear cast in vain by a son of Atreus: *Atreïdês men hamarte, parai de hoi etrapet' enchos* (11.233 = 13.605). There are about 100 occurrences of 18 patronymics that fit this general pattern. There are 15 instances of repeated phrases, but there are only three Iliadic instances of a phrase being repeated with a different patronymic. In the Catalogue of the Ships we find a line that begins with either *Atreïdês* or *Priamidês* (2.577 ~ 2.817). In the aristeia of Achilles, there are two passages where *Pêleidês* substitutes for *Atreïdês* in passages from *Iliad* 3 and 11 (11.169 ~ 20.503, 3.364 ~ 21.272). Thus it appears that particular phrases are much more tightly coupled with particular names than one would expect in a mix-and-match mode of composition that allows for unrestricted combinations of phrases with name variables.

The Composition of the *Iliad*

The development of the epic poet

How did the *Iliad* come into being? I ask the question in a modified form: What processes of composition can plausibly account for the large-scale architectural coherence that critics since Aristotle have noticed as a distinctive feature of the *Iliad* and *Odyssey*? This version of the question has a strong 'unitarian' bias and reveals my affinity with those scholars who use the unified nature of our *Iliad* as their main argument for the position that it must have been the work of a single poet.

A plausible account of the composition of the *Iliad* must respect the constraints that different aspects of our knowledge of the poem exercise on each other. It must do justice to Parry's demonstration that the *Iliad* is rooted in a tradition of formulaic language and must respect more generally those aspects of Homeric art that 'oral criticism' has taught us to see. At the same time, the web of interdependent repetitions shows that some version of a 'cut and paste' mode of composition played an important role in the genesis of the poems as we read them today.

Oral poetry and the 'cut and paste' mode of composition are in themselves equally compatible with theories of single or multiple authorship. The large-scale structural coherence of the work is a strong 'argument from design' for single authorship. But it is hardly compelling. Analysts are fond of pointing to Gothic cathedrals, in which the work of many hands over centuries has elaborated a single design. The honest unitarian should admit that there is an element of faith in his position.

The mutual constraints of these elements point to a process of gradual composition, the stages of which are to some extent recoverable. The author of the *Iliad* – whom I continue to call 'Homer', although that was almost certainly not his name – grew up in a tradition of oral verse-making that provided him with an extraordinarily capable instrument, the language of hexametric narrative. He learnt his craft and assembled a repertoire of familiar stories to be recited on festive occasions of various kinds. A typical performance would last an hour or two; perhaps some were as long as Odysseus' narrative at the court of the Phaeacians. But it is difficult to imagine an institutional context that would support more extended narratives. The poet's repertoire in all probability did not consist of fixed texts, but we may also assume that two performances by him of a given story would resemble one another more closely than either one would a telling of the 'same' story by another singer. Such resemblances would include the scope of the story as a part of the total repertoire, the weighting of elements within that scope, and aspects of diction and style. Howard Gardner in his appealing 'anatomy of creativity' has pointed to a latent decade as a recurring element in the careers of highly creative individuals. We should allow the young poet at least a decade to develop into a master of his craft, with a complete repertoire and a style and excellence recognisable by his audience.

Whether or not we want to attribute 'innovative' tendencies to Homer, we must think of him not only as a master of his craft but also as a supremely gifted individual who, like Shakespeare, Bach or Mozart, could not help transforming whatever he touched. Aristotle saw the particular excellence of the Homeric poems in their control of large-scale narrative, and since this quality distinguishes them from all other predominantly oral poems it is reasonable to look for the specific quality of Homer's genius in his sense for large-scale narrative. We arrive thus at the situation of a master-poet who 'decides' at a certain point to extend the scope of heroic narrative and to compose a work of encyclopaedic dimensions that would incorporate much of his repertoire. The context and motives of that decision are shrouded in darkness, but some speculation may be permitted. One aspect of a poet's greatness is his ability to give authoritative expression to the deepest concerns of his age. Dante and Milton, the most autobiographical of the great epic poets, were open about the relationship of their poetic ambition to the religious and political conflicts of medieval Florence and seventeenth-century England. Did Homer respond similarly to the sense of pan-Hellenic identity of which we find other traces in the eighth century BC? Did this response trigger the break with the tradition that led to the *Iliad* as a poem much longer and more complex than any of its predecessors, or should we look for the cause of this transformation merely in the individual excellence and ambition of a 'monumental composer' (Kirk, 1962, 280)? Was the Ionian poet from Asia Minor attracted to the story of Troy because, like the author of the *Aeneid*, he wanted to account for his cultural indebtedness to a homeland beyond the sea? Such questions are of course unanswerable, but it is a fact that within a generation or two of its composition the *Iliad* became a founding text of Greek culture. It is tempting to relate this historical achievement to an intention and to see Homer's ambitious design for a monumental poem prompted by the desire to give shape to the growing Hellenic consciousness of his age. At the very least, there is no reason to use his status as an oral poet to deny the presence in his career of motives that are more clearly articulated and more easily traced against a known historical background in the works of Vergil, Dante and Milton.

If it took Homer at least a decade to become a master-poet, the execution of his design for a grand poem must have been the work of further years, perhaps decades. Let us assume, for argument's sake, that the composition of the *Iliad* lasted as long as the Trojan War. We can hardly imagine Homer delaying 'publication' to the moment of perfection. Nor can we imagine him reciting from work in progress, as Vergil did with the *Aeneid*. Neither of these alternatives is easily reconciled with what we know from the *Odyssey* and other heroic traditions about the circumstances of a professional singer. Instead we should think of a gradual process of composition in which the poem was always complete after a fashion, having a beginning, a middle and an end. Thus, during Homer's maturity there was always something like a 'complete *Iliad*', but it was always expanding. A distant analogue would be the composition of Goethe's *Faust*, of which there also was a complete/incomplete version over a period of fifty years. We may assume that the plan and scope of the work underwent modifications over the years but that it was part of the poet's genius to have conceived of a design capable of such expansion.

The assumption of an evolutionary process in which an always complete *Iliad* was always expanding is eminently compatible with the one distinctly oral feature of

Homeric narrative that may justly be said to operate with equal force at all narrative levels. G.S. Kirk (1976, 78), who has given the best description of this feature, calls it the 'cumulative style' (other names for it are 'additive' or 'paratactic'). Unlike a Latin period, the Homeric sentence is complete from a very early stage but can be greatly elaborated through additions. The first paragraph of the *Iliad* is a good example.

Mênin aeide thea is a complete sentence to which the poet adds elements each of which leaves the sentence complete but capable of further expansion:

mênin aeide thea Pêlêïadeô Achilêos oulomenên	Sing, goddess, the anger of Peleus' son Achilleus and its devastation
hê muri' Achaiois alge' ethêke	which put pains thousandfold upon the Achaians
pollas d' iphthimous psuchas Aïdi proïapsen hêrôôn,	hurled in their multitudes to the house of Hades strong souls of heroes
autous de helôria teuche kunessin oiônoisi te pasi	but gave their bodies to be the delicate feasting of dogs, of all birds,
Dios d' eteleieto boulê,	and the will of Zeus was accomplished
ex hou dê ta prôta diastêtên erisante	since that time when first there stood in division of conflict
Atreïdês te anax andrôn kai dios Achilleus.	Atreus' son the lord of men and brilliant Achilleus.

The forward surge and cumulative force of this magnificent paragraph are not arrested by any suspension of meaning except for the very end, where the postponement of the subject into the next line creates a two-line semantic unit with great closing force. This procedure, in which modification is achieved without 'revision' or loss of forward motion, clearly has its origin in a technique of oral verse-making.

A procedure that allows for continuous forward composition also tolerates subsequent insertions of additional materials: the joints of a narrative stretch composed in this fashion are rarely so tight that something cannot be squeezed in. Take the example of the Catalogue of the Ships, which shows the technique operating at several levels. This is almost certainly a piece of narrative that existed once in a somewhat different form and was inserted in its present place after minor modifications that themselves took the form of additions. At one time the Catalogue may have been a simple muster of troops. The text acquires its naval character through the addition after each contingent of a line specifying the number of ships. We would not miss these lines if they had not been transmitted. Moreover, at the beginning of the Catalogue the poet invokes the Muse to tell him the names of the leaders rather than the crowd, but the invocation ends with a detachable specification of the leaders as the leaders of the ships (2.493).

The Catalogue certainly was composed to reflect the Achaean forces at the beginning rather than at the end of the war. For instance, it lists Protesilaos, the first man to die on Trojan soil, and Philoktetes, who was left behind on Lemnos. The resulting editorial problem was solved by addition rather than subtraction: to the mention of these two leaders is in each case added a detachable commentary (2.699-709, 721-8) that brings the story up to date. Once adjusted by means of appropriate additions, the whole Catalogue becomes an addition that is inserted at a joint in the narrative.

The epic that accumulated over ten or more years as a consequence of the poet's expansion of an elastic design differed from his previous repertoire in gradually turning into a fixed text to be recited verbatim rather than composed anew with each performance. It is very likely that the concept of a fixed text entered Greek culture through the creation of the *Iliad* as a poem of such scope, excellence and complexity that it had to be protected from the vagaries of performance. Many Homeric scholars believe – and, I think, rightly – that the existence of the *Iliad* as a fixed text is closely related to the introduction of writing into Greek culture some two generations before the life of Homer. But the concept of a fixed text does not depend on writing, and it would be misleading to think of the availability of writing as the chief cause of the transformation of an oral tradition into the monumental epic.

Shortly after Homer, the heroic tradition went into a tailspin from which it never recovered. Following a line of argument that W.J. Bate in *The Burden of the Past* (p. 82) has traced back to Velleius Paterculus, G.S. Kirk (1976, 2-3) has argued that the cause of that decline lies in the very excellence of the *Iliad* and *Odyssey*. These poems exhausted the possibilities of the genre, discouraged creative imitation, and replaced innovation with preservation. Like tragedy three centuries later, the epic died after a burst of stupendous energy only to survive as a fixed monument. If we accept this plausible analysis, for which the history of culture provides many analogues, the concept of a fixed text is the product of a collusion between Homer and his audience. The author, after developing from the fluid tradition a repertoire that over the years had grown more stable, took the further step of refashioning and freezing this repertoire into a monumental poem. The audience responded to this extraordinary ambition and recognised the poem as a 'classic' in need of preservation. The birth of the *Iliad* was the death of the heroic tradition.

It is likely that Homer saw the possibility that writing offered to his ambitions and that he used it to create a text that differed from earlier heroic poetry in being longer, more complex, and fixed. But Homer the writer did not unlearn the skills of oral verse-making. On the contrary, the technical constraints of writing in his days reinforced the procedure of cumulative composition. Even in an age of Xerox machines and word processors revision of a text in the light of subsequent changes is a tedious, complicated and error-prone business. In Homer's day, when papyrus must have been scarce and writing laborious, a text once written represented an investment one would touch only with reluctance. On the basis of such considerations G.P. Goold has developed a model of the 'progressive fixation' of the Homeric texts, and some such procedure most readily accounts for the abundance of doublets in the text. Above all, such a hypothesis resolves the paradox that the *Iliad* is both a magnificently designed and, by our standards, a 'poorly edited' poem.

Homer possessed a copy of the *Iliad*, to which he added over the years until it reached its present shape. The existence of a text that was at any one time fixed but subject to further additions had an effect on the nature of the additions. The poet did not mind repeating himself. Oral verse-making had accustomed him to a very high level of tolerance to repetition at the phrase level, and such conventions as the verbatim repetition of messages established precedents for the repetition of longer passages. The move to a fixed text did not immediately diminish the tolerance to repetition, but created new forms of it. The poet who had composed one speech by a discouraged Agamemnon had no scruples in using a cut version of it when he needed a similar speech for the subordinate purpose of introducing the Embassy. On many other occasions, the poet unconsciously remembered his own combinations of formulaic phrases. Through convenience and inertia, the fixed text replaced the formulaic repertoire as the source of new lines, and the force of that development increased with time. Let us imagine Homer in the eighth year of his *Iliad*, with a text that has grown to 12,000 lines, or 75% of its final length. For the poet at this stage of his career, the existing *Iliad* was a much more powerful determinant than the heroic tradition. The last 4,000 lines of the *Iliad* are Iliadic rather than heroic hexameters, composed for a specific place in a *magnum opus* and reflecting the pressures of that work both in their sameness and difference. But Homer the writer did not yet face any incentives to avoid repetition, and the conditions of recitation ensured that even extended doublets would, for the most part, lie below the threshold of recognition.

The bulk of doublets, including some very long ones, are most readily understood as a carry-over of oral habits into a new mode of composition. Of the splendid lines portraying the clash of armies (4.446-51 = 8.60-5) one can only say that the poet used them again, presumably because he thought well of them. Nothing is gained by reading one context in the light of the other. Sometimes the contexts get in each other's way. The famous prophecy about the fall of Troy is spoken by Agamemnon to Menelaos and by Hektor to Andromache (4.163-5 = 6.447-9). Most modern readers will find the echo disturbing and wish the words had been reserved for Hektor, in whose mouth they resonate with pathos and irony, an effect that is undercut by the vindictive certainty of the hysterical Agamemnon. But as we have seen in earlier chapters, there are many occasions when the doublets establish a significant link between their contexts. Whether the poet intended these links or whether they are a by-product of his associative memory we cannot tell, but the effects yield to interpretation. While such semantically charged doublets are a minority it would be a mistake to disregard them simply because the majority of repetitions are inert.

The stages of the *Iliad*: a rough sketch

The evidence of the doublets, together with our knowledge of the poetic craft in which Homer's artistry is rooted, suggests that the *Iliad* grew over a period of many years and in a cumulative fashion. Is it possible to go farther and to reconstruct the stages of its genesis? The answer depends on the extent to which we believe that Goold's 'progressive fixation of the text' took place without revision of previous elements. If the text grew simply by addition, then it should in principle be possible to recover earlier stages through a process of subtraction, using as evidence the narrative discontinuities to be expected when insertions strain the original narrative joints. On the other hand, there is a great difference between no revision and some revision. We may well believe that the poet was reluctant to adjust his earlier narrative in the light of subsequent additions. We may also concede, without calling into question the excellence of his design or brilliance of its execution, that he was not a very good nuts-and bolts editor of his own work. But given the size and complexity of the work it is highly improbable that the progressive fixation of the text proceeded entirely without deletion or revision. Since even a modest amount of deletion and revision, with its possibilities for feedback between early and late passages, can effectively block the path to the origin of the text, precise reconstruction, the dream of much nineteenth- and twentieth-century German scholarship, is a chimerical enterprise. On the other hand, the rough stages of the poem's growth are visible and have been well known since the nineteenth century, although scholars of that period invariably attributed the stages to different hands. Gottfried Hermann was the first scholar to develop a systematic expansionist theory early in the nineteenth century. In the English-speaking world, the theory gained currency through its inclusion in Grote's *History of Greece* and through the great commentary by Walter Leaf, which is now freely available on the Web and still provides a sane and comprehensive guide through the narrative stumbling-blocks that have given rise to theories of multiple authorship.

In addition to uncertainty about the extent of revision, the task of reconstruction is made more difficult by the nature of the evidence. Homer's language is a linguistic and cultural amalgam of several centuries. It is possible to identify 'early' and 'late' elements in this amalgam with some confidence, but of course the evidence thus obtained is quite irrelevant to the task of identifying individual strata in a work that may have grown into its current form over the much shorter span of a single lifetime. Linguistic evidence may be helpful in identifying some limited post-Homeric interpolations, but for the bulk of the *Iliad* we must assume that the amalgam did not change significantly during the poet's life.

The evidence for different stages of the *Iliad* lies in various forms of narrative discontinuity resulting from the poet's indifference to some unintended consequences of his additions to the text. There are two difficulties with such evidence. First, it is much more difficult to reach agreement on what counts as a narrative discontinuity than to identify a Mycenaean relic or an Aeolian morphological form. Second, narrative discontinuity engenders critical ingenuity. Interpretative strategies of all kinds, from allegorical exegesis onward, have been developed to make sense of textual difficulties. There is no narrative discontinuity that a skilled interpreter cannot fill with meaning; whether it should be filled is a matter of judgement and rests on one's assessment of the range of narrative conventions operative in the work. My own sense is that Homeric narrative, while very subtle in its use of juxtaposition and implicit contrasts, is very straightforward in its concern for causes and consequences – witness the opening lines of the *Iliad*. Any interpretation that violates the straightforwardness of Homeric narrative may miss the mark as easily as one that shrugs off problems of coherence as inevitable by-products of oral composition.

The two major forms of discontinuity are 'cracks' in the narrative joints and poor cross-references. With both forms, there are many instances in the *Iliad* where 'interpretation' puts a much greater strain on the conventions of Homeric narrative than does the assumption that the discontinuity results from the poet's deficiency as an editor. The opening of the second book is a cardinal example of a crack in the narrative. Zeus has taken steps to honour his promise to Achilles and has sent a dream promising victory to Agamemnon. One expects that Agamemnon will act on this deceptive dream and will come to grief, but nothing of the kind happens. Instead he calls a council of his elders and informs them that he will first test the army 'as is proper' (2.73) and make a speech urging them to go home. The failure of this plan, the mutiny of the army and Odysseus' restoration of order lead to a new beginning of the war in which, as countless critics have pointed out, we move back in time to the first year. The derailment of narrative at the beginning of Book 2 corresponds to some odd features of what may have been the other end of the original joint. Book 11, the third day of battle, marks a very strong beginning. It is, to be sure, appropriate as the overture to this decisive day of fighting, but a number of correspondences between Books 11 and 1 and 2 suggest that the third day of fighting was once the first and that with Book 11 the narrative returns to the position at which it had been interrupted at the beginning of the second book.

Another crack in the narrative is remarkable for showing signs of careful splicing on the surface. Book 13 ends with a description of the noise of battle. In the opening lines of Book 14, Nestor responds to the noise of battle, leaves his tent, and shortly encounters the injured warriors Agamemnon, Diomedes and Odysseus. Their ensuing conversation, however, does not reflect the situation at the end of Book 13, where the Achaeans have the upper hand; rather, it responds to the crisis of Book 12, when Hektor smashes the gates of the wall. Thus Nestor's response to the battle noise covers up a significant discontinuity. If we return now to the end of Book 13, we see that an encounter of Aias and Hektor is elaborately prepared through an exchange of flyting speeches, but is left dangling in the air. On the other hand, towards the end of Book 14, there is an encounter of Aias and Hektor that begins unusually abruptly (14.402).

A third and very glaring example occurs in Book 20. The book opens with an assembly of the gods in which Zeus urges the gods to take sides in the imminent battle. The gods line up on the battlefield, and there is an expectation of cosmic terror as sky and earth are shaken and Hades fears for the safety of his infernal realm. But nothing happens. Instead the narrative turns to the unusually digressive encounter of Achilles and Aeneas, which does contain the structurally important lion simile that concludes the chain of Iliadic lion similes but is otherwise only loosely related to the narrative (20.164; above, p. 111). If we look for a continuation of the narrative that pitches the gods against each other, we must go to the second half of Book 21, where we can very clearly see the poet's splicing of different pieces. Hera sends Hephaistos to assist Achilles in his fight with the river (21.330); this confrontation of water and fire in their most elemental form leads to the free-for-all of the gods that was expected (if not quite in this style) after the impressive line-up of Book 20. The transition is smooth enough, but in retrospect the concluding line of the prologue looks strange (20.73-4):

> and against Hephaistos stood the great deep-eddying river
> who is called Xanthos by the gods, but by mortals Skamandros.

If they are poised to battle already, why does it take Hera to set Hephaistos against Skamandros? More fundamentally, what business does the lowly local river have among the immortal gods in the first place? The answer is that the lines were added to the prologue in the light of changes that (a) separated it from its original continuation and (b) merged the river fight with the fight of the gods.

Many students of Homer attribute the problem of odd, absent or inaccurate cross-references to the imagination of pedantic readers and appeal to an alleged rule of oral poetics under which the attention span of the poet and his audience is limited to the immediate narrative context. For instance, in Book 8, Zeus predicts that there will be fighting over the body of Patroklos *epi prumnêisi … steinêi en ainotatêi* (8.475-6).

Aristarchus deleted the line on the grounds that the prediction does not come true: the fighting over the body of Patroklos does not take place 'near the bows of the ships', let alone 'in a very narrow place'. Schadewaldt (1943, 110n) excused such inaccuracies by postulating an 'uncertainty principle' that results partly from the poet's desire for progressive revelation and partly from the exigencies of traditional diction, which did not always permit the required precision. But the trouble with the phrase is not that it is insufficiently accurate; rather, it is falsely specific, and there is no evidence that it is formulaic. We may not want to make much of the discrepancy, but it will not do to see in such instances an unproblematic by-product of oral composition. Precise cross-references are not uncommon in the Iliad. Thus Antenor and Hektor refer to the broken truce (7.69, 7.351), Hektor (8.177) and Achilles (9.349) to the recent building of the wall. Athene refers to Thetis' interview with Zeus (8.370), and Poulydamas remembers yesterday's defeat (13.745). Similarly, Hektor remembers his flouting of Poulydamas' advice on the previous night (22.100). Patroklos describes Sarpedon as the man who first breached the wall (16.558), and with a precision that borders on pedantry Glaukos, after the death of Sarpedon, prays to Apollo to heal the hand-wound he had suffered 2,500 lines earlier (16.511, 12.387). Who would have noticed had Homer nodded on this occasion? Given the frequency of quite precise cross-references, false connections and the conspicuous absence of expected connections pose a problem that requires explanation.

A very instructive case of missing or misleading cross-references occurs in the career of Pandaros, which spans Books 4 and 5. Armed with the weapon of Paris, he re-enacts the original offence and wounds Menelaos. His death, on the other hand, resembles that of Hektor: he is the victim of Diomedes' spear guided by Athene. His career has thematic coherence as a foreshortened version of the war which begins with Paris and ends with Hektor. Against the strong presence of this pattern we must set the spectacular absence of any explicit statement to the effect that his death is the punishment for his foolish transgression. When Pandaros reappears in Book 5, introduced by his patronym, he injures Diomedes, who prays to Athene that she may assist him in his revenge. The goddess grants the prayer, and we see its fulfilment 160 lines later when she guides Diomedes' spear (5.290). This is an intelligible sequence of promise and implicit fulfilment, and it tells a story that concerns only Diomedes and Pandaros.

The second encounter of the two has an unusually broad prelude. Aeneas goes in search of Pandaros and scolds him for not using his bow. Pandaros gives a lengthy answer in which he describes this unsuccessful attack on Diomedes, whom he correctly supposes to stand under the protection of some god. Arguing that he foolishly took his bow when he should have followed his father's advice and come to Troy with his horses, he continues (5.206-8):

> For now I have drawn it against two of their best men, Tydeus'
> son, and the son of Atreus, and both of these I hit
> and drew visible blood, yet only wakened their anger.

These lines are doubly problematic. First, Pandaros refers to Diomedes as if he had not told the story of their previous encounter twenty lines earlier in the same speech. Second, the reference to Menelaos is assimilated to the Diomedes scene as if it had been an injury in open battle. Thus lines 206-8 are both redundant and inaccurate, but together with the general fuss Pandaros makes about his bow they strongly link the Pandaros of Books 4 and 5. Why did the poet not take the obvious step and have Diomedes exult over the body of Pandaros, saying something like: 'There you are, you foolish braggart, and may other truce-breakers come to no better end'? The gloating speeches of Book 13 (above, p. 89) show that such words are entirely within the conventions of Homeric narrative. Why are they absent here? The most plausible answer is that the poet developed the role of Pandaros in our *Iliad* from a simpler version that survives in Book 5 but saw no need to make explicit the changed significance the death of Pandaros acquired in the elaborated version.

Inadequate cross-references also appear between the duel of Paris and Menelaos and the Paris-Hektor scene of Book 6, where Hektor accuses his brother of dodging war because of an unspecified *cholos* or anger (6.326). This allusion to an event not reported in the *Iliad* is especially odd since we might reasonably expect Hektor to say something about the fiasco of the duel in Book 3. Some scholars have heard such a reference in Paris' reply in which he says that he is full of grief rather than anger but will go and fight since 'victory passes back and forth between men' (6.339). Such an echo requires very subtle ears, and the fact remains that Hektor's visit to Paris does not in any real sense 'follow' on the events of Book 3 (Heitsch).

A somewhat similar problem is raised by the duel of Hektor and Aias and its relation to the duel of Paris and Menelaos. Here there are several passages that refer explicitly to the breaking of the truce, but the links are perfunctory, and do not answer the question how anything like the Hektor-Aias duel is at all possible following the disaster of the broken truce (Kirk, 1978).

Yet another problem appears in the assembly of the gods in Book 20, where Zeus tells the gods to join the fighting. This is usually taken as the lifting of his earlier order in which he forbade the gods to join the fighting. But Zeus does not say: 'I hereby revoke my previous order.' Indeed, nothing in the scene compels us to assume that the gods previously were absent from the fighting for an extended period – a strange fact in view of the occasional references to the enforced idleness of the gods elsewhere in the poem (11.73, 13.523, 15.113). It is not even possible to say that the scene by its structure implicitly refers to the earlier injunction. Homeric scenes will sometimes recall one another through a set of correspondences and reversals. Thus, the oblivious Andromache of Book 22 reverses the solicitous Andromache of Book 6; the boasts of Hektor in the council of the third night recall those of the second night, etc. But the opening of Book 20 neither refers to nor corresponds to the opening of Book 8, and this absence is all the more conspicuous since in the battle of the gods in Book 21 there is a very explicit cross-reference on a much less important matter: Ares attacks Athene with the express purpose of avenging his defeat at her hands in Book 5 (21.394).

From a structural perspective the most striking discontinuity is the absence of any back-references to the Embassy at places where such a reference would seem a good deal more functional than Glaukos' memory of his injured hand. Indeed, in Books 11 and 16 the text is in open conflict with the Embassy. In Book 11, Achilles says to Patroklos (608-10):

> son of Menoitios, you who delight my heart, o great one,
> now I think the Achaians will come to my knees and stay there
> in supplication, for a need past endurance has come to them.

In Book 16 he says that the Trojans would not be victorious 'if powerful Agamemnon treated me kindly' (16.72) but urges Patroklos to (84-6):

> win, for me, great honour and glory
> in the sight of all the Danaans, so they will bring back to me
> the lovely girl, and give me shining gifts in addition.

These words are not easily construed as the words of a man who had on the previous night rejected a most elaborate attempt at reconciliation. A whole literature has grown up around attempts to explain Achilles' silence on various grounds, none of them persuasive. Schadewaldt (1943, 81) argued that when Achilles imagines the Achaeans' supplication he implicitly contrasts this with the Embassy in which Aias and Odysseus merely asked him to settle out of court. As for the phrase 'if powerful Agamemnon treated me kindly', he sees it as referring to a fundamental attitude unaffected by recent events. And he points out rightly that the same speech that appears to ignore Agamemnon's offer contains another statement that has a passage in Book 9 as its antecedent. When Achilles says (16.61-3):

> and yet I have said
> I would not give over my anger until that time came
> when the fighting with all its clamour came up to my own ships.

his words refer as plainly as anything in the *Iliad* to his final words to Aias (9.650-2):

> that I shall not think again of the bloody fighting
> until such time as the son of wise Priam, Hektor the brilliant,
> comes all the way to the ships of the Myrmidons, and their shelters,

But the silence of Achilles about the offer of Agamemnon does not yield to any interpretation that is compatible with the conventions of Iliadic narrative, and we may conclude that his silence is not an intentional and interpretable aspect of the narrative but a by-product of the cumulative process of composition. More generally speaking, discontinuities in the joints and cross-references of the *Iliad* are the result of an editing technique that did not keep pace with the poet's architectonic ambition. The creative genius and the wretched editor of the scholar's imagination are one and the same person, composing a major work at an intersection of two modes of textual production.

Editorial deficiencies, however, are not structural flaws. This is the point usually overlooked by the analysts in whose scheme of values editorial neatness ranks next to, perhaps even above, godliness. It is a characteristic experience of reading the *Iliad* that as soon as the reader adjusts to the 'sloppy tolerances' of the text its most glaring cracks disappear and its structural coherence comes into full view. But because Homer was not, by our standards, a very good editor of his text, we can sketch the development of the *Iliad* through several phases. He began his career by developing a repertoire of songs, which existed in his memory in a fluid or semi-fluid form. The earliest '*Iliad*' is that structure which eventually proved capable of absorbing much of his repertoire into the fixed text of a grand epic. This 'Ur-*Iliad*' was very much like the hypothetical *mênis*-poem of the nineteenth-century analysts. It moved from the quarrel of Agamemnon and Achilles and Achilles' prayer to Zeus to the defeat of the

Achaean heroes in what is now the battle of the third day. It continued with Hektor's attack on the ships, the Patrokleia, and the return of Achilles to battle. This earliest version did not have the elaborate and expansive finale of our *Iliad*. Perhaps in it Hermes did steal the corpse of Hektor – a possibility that is raised by the gods in our text, only to be discarded as inappropriate (24.24, 71). It is an attractive speculation that the role of Hermes in the last book of the *Iliad* as we now have it is a transformation of that traditional story into what Karl Reinhardt called an 'epic situation'.

The poet expanded this 'Ur-*Iliad*' by adding two large blocks of narrative, roughly Books 2-7 and 12-15 in our *Iliad*. Each block shows traces of internal stratification. The derailment of narrative at the opening of the second book is the chief evidence for the addition of the first block, but the relation of Paris-Menelaos to Aias-Hektor, Paris and Hektor in Books 3 and 6, the oddities in the career of Pandaros, and numerous other features make it certain that the first day of fighting reached its final shape in several stages. The fact that key scenes in this block are 'dated' early in the war is the strongest argument for the hypothesis that these books existed in some form prior to their inclusion in the *Iliad*. It is very easy to see how a poet would shrug off as insignificant the anachronism that results from putting scenes from the beginning of the war at the beginning of his poem, even though it begins late. It is much harder to see why a poet would invent such anachronisms. (It is tempting to see in the flashback narrative of the *Odyssey* a solution to technical problems of narrative raised by the construction of the *Iliad*.) The books were part of the poet's repertoire. When he recast them for inclusion in his epic he probably gave them for the first time a genuine fixed shape, but his version of, say, Helen on the walls had sufficiently solidified over the years to resist a seamless incorporation into the fixed text.

The second block of narrative is identified as a later insertion by the opening of the Patrokleia. When Patroklos returns to Achilles he reports to him the situation of the war as it existed at the end of Book 11. It could be argued that since Patroklos had spent his time tending to the wounded Eurypylos his report accurately reflects the limited knowledge he has of the war. But it is not like Homer to distinguish between his own and his characters' knowledge of plain facts, and what, in any event, would be the point of such perspectivism? Patroklos' report at the opening of Book 16 is out of date because it was composed at a time when Books 12-15 did not yet exist. The curious splicing of Books 13 and 14 is only one of many features pointing to the internal layering of this block.

Book 9 represents a late stage in the growth of the *Iliad*, as is shown by the lack of back-references in Books 11 and 16. The impulse for the composition of this book may have come from the poet's recognition that in his transformation of a *mênis* poem into an '*Iliad*' he was beginning to lose sight of Achilles, whose absence from battle threatened to turn into disappearance from the poem. Hence the decision to foreground the absence of the protagonist by his renewed refusal to fight (above, p. 48). It is quite in keeping with the assignment of Book 9 to a late stage that Adam Parry (1956) has found in the speech of Achilles evidence of a personal Achillean and Homeric style.

The addition of the Embassy required the creation of a situation that would plausibly motivate it. It is an old insight of analytical criticism that Book 8 serves this function. The second day of fighting in the *Iliad* is remarkable for the brevity of description and for the extremely high percentage of repeated lines. Given the previous elaborations of the first and third days of fighting the poem did not stand in need of further fighting scenes. Thus the poet composed a minimal version of a major Achaean defeat. Only the end of the book rises above a utilitarian minimum: the famous tableau showing the Trojans outside the wall is carefully composed with a view to the contrasting despair of the Achaeans, and the transition from Book 8 to Book 9 is the most artful and deliberate in the whole poem.

There is powerful evidence that our version of Book 9 is itself an elaboration of an earlier form in which Aias and Odysseus were the only delegates. When the delegates walk to the tent of Achilles, the poet repeatedly uses dual forms of pronouns and verbs. There are some dozen instances in the *Iliad* in which dual verb forms are used with plural nouns, sometimes because there is a residual notion of pairs and sometimes for no apparent reason at all. But in Book 9 dual pronouns and verbs reinforce each other and continue for some twenty lines so as to convey a strong vision of two delegates. There are, however, three delegates: Aias, Odysseus and Phoinix, the old tutor of Achilles. Further oddities in the narrative relate to the manner in which Phoinix is introduced. There are many attempts to 'interpret' the dual forms, but they are all counsels of despair and do not explain the flagrant violation of ordinary narrative norms, for which much the simplest explanation is that the poet wanted to add the more intimate appeal of the old tutor and did not bother to revise his previous narrative in the light of his addition.

Book 9 is evidence of Homer's growing interest in the consciousness of his protagonist. The same interest transformed the death of Patroklos without completely obliterating traces of an earlier version. The narrative oddities of Patroklos' death concern the fate of his armour and the relationship of Kebriones and Sarpedon as his major victims. Like the death of Hektor, the Patrokleia enacts the rule that the killer is killed: Patroklos kills Kebriones, Hektor's charioteer, and after a bitter fight over the body Hektor kills Patroklos. The Patroklos-Kebriones-Hektor triangle is supported by a sequence of two similes. Hektor and Patroklos fight over the body of Kebriones like two lions over a dead deer (16.756). When Hektor kills Patroklos he is like a lion who has defeated a boar after a long fight over a spring (16.823). In this triangle Patroklos is a strong warrior who loses in the end to an even stronger one. But this version of Patroklos' death is overlaid by another version in which Patroklos is the helpless victim struck by a god. In this version his major antagonist is Sarpedon, who supersedes Kebriones as a warrior of greater stature and whose death brings greater glory to Patroklos. That Sarpedon is an addition to Book 16 is apparent among other things from the overly explicit cross-references that refer to his presence in Book 12, where he is also a latecomer. There are also inconsistencies about the armour of Patroklos, sometimes explained by attributing the entire motif of the exchange of armour to another poet who wanted to insert his poem about the shield of Achilles. G.S. Kirk (1962, 220) attributed the loose ends to the oral composer's weaving of narrative fabric with the threads of different traditions. More probably, the loose ends result from a reinterpretation of the Patrokleia in the light of the deeper purpose visible in the Embassy: the poet developed the theme of Patroklos as the 'alter ego' of Achilles (the exchange of armour) and chose for Patroklos a mode of death that would be reflected with greater pain in the consciousness of Achilles.

The expansion of the *Iliad* also reflected the aristeia of Achilles. It is a peculiar feature of the *Iliad* that some of its most awkward narrative joints occur in this section. Nowhere in the *Iliad* is narrative continuity as poor as in Books 20 and 21, the sequence of events that moves from the assembly of the gods via the 'Aeneid' to the scenes of mass slaughter, from there to the curious doublets of Lykaon and Asteropaios (the former one of the most magnificent scenes in the *Iliad*), and then to the river fight and theomachy. Why this should be so is hard to tell, but the fact is worth noting.

The first and last books of the *Iliad* were probably among the last sections of the work to receive their present shape. As time went on the poet faced the problem that Henry James lamented when he termed the novel a 'baggy monster'. To counteract the sprawling tendencies of his epic, the poet designed a narrative frame, an elaborate set of correspondences that relate beginning to end. The design is deeply rooted in the poet's vision of the world as a cosmos of polar opposites, which led Whitman to analyse the entire *Iliad* as a geometric structure in which every part is balanced by a counterpart in a pattern of elaborate and total symmetry. But the geometric structure is much more apparent in the outer than in the middles sections of the work, and it reaches a peak of formalism in the virtual mirror images of beginning and end (above, p. 71).

It is an odd feature of the framing books of the *Iliad* that they share many phrases with the *Odyssey*. If we count shared bigrams in sliding text windows of 100 lines, the segments that lie 2.5 or more standard deviations above the average are all found in the first and last books, except for two segments in *Iliad* 18. The most Odyssean sections of the *Iliad* are the voyage to Chryse, Priam's visit to Achilles' tent, and Thetis' visit to Hephaistos. By contrast, while the statistical results are striking and square with philological observations that have often been made since the nineteenth century, there is no obvious way of interpreting them.

Some useful hints can be gleaned from a table that shows a few top and bottom values from 626 text segments arranged around the median value, which is very close to the average. It is not surprising that the Catalogue of the Ships and some fighting sections in Book 16 are the least Odyssean parts of the *Iliad*. We might say with Horatio that it needs no statistician or ghost 'come from the grave to tell us this,' since by just about any criterion the Catalogue of the Ships differs substantially from all other Homeric lines. On the other hand, the standard deviations tell us that *Iliad* 1 and 24 stand out even more on the plus side than the Catalogue of Ships stands out on the minus side.

It is safe to say that the Odyssean repetitions of the framing books of the *Iliad* are not by-products of oral composition. There are also difficulties with the explanation that the poet of the *Odyssey* took over Iliadic lines or passages. The bulk of shared passages in *Iliad* 1, for instance, involves passages that are repeated across the *Iliad* in a manner somewhat reminiscent of Odyssean patterns of repetition. For instance, the close repetition of a long meal scene in Iliad 1 and 2 would not be unusual in the *Odyssey*, but is quite untypical of the *Iliad*. There is a substantial amount of evidence that would support an argument for significant and specific links between the ways in which the *Odyssey* and the framing books of the *Iliad* were composed. But there is not enough evidence to prove it or to develop more specific hypotheses about how this interaction might have worked.

That the *Iliad* developed roughly in the manner sketched above is plausible, but the nature of the evidence does not permit firmer conclusions. Additional support for the hypothesis of a single composer for the *Iliad*, however, comes from the virtual sholarly consensus that Book 10 of the *Iliad*, the so-called Doloneia, is a later addition.

Table 16. *Iliad* segments with most and fewest Odyssean bigrams

Rank	Start line	Bigram count	Standard deviation
1	1.426	351	4.03299
4	24.337	324	3.25814
9	18.329	297	2.48329
11	18.379	293	2.36849
12	24.562	293	2.36849
312	11.106	210	-0.01345
614	16.307	141	-1.99363
616	16.282	138	-2.07972
619	2.465	134	-2.19451
622	2.790	128	-2.36670
626	2.490	107	-2.96936

The 579 lines of his book relate how after the failure of the Embassy both the Achaeans and Trojans engage in spying missions, how Diomedes and Odysseus trap the Trojan spy Dolon, extract a confession from him, kill him despite their promises to the contrary, and conclude their mission with a massacre of the sleeping Thracians. The book is full of odd words and things, such as the boar helmet or the animal skins worn by the Achaeans, and it delights in a complex parallelism of scenes that has struck many scholars as mannered. The emphasis on the ruthless cunning of Diomedes and Odysseus differs markedly from the ethos of fighting that prevails elsewhere in the poem. Even in translation the reader senses that the Doloneia takes him into another world and speaks with a different voice. One could of course argue that the Doloneia is in more ways than one a night piece and that it contrasts intentionally with the remainder of the work. On the other hand, there is no reference to the events of the Doloneia anywhere in the *Iliad*, and the narrative moves without disturbance from the last line of Book 9 to the first line of Book 11. No other passage of comparable length can be cut from the *Iliad* without any consequences to the structure of the rest.

The Doloneia is the only part of the *Iliad* whose authenticity has been doubted since antiquity, and modern scholars agree for the most part with the position attributed by Eustathius to ancient critics that it was composed after the completion of the *Iliad* for inclusion in its present place. This scholarly consensus contrasts sharply with the notorious disagreements analysts have about the rest of the *Iliad*. In particular, there is no comparable agreement about differences of voice and narrative technique in other parts of the *Iliad*. The Doloneia thus is a test case: it shows what types of evidence or degree of convergence between such types is required to make a forceful claim that something has been added to a complete text. Since no other part of the *Iliad* comes close to meeting those requirements, the consensus about the Doloneia is an acknowledgement of sorts that the assumption of a single author working over a lifetime is the most plausible hypothesis to account for the co-existence in the *Iliad* of narrative discontinuities with an overriding coherence of voice, design and purpose.

The Life of the *Iliad*

The completion of a text is the beginning of a life that is sustained through the ages as long as there are readers to construe the meaning of the words. Readers respond to the text in different ways, and from the traces of their response one may reconstruct the life of the text. Responses take many forms. Direct comment constitutes a body of scholarship and criticism, which in the case of important texts develops a coherence and authority of its own, guiding or even prescribing appropriate questions and responses. But commentary is neither the only nor the most important form of response. Imitation, adaptation, translation and such negative responses as evasion or neglect bear equally on the life of a text and form a tradition of implicit commentary. Moreover, explicit and implicit responses interact through the ages. Vergil's reading of Homer, to give the most celebrated example, draws on a rich tradition of explicit commentary, and the *Aeneid* in turn, although not a commentary, has done more than any other text to shape the responses of readers to Homer.

No Western text boasts a life as long as the *Iliad* and few can match its energy and glory. To tell the life-story of the *Iliad* is far beyond the scope of this modest epilogue, which can only sketch in the broadest terms the stages of its life as it appears in the succession and interaction of different forms of reader response.

The oldest form of criticism is allegorical and can be traced back to Theagenes of Rhegium in the sixth century BCE. Allegory is a procedure for dealing with objectionable features of a text by claiming that they 'say something else' (the literal meaning of 'all-egoria'). Allegorical exegesis arose out of the need to deal with the scandals of Homeric theology. It flourished among Stoic thinkers and later merged with similar Judaeo-Christian procedures to become the favoured method for 'saving' the ancient gods in a Christian world. The most famow and most productive allegorical interpretation of an Iliadic passage transforms the golden chain by which Zeus threatens to hang the other gods into the 'Great Chain of Being'.

Plato in his *Ion* is our main source for the professional interpretation of Homer in classical times. Ion is a rhapsode, a man who makes a living reciting and explaining Homer and by virtue of his knowledge of the poems thinks of himself as a walking encyclopaedia. But while Plato exposes the pretensions of such knowledge he does not give us enough evidence to say very much about patterns of interpretation and explanation common in his day.

We are on firmer ground with the Alexandrians. They had no encyclopaedic ambitions and they wanted no truck with allegory. They were professional scholars in our sense, interested in employing philological techniques to establish and elucidate the text. 'Explaining Homer out of Homer' was Aristarchus' anti-allegorical slogan. Much of the work of the Alexandrians has come down to us via a devious route and survives in the marginal notes of Byzantine manuscripts, the 'scholia'. It is in the nature of such 'notes and queries' that they do not easily convey a comprehensive view of the poem. But scholars who, like Jasper Griffin, have made a point of systematically consulting the scholia have found in them a treasure of acute and sensitive observation that reveals much about the ancient understanding of the *Iliad*. In addition to the scholia, parts of ancient Homeric scholarship survive in the discursive commentary of the twelfth-century Byzantine scholar Eustathius, Bishop of Thessalonika, which for centuries to come remained a basic reference tool for Homeric scholars.

Although Homer was a much edited author during the Renaissance, there are no significant advances in textual and philological scholarship between Alexandrian times and the early eighteenth century, when Richard Bentley discovered the 'digamma', the sound that had disappeared from Greek by Homer's day, but had left its traces behind in certain features of Homeric prosody. This discovery led the way to a systematic and exhaustive analysis of Homeric language: a modern scholar can say with justice that there are many features of Homer's poetry that he understands more fully than any ancient reader, including perhaps Homer himself. Another milestone in the philological criticism of Homer is the publication in 1788 by the French scholar Villoison of the Venetus A manuscript, which dates from the tenth century and is the best manuscript of the *Iliad*. The manuscript also includes a set of scholia that provide more valuable and extensive evidence for Alexandrian scholarship than had been previously available. Modern textual scholarship of the *Iliad* (1920), dates from the publication of that manuscript. The late eighteenth century also saw the beginning of the analytical criticism of Homer, which had precursors in the work of d'Aubignac and in casual remarks by Vico and Richard Bentley, but may be said to begin properly with the publication of Friedrich Wolf's *Prolegomena* in 1795 (above, p. 7).

Travellers and gentlemen scholars of the eighteenth century had begun to cultivate the pleasant pastime of taking ancient authors – above all, Homer – out of the world of thickly annotated folio volumes and placing them in their real and original habitat of Greece. 'We proposed to read the *Iliad* and *Odyssey* in the countries, where Achilles … fought and where Homer sung', Robert Wood wrote in his *Essay on the Original Genius and Writings of Homer*, the most influential book to popularise this new approach (Jenkyns, 8). A century later, Heinrich Schliemann thought that he had discovered Homer's Troy. The systematic excavations of Troy, Knossos and Mycenae that have continued since the late nineteenth century have given us a much fuller understanding of the material base of Homeric culture. But the dream of explaining Homer out of the ruins has not come true: the more we have learnt about the world of early Greece, the more sceptical we have become about assuming a simple relationship between the world of the poetry and any historical reality (above, p. 1).

First reflections of the *Iliad*: the *Odyssey*, tragedy and Plato

Textual scholarship and its related disciplines distrust interpretation and are made possible by the belief in the fiction that restoration is possible and will ultimately make interpretation redundant. The text of the *Iliad* we read today is the valid product of that noble delusion. But the life of the *Iliad* is not limited by the history of that text and its explanations; it is a story of misreadings, most lively and influential where it is least hampered by an ethos of faithful explication.

8. The Life of the Iliad

The first major stage in the life of the *Iliad* is the *Odyssey*. Whether it was work of the same poet or of a younger contemporary or disciple, it was conceived as a complementary sequel to the *Iliad*. The *Odyssey* completes the story of the *Iliad*. Through the return of Odysseus, it tells of the return of the other Achaeans as well. Demodokos' story of the Wooden Horse (*Od.* 8.486) shows the narrator's effort to create seamless narrative continuity from the beginning of the *Iliad* to the end of the *Odyssey*. Whether or not the *Iliad* and *Odyssey* are the work of the same poet, their systematic complementarily created 'Homer' as an oeuvre that established the forms and modes of Western literature, and in particular the recurring polarisation of human experience into a tragic and a comic vision. Because of the *Odyssey* it becomes an impossible enterprise to tell the life of the *Iliad* apart from that of 'Homer', a term that refers sometimes to a man, sometimes to a body of works, and frequently to whatever the speaker understands by the principle of poetry.

If we look in Greek literature for those traces that lead us specifically to the *Iliad*, we encounter tragedy. The plot of the *Iliad*, with its concatenation of the fates of Hektor, Patroklos and Achilles, provided the great exemplar that allowed the Attic playwrights to refine the art of plot construction and to achieve in their best plays a degree of concentration that led Aristotle to rank tragedy above epic. We know that Aeschylus wrote a trilogy about Achilles, but the corpus of extant plays accurately reflects the fact that the great dramatists acknowledged the primacy of the *Iliad* by keeping their distance from it. Of the thirty-odd plays that have survived from antiquity, only one, the *Rhesus*, deals with an event directly narrated in the *Iliad*. (This play, although attributed to Euripides, probably originates in the fourth century BCE, and it is telling that its subject, the Doloneia, is a peripheral part of the *Iliad*.) The fall of Troy and the aftermath of the war, on the other hand, were favoured because the *Iliad* gave to these subjects a special weight and interest without preempting their treatment. Aeschylus' most majestic work, the *Oresteia*, is a sequel of sorts to the *Iliad*. It sharpens the paradox of defeat in victory and challenges the theology of the *Iliad* by showing the power of the chthonic forces that the Olympian vision had banished from its ken. Sophocles' *Aias*, his earliest surviving play, similarly uses a post-Iliadic event to deepen the dilemma of the warrior code. Because the arms of Achilles were awarded to Odysseus rather than to him, Aias is seized by an implacable hatred for Agamemnon, a *mênis oulomenê* that leads to slaughter and self-destruction without a compensating heroic achievement. The scene between Aias, his war-bride Tekmessa and their son Eurysakes is a transposition of the Hektor-Andromache scene of Book 6 of the *Iliad* into a harsher key – the only instance in Attic tragedy of a direct imitative challenge to the *Iliad*. The *Philoctetes*, Sophocles' other play about the Trojan War, is a bitter vision of a post-Iliadic and post-heroic world in which the good have died and the likes of Thersites prosper. A similar vision informs Euripides' plays about the aftermath of the Trojan War.

Tragedy is one great trace of the life of the *Iliad* in Greek culture; the other is Plato. The Republic is the *locus classicus* for the war of poetry and philosophy. Plato of course attacks all poets rather than Homer or the *Iliad*, and Homer is singled out simply because he enjoys pride of place. None the less, the scandal in Plato's eyes is not this or that aberration from moral standards but the fundamentally ambiguous relationship of poetry to morality. Despite its *risqué* story of Ares and Aphrodite the *Odyssey* shows few traces of that ambiguity. *The Iliad*, on the other hand, is deeply imbued with it; or, to put it differently, at their most serious moments Plato and the author of the *Iliad* live in different worlds. For this reason there is some justice in seeing Plato's attack on poetry as fundamentally a response to the *Iliad*.

Homer and Vergil

With the *Odyssey*, the *Iliad* becomes part of Homer; with Vergil it becomes part of the 'epic tradition'. The stance of the *Aeneid* vis-à-vis the *Iliad* and *Odyssey* established an exemplary relationship of admiration and rivalry: the history of its repetition in different times and places is the history of the epic tradition. The *Aeneid* has been far more important than any other text in identifying the criteria and questions that have dominated Homeric criticism through the ages. If the *Odyssey* creates 'Homer' by joining itself to the *Iliad*, the *Aeneid*, by distancing itself from Homer, creates the 'Homeric', the elusive category whose definition always turns out to be some version of the difference between Homer and Vergil.

Vergil's poetic ambition was to create a work that would do for Rome what the *Iliad* and *Odyssey* had done for Greece. The first point to note about Vergil's achievement is that he wrote in Latin rather than in Greek. The *Aeneid* appropriates and emancipates itself from a foreign paradigm, thereby establishing for its Greek precursor a climate of remote primacy. Second, Vergil conceived the *Aeneid* as an equivalent that self-consciously and explicitly proclaims its dependence on its models at every step. Vergil's attitude is filial in the extreme: Aeneas carrying Anchises away from the burning Troy may stand as an image for the poet as well. This self-proclaimed dependence turns the *Iliad* into a poem without origins or, rather, a poem created *ex nihilo* by the original genius of Homer.

The *Aeneid* comprehends, supersedes and reverses the events of the *Iliad* and *Odyssey*. To the destruction of a city and the subsequent wanderings of the conquerors it opposes the wanderings of a refugee whose descendants will in time found Rome. The burning Troy, dimly envisaged at the end of the *Iliad*, is fully described, but it functions as a beginning. And the Homeric bias for the Achaeans is replaced by the Roman poet's bias for the Trojans who are his ancestors, for it is from Aeneas that Caesar and Augustus, the greatest Roman rulers, trace their descent.

This reversal is only the most visible form of a critique of Homer that despite its tone of filial deference leaves no aspect of the model untouched. The critique is easiest to see on the moral level, where Vergil is the heir to centuries of philosophy. Plato had complained in the *Republic* about the moral deficiencies of Achilles, calling him greedy, brutal, uncontrolled, and generally lacking in the virtues that result from a proper education and find their embodiment in the Philosopher King (*Republic* 390e). Aristotle in the *Nicomachean Ethics* projected the ideal of the magnanimous man. Such embodiment of virtues in images of human perfection appealed to the Romans. It appears, for instance, in Cicero's attempts to capture the excellences of rhetoric through an image of the perfect orator. It is not surprising, therefore, that the protagonist of the *Aeneid*, unlike his predecessor in the *Iliad*, is an epic hero embodying the virtues of the soldier Achilles and the statesman Agamemnon without any of their shortcomings. In addition to the specifically heroic virtues of courage and wisdom, Aeneas also embodies the remaining cardinal virtues: piety and, despite his entanglement with Dido, temperance.

190

The list of Vergilian corrections of moral lapses in the *Iliad* is a long one. Aeneas does not withdraw from battle in anger; rather, his absence is the inevitable consequence of his attempt to secure allies. Far from mutilating the body of his opponent, he is even reluctant to kill him. And so it continues in a thorough revision of Iliadic scenes in which motives and actions that appear blameworthy to Vergil are either transformed or attributed to bad characters.

Since moral, social and aesthetic criteria are inextricably intertwined in the ancient world, the Vergilian critique of Homer extends to matters of social and stylistic decorum. The *Aeneid* reflects the greater social stratification of the Roman world, and our familiarity with its sense of protocol inevitably moulds our reading of Homer. Odysseus shoots a deer on Circe's island, makes a crude sling from branches, and lugs the animal on his back to his sole remaining ship (*Od.* 10.157). Aeneas even in distress remains the admiral of a fleet. On his arrival in Libya, he climbs a hill and sees a herd of deer led by three stags. He takes the bow and arrow carried for him by his faithful Achates (more servant than companion) and shoots first the 'leaders', then the 'common crowd', until he has killed one animal for each ship. As to how these were transported back to the ships, it is beneath the epic poet's dignity to attend to such detail: certainly Aeneas did not carry them himself (*Aen.* 1.184). He carried his father and the house gods out of the burning Troy, and he will later put on the 'shield and destiny of his descendants' (2.707, 8.731). But an epic hero does not lug dead animals on his back.

Social stratification goes hand in hand with a hierarchy of styles. In theories of style since the Hellenistic period epic and tragedy are the prime literary examples of the high style. Vergil made such theories canonical through the example of his poetic career, which he understood as a self-conscious progress from the humble beginnings of pastoral to the exalted form of the epic. We may have tired of the soaring epic ambition with its quest for an 'answerable style', and we may find greater delight in the rugged practicality of Odysseus and in the vivid concreteness with which it is described. But what we like to think of as an immediate response to the quintessentially Homeric world and style has its origin, directly or indirectly, in the Vergilian response to Homer.

In talking about the critical recension of Homer that is implicit in the *Aeneid* and makes Vergil the greatest of all Homeric critics, we must not neglect the sense of doubt and inadequacy that besets the Vergilian enterprise at every step and has left its traces both in the text and in some telling anecdotes. Vergil said that 'borrowing a line from Homer was like stealing the club of Hercules', forbade the publication of the *Aeneid* and wanted to burn it on his deathbed. His personal shyness gave him the nickname Parthenias, 'the Maiden'. Since Vergil's day, an acute sense of the 'anxiety of influence' has been *de rigueur* for the epic poet – a fact well known to Dante. The figure of the epic poet approaching his great task with an equal sense of inferiority and superiority bears on the *Iliad* precisely because its author alone of all poets is seen as exempt from this contradiction.

The matter of Troy, Chapman, and Shakespeare

Despite the misgivings of its author, the *Aeneid* was an immediate triumph. It became the national epic of Rome, and it marked the maturity of Latin as the language of a distinct literary culture that came to dominate the West and turned Greek into a foreign language not even known by the educated elite. As the *Aeneid* triumphed, the *Iliad* went into hibernation. Poems about Troy, however, remained popular. One of these was the *Ilias Latina*, a poem of a thousand hexameters that summarises the events of the *Iliad*. It belongs in the first century CE, but the Middle Ages falsely saw in it the work of Pindar. More influential was the *Historia de excidio Troiae*, which is a fifth-century version of an earlier Greek poem that attributes itself to the Phrygian Dares, a counsellor of Hektor. This history by an 'eyewitness' with a Trojan bias was very popular in the Middle Ages and, together with another 'eyewitness report' by the Cretan Dictys, a companion of Idomeneus, it provided the main source for the vast literature of Troy that flourished in the Middle Ages. In the twelfth century Benoit de Sainte-Maure combined and expanded these accounts; a century later Guido delle Colonne paraphrased Benoit in a Latin 'history', which, translated into French (1464), and back from French into English, became the first book printed in England, Caxton's *Recuyell of the Historyes of Troye*. An episode from this cycle was elaborated by Boccaccio, and in its English adaptation became the greatest of all medieval works about Troy: Chaucer's *Troilus and Criseyde*. The point to be made about this poem and about the tradition from which it derives is that they have nothing to do with the *Iliad* but completely supersede it. Chaucer's narrator early disclaims any intention to relate the story of the war and tells his readers that they may find the 'Troian gestes, as they felle, in Omer, or in Dares, or in Dite' (1.146).

In the envoi 'Omer' is listed once more, together with Vergil, Ovid, Lucan and Statius, as one of the poets whose footsteps the author's 'litel' book is to kiss (5.1792). But here, as in the fourth canto of the Inferno, Homer is a mere shade. And so he remained for an early Humanist writer like Petrarch, who acquired a Greek manuscript of Homer but was unable to read it.

The revival of the *Iliad* in the West is part of the revival of Greek studies that began in the fifteenth century for many reasons, including the influx of Byzantine scholars into Italy as a consequence of the fall of Constantinople. The sixteenth century, in particular, was an age in which a knowledge of Greek, while precious, spread beyond an exclusive group of scholars. An interest in Greek literature is characteristic of the learned poets of sixteenth-century France, especially of Ronsard. But one should not imagine that the revived *Iliad* superseded the medieval Troy literature. It would be more correct to think of the Renaissance *Iliad* as another, though highly prestigious, item in that literature, which retained its hold on the European imagination, perhaps even strengthened it when new national monarchies, as in France and England, legitimated their origins by myths of descent from Troy. Take the 1583 edition of Homer by the French poet Jean de Sponde (Spondanus), the work of a man then in his mid-twenties. It is not a work of great scholarly merit, but interesting for that very reason since it reflects accurately the knowledge and interests of a highly educated literary man in the late sixteenth century. The work includes not only the *Iliad* and *Odyssey* in Greek with facing Latin prose translations but also the *Ilias Latina* and Dares. In other words, it is as much an encyclopaedia of Troy poems as it is an edition of Homer.

If the reading of Homer was in part shaped by the literature of Troy, it was much more powerfully affected by Renaissance theories of the epic. Much Homeric criticism between 1500 and 1700 is found in commentaries of Aristotle's *Poetics* or Horace's *Ars Poetica* and in the innumerable vernacular poetic treatises based on them. This criticism operates at considerable distance from the Homeric texts and deals in generalities that stay within the bounds of the Vergilian recension. It often takes the form of adjudicating competing claims or answering specific charges such as 'Is Plato right in attacking poets?', 'Is Aristotle right in preferring tragedy to epic?', 'Is Vergil greater than Homer?' The most influential of these discussions are shaped by an exalted notion of the moral power of poetry, by a belief in the supremacy of epic poetry, and by a celebration of the epic hero as the pinnacle of human perfection. It did not escape Renaissance readers that in the context of such assumptions the *Iliad* is a problematical text. In particular, it was difficult to see Achilles as an epic hero: Tasso's Rinaldo and other 'improved' Achilles figures of Renaissance epics bear clear witness to these difficulties (Steadman). The greater compliance of the *Aeneid* with the ideals of epic perfection led Julius Caesar Scaliger in his *Poetics* to proclaim its superiority over Homer – a judgement that repeats Vergil without his characteristic diffidence.

The Renaissance response to the *Iliad* finds a unique and representative expression in Chapman's translation and in Shakespeare's *Troilus and Cressida*. Readers during the 1590s took a special interest in the literature of Troy. A reprint of Caxton appeared in 1596; Chaucer's works, including Henryson's *Testament of Cresseid*, were reprinted in 1598, and we know of several lost Troy plays from this period. When George Chapman published his *Seaven Bookes of the Iliades of Homer, Prince of Poets* (*Iliad* 1-2, 7-11), this publication was, from one perspective, just another book about Troy, and the translation joined an established library. But it is more important to an understanding of Chapman's enterprise to see it as a powerful and strained expression of the Renaissance quest for heroic greatness. A key to the cast of this work is found in the translation of these lines from the opening passage (1.3-5):

> *pollas d'iphthimous psuchas Aïdi proiapsen*
> *hêrôôn, autous de helôria teuche kunessin*
> *oiônoisi te pasi.*

> and many brave soules load
> From breasts Heroique – sent them farre, to the invisible cave
> That no light comforts; and their lims to dogs and vultures gave.

Hêrôs in Homeric Greek means *warrior*, and *iphthimous psuchas hêrôôn* means something like *the strong life spirits of warriors*. But in 'brave soules load/ From breasts Heroique' the postpositive and capitalised adjective has a climactic force and points towards the category of the 'Heroic'. If 'breasts Heroique' moves away from Homer in one direction, the periphrastic expression for Hades shows not only a penchant for elaboration but also a taste for metaphysical speculation that is foreign to Homer and reflects a conviction that the epic poem must be profound. Pope in the preface to his own translation accuses Chapman of a 'strong Affectation of extracting new Meanings out of his Author', but also credits him with a 'daring fiery spirit that animates his Translation' (7.21). Chapman's work is a milestone in the history of translation, and Keats in his famous sonnet paid it as handsome a compliment as one poet ever received from another. But the tortuous nature of the translation prevented it from finding a wide readership, and in this respect it differs not only from Pope's Homer but also from such Elizabethan classics of translation as North's Plutarch.

Chapman completed his translation of the *Iliad* in 1611 and in 1614 added a version of the *Odyssey*. But his *Seaven Bookes* is the most influential part of his translation, for it inspired *Troilus and Cressida*, one of the most curious episodes in the life of the *Iliad*. Shakespeare's play intertwines a love plot and a war plot. The love plot is clearly medieval, but the war plot follows the contours of the *Iliad* and is framed by the withdrawal of Achilles and the death of Hektor. Moreover, the war plot elaborates precisely the narrative motifs that figure prominently in the *Seaven Bookes*: the council of the desperate Achaeans (Book 2), the duel of Hektor and Aias (Book 7), and the Embassy (Book 9). *Troilus and Cressida* is an unchecked outburst of the deflationary and corrosive perspective that Shakespeare in his tragedies always keeps under control. The play focuses on the *Iliad* as its target because Chapman had recently reaffirmed its status as the paradigm of heroic poetry not only in his translation but also in the effusive prefatory matter.

In the *Iliad* Thersites had been introduced for the express purpose of being kicked out: with the expulsion of this loudmouth and coward, the Achaeans reassert their commitment to the warrior code. Expelled from the *Iliad*, Thersites found a niche in handbooks of rhetoric, where he survived through the ages: a medieval schoolboy might run across Thersites as the type of railing detractor without ever hearing of the *Iliad*. Shakespeare's version of this Thersites re-enters the world of the *Iliad*; indeed, he becomes the filter through which its characters and events are seen in *Troilus and Cressida*. The privileged position given to him reflects an implicit understanding on Shakespeare's part of what is not found in the *Iliad*. The return of Thersites, which has a parallel in the celebration of Thersites as the arch-survivor in Sophocles' *Philoctetes*, allows us to draw a suggestive analogue between one of Shakespeare's most problematic plays and a number of plays of the fifth century BCE in which a mood of disillusionment and weary cynicism likewise defines itself against the heroic world of the *Iliad*. Some of these plays – e.g. Euripides' *Orestes* – raise questions of classification that are similar to the curious status of *Troilus and Cressida* as a problem play. To treat such works as episodes in the life of the *Iliad* is helpful in clarifying their mode and purpose. There remains, however, the question whether we should call a work like *Troilus and Cressida* a critique of the *Iliad* or whether we should see it as a subversion or rejection of the values implicit in the Vergilian recension of Homer and to their inflationary tendencies.

Milton and Pope

A very different critique of the *Iliad*, and one that clearly by-passes the *Aeneid*, appears in *Paradise Lost*. By the standards of his age, and indeed by modern professional standards, Milton had an exceptionally thorough knowledge of Greek, and Homer was one of three authors – Ovid and Isaiah were the others – that his daughters read most frequently to their blind father in the original. The opening lines of the epic closely follow the *Iliad*:

Of Man's first Disobedience and the fruit
Of that forbidden Tree whose mortal taste
Brought Death into the world and all our woe ...

'Man's first Disobedience' echoes *mênin Pêlêiadeô Achilêos* in its syntactic structure, and both openings explore the polarity of a central event and its disastrous consequences. The Iliadic echoes point to larger structural resemblances. Milton copies the distinctive structural feature of the *Iliad*, its way of telling a larger story by means of a central incident. The wrath of Achilles and the fall of man are episodes in much larger cycles of events, the Trojan War and the Celestial Cycle, which begins with Creation and ends with the Last Judgement. This relationship of plot to story led Milton to think of the triangle of Adam, Eve and Satan in terms of Achilles, Patroklos and Hektor-Apollo (perhaps prompted by the not uncommon identification of Apollo with Satan via *Apollyon*, 'destroyer', a Greek word for the devil). In elaborating the story of the Fall, Milton had available to him a rich narrative tradition. While he used it freely, he departed from it in the scene that accounts for Eve's meeting Satan by herself. His Eve asks Adam's permission to work by herself, and when she returns to him Adam recognises her fall as the consequence of his failure to protect her. In other words, Milton uses the Patrokleia both to motivate Eve's separation and to articulate a moment of tragic recognition in which Adam, like Achilles, sees his own doom in that of his dead beloved. One of Milton's most powerful Homeric allusions further emphasises the moment of tragic recognition. When Hektor dies, Andromache is at home working a piece of embroidery. As she hears the shouts of woe, she rushes to the towers and faints at the sight of the dead Hektor. Her headgear, a precious wedding present, falls to the ground. When she recovers, she expresses her loss in words. This sequence is closely followed by Milton in leading up to Adam's sight of the fallen Eve. He had been weaving a wreath of flowers in anticipation of her return, but when he sees her he is horror-struck and (9.892-3)

> From his slack hand the garland wreathed for Eve
> Down dropped, and all the faded roses shed.

In the ensuing speech he expresses the meaning of the gesture and calls Eve 'defaced, deflowered, and to death devote' (9.901). Milton's fusion of the two great Iliadic recognitions of tragic loss rests on an apprehension of the dramatic structure of his model that has its only parallel among the Attic playwrights. But Milton rejects the premises on which that structure rests and offers a powerful critique of tragic consciousness. Knowledge brings disaster in the *Iliad* (and in Greek tragedy), but it also provides the ground for identity and self-assertion. Milton takes over the structure of tragic recognition but rejects its metaphysical implications. Whereas the blind Achilles had been transformed into the seeing Achilles by the death of Patroklos, Adam falls into blindness. His tragic consciousness of Eve's doom is false, and the situation of tragic recognition becomes the scene in which man wilfully isolates himself from divine grace. Tragic necessity in *Paradise Lost* is an illusion, and the poem's true recognition occurs beyond the fall when Adam and Eve discover their dependence on one another and divine grace. Through his use of the *Iliad*, and by placing and transcending the situation of tragic recognition, Milton discovered the conditions of Christian tragedy, and his work is the most sustained reflection on the relationship of Christian tragedy to its ancient sources.

Milton's use and understanding of the *Iliad* rest very much on his own reading and have no parallel in his day. With Alexander Pope, on the other hand, we come to an author whose response to Homer subsumes that of an entire age, in England and beyond. Between 1715 and 1720, Pope published his translation of the *Iliad* in six volumes, each containing four books of the original. Bentley, the greatest classical scholar of his age, was contemptuous: 'it is a pretty poem, Mr. Pope, but you must not call it Homer'. The polite world for whom it was intended thought otherwise. Pope's Homer was widely read and quickly established itself as one of the few translations to become originals in their own right. Pope's *Iliad* is arguably the finest English poem in heroic couplets, and outside the Greek world more readers got to know Homer through Pope than had ever read him in any version.

Pope's interest in Homer dates back to his childhood when he read the *Iliad* in Ogilby's version, published in a richly illustrated folio version. A mediocre work, it more than justified its existence by the spark it lit in the eight-year-old boy. The more immediate cause of Pope's *Iliad* was the precarious state of the author's fortunes. Pope conceived of his translation as a commercial venture that would bring him financial security, and in this regard, as in many others, the translation was a resounding success that permitted the poet to buy the small estate at Twickenham, where he spent the rest of his life.

Like Chapman, Pope endows Homer with a heroic patina. If Homer does not live up to 'the Majesty of Epic Poetry where everything ought to be great and magnificent' (7.lii), Pope will improve his original, sometimes apologetically. Thus, when Athene gives Menelaos the bloodthirsty courage of a fly, Pope in his note acknowledges the just precision of the original, but in the translation changes the animal into a 'vengeful hornet' because our 'present Idea of the Fly is indeed very low as taken from the littleness and insignificancy of this Creature' (*Il.* 17.570; 17.642 in the translation). But Pope will have nothing to do with Chapman's abstruseness. On the contrary, he is an ardent apostle of Homeric simplicity and among the most important critics to unfold what is implicit in the Vergilian recension: that Homer is characterised by a lack of art.

The modern roots of that view are found in the battle of the ancients and moderns, the favourite parlour game of the literary elite in late seventeenth-century France, where Homer took his knocks as the standard-bearer of antiquity but also had begun to be worshipped as the only poet to whom it was given to exist in pristine and prelapsarian grandeur. Dryden gives an early and important expression of this view when in his *Essay of Dramatic Poesy* he lines up Homer and Vergil with Shakespeare and Jonson: 'Shakespeare was the Homer, or father of our dramatic poets; Jonson was the Virgil, the pattern of elaborate writing; I admire him but I love Shakespeare.' Pope contrasts Homer and Vergil in terms of invention and judgement. The 'fire' of invention is visible in Vergil, 'but discern'd as through a Glass reflected from Homer, more shining than fierce, but everywhere equal and constant'. Pope elaborates this conceit by first lining up Milton and Shakespeare with Vergil and Homer and then making Homer transcend even Shakespeare, a double comparison that was echoed by Matthew Arnold and was indeed something of a commonplace in Victorian criticism (Jenkyns, 192): 'In Milton it glows like a Furnace kept up to an uncommon ardor by the Force of Art; in Shakespeare, it strikes before we are aware, like an accidental fire from Heaven: But in Homer, and in him only, it burns everywhere clearly, and everywhere irresistibly' (Pope, VII, 4-5).

Homer's only rival is Scripture and, in a phrase that looks forward to Winckelmann's phil-Hellenic slogan of 'noble simplicity and silent grandeur', Pope speaks of the 'pure and noble simplicity of Scripture and Homer'. This Homeric simplicity, however, is a very eighteenth-century plainness that values abstraction. An age can be defined by the purple passages its finds in the classics: the most frequently translated and anthologised Iliadic passage in Pope's day was Sarpedon's speech to Glaukos. Pope translated it at the age of 19 and later used it as the model for Clarissa's speech in *The Rape of the Lock*. Taken from its context, the speech becomes a creed, an example of Pope's habit, as Maynard Mack puts it, of 'teasing the unique fictions of his original toward something more generic and therefore more easily recognizable' (Pope, 7.viii).

Grand and general, Pope's *Iliad* also has a high-gloss finish and a tendency towards the epigrammatic, two qualities that derive from the medium of the heroic couplet. The end of Sarpedon's speech shows these qualities in their most brilliant and attractive light:

> The Life which others pay, let us bestow,
> And give to Fame what we to Nature owe;
> Brave tho' we fall, and honour'd if we live.

The *Iliad* in a world of prose

Pope's Homer was the most successful of many attempts, especially in England and France, to make Homer available to a polite and not necessarily very learned audience. For this audience the epic was no longer a living vernacular genre but existed in differently displaced forms: *Paradise Lost* was a classic, *The Rape of the Lock* a parody, the *Iliad* a translation. The audience of Pope's *Iliad* was to find its authentic literary form in the novel. Fénelon in his *Télémaque*, a kind of *Bildungsroman* based on the opening books of the *Odyssey*, had anticipated this development. Fielding confirmed it by calling *Joseph Andrews* a 'comic epic poem in prose' and by using a technique of allusion that recalls the epic tradition, and in particular Homer, only to distance itself from it. The establishment of the novel as the dominant form of narrative coincides roughly with the development of modern Homeric scholarship and criticism, and it is surely a cardinal fact about the life of the *Iliad* since the eighteenth century that its readers have defined its genre in opposition to prose fiction. For Hegel, the novel is the appropriate expression of a prosaic and bourgeois world. Like the epic, it mirrors the totality of the world, but with a crucial loss of poetic substance. Fictional protagonists like Julien Sorel or Dorothea Brooke may have the brilliance and energy of Achilles, but they live in a world where circumstances rule out the achievement of heroic glory, even at the cost of life.

The dominance of the novel has led to a changing perception of the relationship of the *Iliad* and *Odyssey*. The latter has often been seen as a proto-novel, a perspective that ultimately accounts for *Ulysses*. The *Iliad* by contrast has been increasingly aligned with the stark world that readers discovered in other forms of 'heroic poetry', and especially in Germanic mythology. This vision of the heroic differs significantly from the Renaissance vision and replaces a timeless image of human perfection with an image of splendid and atavistic brutality.

The changing fortunes of Homer as a school author also bear on the understanding of the *Iliad* as a heroic poem. In the nineteenth century, Homer, the great paragon of naïve poetry, the original genius from the childhood of man, becomes an author for boys, specifically public schoolboys at Winchester or Rugby. Richard Jenkyns' fine chapter on the Homeric Ideal in *The Victorians and Ancient Greece* is appropriately divided into sections on 'Homer' and 'Athletics'.

Opposition to the bourgeois novel and the boys' school as the temple for the cult of the heroic are critical facts for an understanding of the life of the *Iliad* in the nineteenth century. The understanding of Homer fostered in such a context may be seen as restating in a different form the Vergilian category of the Homeric. In the *Aeneid* Turnus understands himself as Achilles, but for Vergil Turnus represents violence and the flamboyance of heroic gesture without lasting achievement. Aeneas, the cautious and farsighted leader, on the other hand, lacks glamour. And, while Vergil's art is in the highest degree poetic, *pius Aeneas* is a rather prosaic character. From one perspective Vergilian art and the world of prose provide a similar background for the identification and admiration of the Homeric.

The Vergilian prism has been no less dominant in the twentieth-century criticism of Homer. To return for a moment to the chimerical *homo homericus* discussed in the first chapter, if there is a distinguishing feature of twentieth-century criticism, it lies perhaps in the innocent arrogance with which it has claimed a superior understanding on the basis of radically new insights into the nature of Homer's art or his vision of man. Much Homeric scholarship in the twentieth century was a close cousin of cultural anthropology. I remember reading somewhere that it is the professional disease of anthropologists to overestimate the difference between human cultures. Faced with the competing claims that people are people and people are different they prefer to err on the side of the latter. Combine this with the scholar's territorial instinct to dwell on the distinctness of his subject and sharply mark off its boundaries, and you get a 'real' Homer who is very 'different'. But if you take a longer view, the oral Homer or Snell's characters who do not yet have a concept of a unified self are not so distant cousins of the Homeric naïve, a concept with a very long history indeed. Whether Parry and Snell are 'closer' to the *Iliad* than Ronsard or Pope is by no means an idle question. I do not mean to suggest that to study the life of the *Iliad* is to sort through the junkheap of discarded interpretations: on the contrary, the life has a shape and direction that must guide our own understanding. But criticism is not a progressive art.

If we think of the life of the *Iliad* as revealing to us an identity that can guide our own understanding, we are confronted with a peculiar problem. The most distinctive feature of Homeric criticism has been the recurring attempt to endow the category of the Homeric with a supremacy that elevates it beyond the limits of an individual style and puts it beyond description. For the Greeks, Homer was The Poet. For Ronsard and the Vergilian tradition Homer's 'naïve facilité' identifies the Homeric with the natural. The naive Homer is the modern version of the self-defeating enterprise of combining description with absolute praise. Homer is not the only artist to have suffered this fate: we recognise it in the criticism of Shakespeare and Mozart. But in Homer the dilemma is more central. Is it chronological priority or a peculiar greatness that has created the persistent temptation to dissolve the Homeric as the contours of a specific identity and to equate it with some version of the absolute? To that Homeric Question we may never find an answer.

Bibliography

Adkins, A.W.H. *Merit and Responsibility*. London, 1960. The standard discussion of the Homeric poems as the description of a real society based predominantly on competitive values. See the criticism by Long and the author's defence (Adkins 1971).

Adkins, A.W.H. 'Homeric Values and Homeric Society', *Journal of Hellenic Studies* 91 (1971): 1-14.

Aeschylus. *Die Fragmente der Tragödien des Aischylos*, ed. Hans Joachim Mette. Berlin, 1959.

Arend, Walter. *Die Typischen Scenen bei Homer*. Berlin, 1975. This careful classification of recurring scenes in the Homeric poems, first published in 1933, is still the standard work in its field.

Arnold, Matthew. 'On Translating Homer', in *On the Classical Tradition*. Ann Arbor, 1960.

Austin, J.N.H. 'The Function of Digressions in the *Iliad*', *Greek Roman and Byzantine Studies* 7 (1966): 295-312. A superb essay on the role of descriptive detail in articulating narrative progress and marking moments of significance and suspense.

Austin, N. *Archery at the Dark of the Moon: Poetic Problems in Homer's Odyssey*. Berkeley,1975.

Bakker, Egbert J. *Poetry in Speech: Orality and Homeric Discourse, Myth and Poetics*. Ithaca, NY, 1997.

Bakker, Egbert J. 'Rhapsodes, Bards, and Bricoleurs: Homerizing Literary Theory', in *Classics@*, 3 (2007). Available from http://chs.harvard.edu/chs/issue_3_papers_in_pdf.

Bate, Walter Jackson. *The Burden of the Past and the English Poet*. Cambridge, MA, 1970.

Bloom, Harold. *The Anxiety of Influence: A Theory of Poetry*, 2nd ed. New York, 1997.

Burgess, Jonathan Seth. *The Tradition of the Trojan War in Homer and the Epic Cycle*. Baltimore, MD, 2001.

Burkert, Walter. *Greek Religion*. Cambridge, MA , 1985.

Cairns, Douglas, ed. *Oxford Readings in Homer's Iliad*. Oxford, 2002. A judicious collection of recent approaches to the *Iliad*.

Davison, J.A. 'The Homeric Question', in *A Companion to Homer*, ed. Alan J.B. Wace and Frank Stubbings, 234-65. London, 1962. The most informed and judicious discussion in English of theories about the authorship of the Homeric poems since the late seventeenth century.

Dodds, E.R. *The Greeks and the Irrational*. Berkeley, 1951. The opening chapter, 'Agamemnon's apology', is the classic discussion in English of the problem of double motivation in Homer.

Edwards, Mark W. *Homer. Poet of the Iliad*. Baltimore, 1987. An exceptionally sensitive and level-headed book. The first part on the characteristics of Homeric poetry is very successful at surveying a controversial field in a detailed and non-technical manner.

Eichholz, D. E. 'The Propitiation of Achilles', *American Journal of Philology* 74 (1953): 137-48. The best statement of the case that Agamemnon's offer is inadequate and that Achilles is right to reject it.

Fenik, B. *Typical Battle Scenes in the Iliad: Studies in the Narrative Techniques of Homeric Battle Description*. Wiesbaden, 1968.

Fenik, B. 'Stylization and Variety: Four Monologues in the *Iliad*', in *Tradition and Invention*, ed. B. Fenik, 67-90. Leiden, 1978. This illuminating analysis of scenes of deliberation by Odysseus, Menelaos, Agenor and Hektor points far beyond its immediate topic to larger issues of context sensitive interpretation of conventional materials in Homeric narrative.

Finnegan, Ruth H. *Oral Poetry: Its Nature, Significance, and Social Context*. Cambridge, 1977. This very empirically oriented book shows that oral poetry comes in many stripes, that the relationship between the spoken and the written takes many forms, and that orality *per se* has little evidentiary or explanatory value.

Foley, John Miles. *Homer's Traditional Art*. University Park, PA,1999.

Fränkel, Hermann. *Die Homerischen Gleichnisse*. Göttingen, 1977. First published in 1921. A path-breaking book in its day and still the most interesting, if occasionally fanciful, treatment of its subject. A central section is translated in the anthology by Wright (q.v.).

Freud, Sigmund. 'The Theme of the Three Caskets', in *The Standard Edition of the Complete Psychological Works of Sigmund Freud*, 291-301. London, 1958.

Friedrich, Rainer. *Formular Economy in Homer: The Poetics of the Breaches*. Hermes Einzel-schriften. Stuttgart: Steiner, 2007.

Friedrich, Wolf-Hartmut. *Wounding and Death in the Iliad: Homeric Techniques of Description*, tr. Gabriele Wright and Peter Jones. London, 2003. German edition published in 1956. This ingenious demonstration of differences in the representation of injury and death retains its value even for a reader who does not agree with the author's analytical conclusions.

Gardner, Howard. *Creating Minds: An Anatomy of Creativity Seen Through the Lives of Freud, Einstein, Picasso, Stravinsky, Eliot, Graham, and Gandhi*. New York, 1993.

Goold, G.P. 'The Nature of Homeric Composition', *ICS* 2 (1977): 1-34. A speculative but plausible reconstruction of the progressive fixation of the texts of the *Iliad* and *Odyssey* over the life-time of their poets.

Graziosi, B. *Inventing Homer: The Early Reception of Epic*. Cambridge, 2002.

Griffin, J. *Homer on Life and Death*. Oxford, 1980. A superb general book, which treats the two epics as one oeuvre and discusses a range of narrative and thematic conventions. Especially good on symbolism, setting and characterisation.

Grote, George. *A History of Greece*. London, 1846-56.

Hainsworth, J.B. *The Flexibility of the Homeric Formula*. Oxford, 1968.

Hainsworth, J.B. 'Criticism of an Oral Homer', *Journal of Hellenic Studies* 90 (1970): 90-8. A sceptical survey of attempts to derive a poetics of oral composition from the known facts about formulaic verse-making.

Heitsch, Ernst. 'Der Zorn Des Paris: Zur Deutungsgeschichte eines Homerischen Zetemas', in *Gesammelte Schriften, I: Zum Frühgriechischen Epos*. Munich and Leipzig, 2001. An exemplary discussion from an analytical position of the difficulties involved in reconciling the Paris scenes of Books 3 and 6.

Hoekstra, A. *Homeric Modifications of Formulaic Prototypes. Studies in the Development of Greek Epic Diction*. Amsterdam, 1965.

Homer. *Homeri quae extant omnia ... cum Latina versione ... perpetuis ... in Iliada simul ad Odysseam. Spondani ... Commentariis*, ed. Jean de Sponde. Basel, 1583. A characteristic example of late sixteenth-century scholarship. Used by Chapman for his translation.

Homer. *Homeri Ilias ad veteris codicis Venetifidem recensita. Scholia in eam antiquissima*, ed. J.B.C. d'Annse de Villoison. Venice, 1788. The first printed edition of the Venetus A manuscript, on which all modern editions of the *Iliad* are based.

Homer. *The Iliad, Edited with Apparatus Criticus, Prolegomena, Notes and Appendixes*, ed. Walter Leaf. London, 1900. While largely superseded on archaeological and historical matters, this masterpiece of late nineteenth-century scholarship remains extremely valuable on questions of meaning, usage and narrative structure. Its notes are accessible through the Homer texts at the Perseus site (http://www.perseus.tufts.edu).

Homer. *Homers Ilias. Für den Schulgebrauch erklärt*, ed. C. Hentze and Karl Friedrich Ameis.

Leipzig, 1902-6. The two-volume appendix to this edition is virtually a variorum edition of nineteenth-century analytical scholarship. Very helpful on parallel passages and grammatical explanations.

Homer. *The Iliad of Homer*, tr. Richmond Lattimore. Chicago, 1951.

Homer. *Iliad. Book XXIV*, ed. C.W. MacLeod. Cambridge, 1982. A model commentary that combines philological acumen with literary sophistication.

Homer. *Homeri Ilias*, ed. testimonia by Martin L. West. Stuttgart and Leipzig, 1998. This Teubner edition is now the standard Greek edition. It is particularly valuable for its extensive list of papyri and ancient reference to particular words and lines in the *Iliad*.

Homer. *Homers Ilias Gesamtkommentar: Auf der Grundlage der Ausgabe von Ameis-Hentze-Cauer (1868-1913)*, ed. Joachim Latacz. München, 2000-. This is a complete revision of Ameis-Hentze, but it has not yet progressed beyond the second book of the *Iliad*.

Janko, Richard. *Homer, Hesiod, and the Hymns: Diachronic Development in Epic Diction*. Cambridge, 1982. One of the first studies to make good use of computers to sift evidence for diachronic change in the corpus of Early Greek epic.

Jenkyns, Richard. *The Victorians and Ancient Greece*. Oxford, 1980.

Johnson, Samuel. *Prefaces, Biographical and Critical, to the Works of the English Poets*. London, 1779-81, VII, 295. Cited from the Chadwyck-Healey electronic collection, *Literary Theory*.

Kahane, Ahuvia. *The Interpretation of Order: A Study in the Poetics of Homeric Repetition*. Oxford, 1994.

Kahane, Ahuvia and Martin Mueller. *The Chicago Homer*. http://www.library.northwestern.edu/homer

Kakridis, J.Th. *Homeric Researches*, Lund, 1949.

Kirk, G.S. and J.E. Raven. *The Presocratic Philosophers: A Critical History with a Selection of Texts*. Cambridge, 1957.

Kirk, G.S. *The Songs of Homer*. Cambridge, 1962. Two important themes of this influential book were the emphasis on the sub-Mycenean and relatively impoverished centuries as the breeding ground for Greek epic and the theory of the 'monumental composer' who transformed the conditions of epic without any access to writing.

Kirk, G.S. *Homer and the Oral Tradition*. Cambridge, 1976. This set of essays written over a number of years is an excellent introduction to questions of oral composition in Homer. The later essays especially are less doctrinaire and more persuasive than the sections on oral poetry in *The Songs of Homer*.

Kirk, G.S. 'The Formal Duels in Books 3 and 7 of the *Iliad*', in *Homer: Tradition and Invention*, ed. Bernard Fenik, 18-40. Leiden, 1978. A methodologically significant essay that display a striking rapprochement of 'oral' and 'analytical' approaches in discussing the interdependence of the two duels.

Kirk, G.S., Mark W. Edwards, Richard Janko, Bryan Hainsworth and N.J. Richardson. *The Iliad: A Commentary*. Cambridge, 1985. The six volumes of this commentary echo the interests of their quite different editors. They do not necessarily supersede earlier commentaries.

Knauer, Georg Nicolaus. *Die Aeneis und Homer; Studien zur poetischen Technik Vergils, mit Listen der Homerzitate in der Aeneis*. Göttingen, 1964. The elaborate tables of correspondences between Homer and Vergil make this book an indispensable reference tool, quite apart from its great merit as a critical study.

Latacz, Joachim. *Troy and Homer: Towards a Solution of an Old Mystery*. tr. Kevin Windle and Rosh Ireland. Oxford, 2004. The most recent and very learned, but not uncontroversial, treatment of the question whether and how historical events are reflected in the *Iliad*.

Lesky, Albin. *Göttliche und menschliche Motivation im Homerischen Epos*. Heidelberg, 1961. A measured and perhaps definitive account of the problem of human and divine motivation in Homer. Modifies Snell and Dodds by stressing the links between Homeric and modern experience. A translation of this essay is included in Cairns' *Oxford Readings in Homer's Iliad.*

Lohmann, Dieter. *Die Komposition der Reden in der Ilias.* Berlin, 1970.

Long, A.A. 'Morals and Values in Homer'. *Journal of Hellenic Studies* 90 (1970): 121-39. A trenchant critique of Adkins' theories about the moral values of Homeric society.

Lord, Albert Bates. *The Singer of Tales.* Cambridge, MA, 1960.

Martin, Richard P. *The Language of Heroes: Speech and Performance in the Iliad.* Ithaca, NY, 1989.

Minchin, Elizabeth. *Homer and the Resources of Memory: Some Applications of Cognitive Theory to the Iliad and the Odyssey.* Oxford, 2001.

Moulton, C. *Similes in the Homeric Poems.* Göttingen, 1977.

Mueller, Martin. 'Paradise Lost and the *Iliad*', *Comparative Literature Studies* 6 (1969): 292-316.

Mueller, Martin. 'Knowledge and Delusion in the *Iliad*', *Mosaic* 3 (1970): 86-103.

Muellner, Leonard Charles. *The Anger of Achilles: Menis in Greek Epic, Myth and Poetics.* Ithaca, NY, 1996.

Nagler, Michael. *Spontaneity and Tradition: A Study in the Oral Art of Homer.* Berkeley, California, 1974.

Nagy, Gregory. *The Best of the Achaeans: Concepts of the Hero in Archaic Greek Poetry.* Baltimore, MD, 1979.

Nagy, Gregory. *Poetry as Performance: Homer and Beyond.* Cambridge, 1996.

Ong, Walter. *Orality and Literacy: The Technologizing of the Word.* London, 1982. An excellent introduction to its topic. It avoids nostalgia and describes different language technologies in terms of the gains and losses that are inescapably attached to them.

Otto, Walter F. *The Homeric Gods.* London, 1954. A celebratory account of Greek religion, unmatched for its intuitive power and, if used with caution, a wonderful introduction to the subject.

Page, Sir Denys. *History and the Homeric Iliad.* Berkeley, 1959. A justly famous book, but to be read sceptically because of the author's ability to make quite extravagant speculations appear as truths resting on a bedrock of facts and common sense. Like Latacz, he sees the *Iliad* as an account of specific events that can partly be reconstructed from other historical sources, including Near Eastern materials.

Parry, Adam. 'The Language of Achilles', *Transactions of the American Philological Association* 87 (1956): 1-7.

Parry, Adam. 'Have We Homer's *Iliad*?' *Yale Classical Studies* 20 (1966): 175-216. A classic defence of the unity and design of the *Iliad* as a work rooted in but not defined by oral poetry.

Parry, Milman. *The Making of Homeric Verse: The Collected Papers of Milman Parry*, ed. Adam Parry. Oxford, 1971. The fundamental work on the system of noun-epithet formulas and its role in a tradition of oral poetry. Adam Parry's long introduction is a masterly survey of this branch of scholarship in the wider context of the Homeric Question.

Perrault, Charles. *Parallèle des anciens et des modernes en ce qui regarde les arts et les sciences*, ed. H.R. Jauss and M. Imdahl. Munich, 1964.

Plutarch. *The lives of the noble Grecians and Romanes compared together by that graue learned philosopher and historiographer, Plutarke of Chaeronea; translated out of Greeke into French by Iames Amyot ... ; and out of French into Englishe, by Thomas North.* London, 1579. Cited from Early English Books Online.

Pope, Alexander. *Translations of Homer*, ed. Maynard Mack. The Twickenham Edition, vols 7-10. London 1967.

Powell, Barry B. *Homer and the Origin of the Greek Alphabet.* Cambridge, 1990.

Redfield, James M. *Nature and Culture in the Iliad: The Tragedy of Hector.* Chicago, 1975.

This anthropologically oriented study throws light on many aspects of the Homeric world but is especially persuasive on the themes of food and purification.

Reinhardt, Karl. 'Das Parisurteil', in *Tradition Und Geist*. Göttingen, 1960. This inspired essay, first published in 1938, is unmatched for its illumination of narrative procedure and moral vision in the Iliad. It is the clearest articulation of Reinhardt's very productive concept of the 'epic situation'. Included in Wright, *Homer: German Scholarship in Translation*.

Reinhardt, Karl. *Die Ilias Und Ihr Dichter*, ed. Uvo Hölscher. Göttingen, 1961.

Ronsard, Pierre de. *Oeuvres Complètes*, ed. Paul Laumonier. Paris, 1914.

Schadewaldt, Wolfgang. *Von Homers Welt Und Werk; Aufsätze und Auslegungen zur Homerischen Frage*, 4th rev. edn. Stuttgart, 1965.

Schadewaldt, Wolfgang. *Iliasstudien*. Darmstadt, 1966. This monograph, first published in 1943, uses the methods of analytical criticism to argue for a unitarian position by showing how firmly Book 11 is anchored in the total structure of the *Iliad*. This seminal and very technical work is much superior to the author's later and often quite pretentious essays.

Schadewalt, Wolfgang. 'Aischylos' Achilleis', in *Hellas und Hesperien*. Zurich, 1970.

Schein, S.L. *The Mortal Hero: An Introduction to Homer's Iliad*. Berkeley, 1984.

Schein, S. L. 'Homeric Intertextuality: Two Examples', in *Euphrosyne: Studies in Ancient Epic and its Legacy in Honor of Dimitris N. Maronitis*, ed. John Kazazis and Antonios Rengakos, 349-56. Stuttgart, 1999.

Seaford, Richard. *Reciprocity and Ritual: Homer and Tragedy in the Developing City-State*. New York, 1994.

Segal, Charles. *The Theme of the Mutilation of the Corpse in the Iliad*. Leyden, 1971. A meticulous study with broad implications for the unity and thematic structure of the epic.

Sinclair, John. *Corpus, Concordance, Collocation*. Oxford, 1991.

Snell, Bruno. *The Discovery of the Mind: The Greek Origins of European Thought*, tr. T.G. Rosenmeyer. Oxford, 1953.

Snodgrass, A.M. 'An Historical Homeric Society', *Journal of Hellenic Studies* 94 (1974): 114-25. An eminent historian of archaic Greece expresses scepticism about taking the Homeric poems as descriptions of a real world.

Steadman, John M. 'Achilles and Renaissance Epic: Moral Criticism and Literary Tradition', in *Lebene Antike: Symposium für Rudolf Sühnel*, ed. Horst Meller and Hans-Joachim Zimmermann. Berlin, 1967.

Taplin, Oliver. *Homeric Soundings: The Shaping of the Iliad*. Oxford, 1992.

Vivante, Paolo. *The Homeric Imagination. A Study of Homer's Perception of Reality*. Bloomington, Indiana, 1970.

Webster, T.B.L. *From Mycenae to Homer*. London, 1958.

Weil, Simone. *Simone Weil's The Iliad or the Poem of Force: A Critical Edition*, ed. James P. Holoka. New York, 2003.

West, Martin L. *Greek Metre*. Oxford, 1982.

West, Martin L. 'The Invention of Homer', *Classical Quarterly* 49 (1999): 364-82.

West, Martin L. *Studies in the Text and Transmission of the Iliad*. München, 2001.

Whitman, Cedric Hubbell. *Homer and the Heroic Tradition*. Cambridge, MA, 1958.

Wilamowitz-Moellendorff, Ulrich von. *Die Ilias und Homer*. Berlin, 1920.

Wolf, F.A. *Prolegomena to Homer* (1795), ed. Anthony Grafton, Glenn W. Most and James E.G. Zetzel. Princeton, 1985.

Wood, Robert. *An Essay on the Original Genius and Writings of Homer*. New York, 1971.

Wordsworth, William. *The Prose Works of William Wordsworth*, ed. W.J.B. Owen and J.W. Smyser. Oxford, 1974.

Wright, G.M., and P.V. Jones. *Homer: German Scholarship in Translation*. Oxford, 1997. An excellent selection of influential German essays about Homer from the middle of the twentieth century.

Index

204

Index

Eurypylos, 53, 59, 80, 98, 146, 183
Eurysakes, 189
Eurystheus, 87
Eustathius, 186, 188
Fénelon, François, 197
Fielding, Henry, 197
Finnegan, Ruth, 14
Foley, J.M., 22
Forster, E.M., 59
Fränkel, Hermann, 11, 34
Friedrich, Rainer, 13
Friedrich, W.H., 83
Gibbon, Edward, 10
Glaukos, 29, 57-8, 78, 96, 100, 124, 168-9, 180-1, 197
Goethe, Johann Wolfgang von, 174
Greek alphabet, 6, 8
Griffin, Jasper, 113, 188
Hades, 90, 114, 129, 179, 193
Hainsworth, J.B., 13
Harmonides, 86, 124
Harpalion, 88, 96
Hegel, G.W.F., 197
Hekabe, 43, 64, 66, 69, 120, 122, 134
Hektor, 19, 28-30, 33, 36-7, 41-8, 62-8, 80, 85-6, 94, 98-100, 114, 118, 123-4, 147, 169-71, 181, 183-4, 189, 195, and passim
Helen, 23, 35-6, 67, 74, 113, 117, 119-22, 127, 183, and passim
Helenos, 94, 166
Henryson, 193
Hephaistos, 3, 58, 60, 71, 92, 105, 118-19, 129, 131-2, 158, 179, 185
Hera, 40, 67, 69, 129, 132, 150, 179, and passim
Herakles, 87, 146, 149-51
Herder, Gottfried, 10, 12
Hermes, 25, 74, 90, 124, 128-9, 132, 147, 149-50, 155, 183,
Herodotus, 1, 86
Hesiod, 12, 133-5, 144, 148, 155
hexameter, 6, 20-1, 137, 143, 177, 192
Hippolochos, 82-3, 86
Hippothoös, 81, 166
Hoekstra, A., 13
Homer, 9-19, 173-6, and passim
Homeric Hymns, 12, 135, 144, 148, 155
Horace, 36, 192
Hyperenor, 32
Hypnos, 131
Hypsenor, 80, 90
Idomeneus, 57, 76, 80-3, 90, 96, 99, 118, 165-6, 171, 192
Ilioneus, 82, 88-91,
Imbrios, 82, 88, 100, 111
Iphidamas, 77, 79-80, 82, 89, 93, 95, 167
Iphigenia, 35
Iphition, 80, 87, 91
Iris, 128-9, 140-1, 145, 147, 150
Isos, 88, 109
Janko, Richard, 8, 28, 158,
Jaynes, Julian, 11

Jenkyns, Richard, 188, 196, 198
Johnson, Samuel, 25-6
Jonson, Ben, 10, 34, 196
Joyce, James, 197
Kalchas, 35-6, 38, 117, 128
Kaletor, 96, 99
Kalypso, 17, 133
Kassandra, 88, 90
Kastor and Pollux, 24-6, 35
Kebriones, 56, 60, 82, 84, 90, 94, 100-1, 109-10, 184
Kimon, 5
Kirk, G.S., 1, 3, 8, 28, 133, 159, 163, 174-5, 181, 184
Kleitos, 166
Klytaemnestra, 36
Knossos, 188
Koiranos, 81, 83
Koön, 77, 79, 82, 93, 95-6
Kopreus, 87
Krethon, 95, 111
Kyklops, 134
Laomedon, 129
Latacz, Joachim, 1
Leontes, 91, 98, 106
Lesky, Albin, 1, 120
Leto, 122, 124, 129
Lewis, C.S., 22
Lord, Albert, 8, 13
Lykaon, 24, 60, 70-1, 89, 91-2, 195
Lykomedes, 95
Lykon, 79, 82
Lykophron, 87, 96
Machaon, 53, 98
Maris, 88
Martin, Richard, 15
Meges and Dolops, 77, 79-81
Menelaos, 26-8, 33, 35-6, 40, 42, 67-8, 70, 86, 88, 103-4, 109-11, 147, 166-8, 180-1, and passim
Menestheus, 172
Menoitios, 40
Meriones, 31, 76-7, 80-3, 96, 101, 105, 111, 165-6, 171
Merops, 88
Miltiades, 5
Milton, 10, 42, 114-15, 131, 133, 174, 194-6
Minchin, Elizabeth, 15
Mozart, W.A., 23, 34, 198
Mycenae, 2-3, 6, 35, 129, 178, 188
Myrmidons, 49, 52, 60, 105, 170, 182
Nagy, Gregory, 7-8
Nausikaa, 9-10, 133
Neleus, 44, 125
Nestor, 2, 3, 6, 29, 38-9, 44, 48, 53, 65, 77-8, 98, 147, 160-1, 179, and passim
Odysseus, 26, 33, 37, 39, 49-52, 63, 78, 86, 106, 108, 117, 122, 125, 147, 158, 184, 186, and passim
Odyssey, 3, 8, 16-19, 37, 133-4, 138-40, 185, 189, and passim
Oineus, 119

205

Index